Nell Regan

HELENA MOLONY:
A RADICAL LIFE,
1883–1967

ARLEN
HOUSE

Helena Molony:
A Radical Life, 1883–1967

is published in 2017 by
ARLEN HOUSE
42 Grange Abbey Road
Baldoyle
Dublin 13
Ireland
Phone: +353 86 8207617
Email: arlenhouse@gmail.com

ISBN 978–1–85132–165–0, paperback
ISBN 978–1–85132–166–7, hardback

International distribution by
SYRACUSE UNIVERSITY PRESS
621 Skytop Road, Suite 110
Syracuse, New York
USA 13244–5290
Phone: 315–443–5534/Fax: 315–443–5545
Email: supress@syr.edu
www.syracuseuniversitypress.syr.edu

Typesetting by Arlen House

Cover images: Helena Molony and Maud Gonne MacBride, 1940s;
Detail from *The Devil's Disciple* (1913), with Sidney Gifford,
Countess Markievicz, Helena Molony and Count Markievicz

CONTENTS

7   *Acknowledgements*

9   *List of Illustrations*

13   Foreword
        Jack O'Connor, Gene Mealy, Joe O'Flynn

17   Preface
        Senia Pašeta

25   Introduction

35   Beginnings

39   Radical, 1903–1911

77   Actor, 1911–1915

119   Soldier, 1916

151   Publicist, 1917–1923

183   Trade Unionist, 1923–1941

233   Memoirist, 1941–1967

271   Legacy

277   *Bibliography*

285   *Index*

Acknowledgements

I would like to thank all the people who contributed to this research; Margaret Mac Curtain, Fergus D'Arcy, Mary Daly, Margaret Ward, Mary Jones, Penny Duggan, Mary Cullen, Maria Luddy, Rosemary Cullen Owens, Francis Devine, Hugh O'Connor, Paidrigín Ní Mhurchú, Katherine O'Donnell, Patrick Smyth, Eve Morrison, Clara Conway and Mary Elliott.

For help at an extremely busy time, the archivists Aoife Torpey at Kilmainham Gaol, Mairéad Delany at the Abbey Theatre and staff at the National Library, in particular James Harte and Berni Metcalfe. Also Marian Thérèse Keyes, Senior Executive Librarian with Dún Laoghaire-Rathdown County Council Public Libraries and Karan O'Loughlin, SIPTU Equality Officer. Very special thanks are due to Alan Hayes of Arlen House, to Padraig Yeates and to SIPTU for its essential support of this biography.

My personal thanks are due to labour historian Therese Moriarty for friendship, support, and the perspective that her own work and deep scholarship has provided over the years, both as a colleague in the Labour History Museum and beyond. To Paula Shields for encouragement and to Ronan, for endnotes, tea and love.

LIST OF ILLUSTRATIONS

41   Inghinidhe na hÉireann members. President Maud Gonne MacBride is seated behind a banner wearing a hat. It has been suggested that Molony is to her left
courtesy Kilmainham Gaol Museum, 13PO–IB54–14

43   Anti-Enlistment leaflet, Inghinidhe na hÉireann

48   First *Bean na hÉireann* header
courtesy Kilmainham Gaol Museum, 13NW–IB54–14

52   Front page of *Bean na hÉireann*, January 1909, with editorial by Helena Molony
courtesy Kilmainham Gaol Museum, 13NW–IB54–17

57   Suffrage debate in *Bean na hÉireann*, February 1909, with editorial by Helena Molony
courtesy Kilmainham Gaol Museum, 13NW–IB54–17

58   Front page of *Bean na hÉireann*, February 1909, with editorial on suffrage debate by Helena Molony
courtesy Kilmainham Gaol Museum, 13NW–IB54–17

67   Constance Markievicz, c 1914
private collection

69   Na Fianna with Constance Markievicz. Image donated, described and signed by Bulmer Hobson
courtesy Military Archives, Ireland, P–21–001

78   The cast of *The Devil's Disciple*, George Bernard Shaw. Count Markievicz's Independent Repertory Company, 1913
private collection

79   Detail of *The Devil's Disciple* showing Sidney Gifford and Helena Molony above Constance and Casimir Markievicz
private collection

86 Rosamond Jacob records Molony's views on love and men in her diary on 4 August 1911
courtesy Jacob Estate and National Library of Ireland

87 Rosamond Jacob records in her diary on 5 August 1911 how Molony, 'Emer', was ill
courtesy Jacob Estate and National Library of Ireland

99 First Abbey Company production of *The Magnanimous Lover*, Royal Court, London, June 1913
courtesy Abbey Theatre Archive

101 Second Abbey Company production of *The Mineral Workers* at the start of the 1913 Lockout
courtesy Abbey Theatre Archive

107 Cover of Abbey Theatre Programmes
courtesy Abbey Theatre Archive

125 *The Dreamers*, February 1916 with Helena Molony, Seán Connolly, Arthur Shields all in the cast
courtesy Abbey Theatre Archive

131 City Hall and Dublin Castle where Molony was posted in Easter 1916
courtesy Military Archives, Ireland, P–33–018

137 Liberty Hall after the destruction of the Rising. Irish Women Workers' Union logo visible
courtesy National Library of Ireland

138 Kilmainham Gaol main entrance
courtesy Kilmainham Gaol Museum, 21PD–1K51–03

141 Helena Molony writing to her cousin Madge from Mountjoy Prison
courtesy National Library of Ireland

144 Helena Molony writing from Aylesbury prison to Ellen Bushell, eager for Abbey gossip and outlining her playwriting ambitions
courtesy National Library of Ireland

153   1917 commemoration, Irish Citizen Army members outside
Liberty Hall, Helena Molony front row, third from
lamppost, in black
courtesy Military Archives, Ireland, BMH CD 119 3 5

157   Liberty Hall, 1917 commemoration, crowds gather to see
banner as Helena Molony, Rosie Hackett and others are
barricaded on the roof
courtesy National Library of Ireland

158   1917 commemoration autograph book, signatures of
Helena Molony, Kathleen Lynn and Madeline ffrench
Mullen
courtesy Kilmainham Gaol Museum, KMGLM 2010.0187

170   Helena Molony to Hanna Sheehy Skeffington re
organisation of domestic servants, 1919
courtesy Sheehy Skeffington Estate and National Library of Ireland

174   Cast list for Abbey Theatre production of *The Round Table*, 1922
courtesy Abbey Theatre Archive

176   Helena Molony giving evidence in 1936 about her activities
during the War of Independence and Civil War
courtesy Military Archives, Ireland, MSP 34REF11739

182   Helena Molony, 1930s
private collection

185   IWWU advertisement, reproduced from the *Dublin Labour
Year Book*

191   Dublin Trades Union and Labour Council Executive
Committee, 1930–31. Helena Molony centre row with dog
Reproduced from the *Dublin Labour Year Book*

192   Detail reproduced from the *Dublin Labour Year Book*

197   Advertisement for the controversial Report of the Russian
Delegation. Reproduced from the *Dublin Labour Year Book*

206 Helena Molony (centre), ITUC delegate to the International
Labour Organisation, Geneva
courtesy Imogen Stuart

211 IWWU delegation to Minister Seán Lemass re Conditions
of Employment Bill, May 1935. Helena Molony back row
left and Louie Bennett front left

217 Helena Molony's Military Service Pension application
courtesy Military Archives, Ireland, MSP 34REF11739

246 Helena Molony and Maud Gonne MacBride, 1940s
courtesy Imogen Stuart

250 Helena Molony's annotated draft statement for the Bureau
of Military History
courtesy Kilmainham Gaol Museum, KMGLM 2011.0283.01

252 Bureau of Military History, Witness Statement 391
courtesy Military Archives, Ireland

256 Helena Molony at a sale of work in St Brendan's,
Grangegorman, 1962
courtesy Kilmainham Gaol Museum, KMGLM 2011.0287

261 Helena Molony
courtesy Imogen Stuart

263 Helena Molony in 1966 at the Abbey Theatre unveiling by
An Taoiseach Seán Lemass of a plaque commemorating
Company and Staff who participated in the 1916 Rising
courtesy Abbey Theatre Archive

265 Application by Eveleen O'Brien following Molony's death
for payment of her outstanding Military Service Pension
courtesy Military Archives, Ireland, MSP 34REF11739

270 Helena Molony, undated
private collection

Foreword

SIPTU is proud to be associated with this, the first biography of Helena Molony, one of the most remarkable members of a remarkable generation that founded the modern Irish State. She was a socialist, campaigner for equality, journalist, actor and, above all, trade union organiser, who dedicated her life to the cause of social justice.

The daughter of a Dublin grocer, Helena joined Inghinidhe na hÉireann in 1903 after hearing a speech by Maud Gonne MacBride. Within a short time, although still in her early twenties, she became its secretary and the editor of its monthly journal *Bean na hÉireann*. It was in the latter role that she first became interested in the trade union movement and started co-writing a 'Labour Notes' column urging women to organise on the factory floor as part of the overall battle for equality. She had the distinction, in 1911, of becoming the first Irishwoman to be arrested for a political offence in twentieth century Ireland after a protest over the forthcoming royal visit of King George V and Queen Mary to Ireland.

During these years she became a close friend of Countess Markievicz, helped her found Na Fianna Éireann and was influential in persuading her, Dr Kathleen Lynn and other women interested in nationalism and female suffrage to take an interest in social and economic issues. Like the Countess, Helena was one of the handful of women to be involved in the Irish Citizen Army, before the Women's Section was formally established.

In 1915 she became secretary of the Irish Women Workers' Union, at James Connolly's request, after its first secretary Delia Larkin returned to England. Helena somehow managed to combine her union work with a successful acting career at the Abbey, helped by the close proximity of the theatre to Liberty Hall, where the union was based. She would literally run between rehearsals, performances and the IWWU offices to ensure members' interests were looked after.

On Easter Monday 1916 she was one of the Citizen Army contingent, commanded by fellow Abbey actor and union activist Seán Connolly that occupied City Hall. She was with him when he died and was one of only five women imprisoned in England after the Rising. On her release she served on the Sinn Féin executive during its reorganisation in 1917 and returned part time to her acting.

However, the main focus of her life became the IWWU and she always put the union first. A terrific organiser and campaigner, she was acutely aware of her own limitations as an administrator and in 1918, Louie Bennett took over as general secretary. Molony continued to serve as effective deputy general secretary and frequently found herself at odds with Bennett and other colleagues because of her more militant stance on many issues.

This was reflected by her continuing involvement with the ICA during the War of Independence. She took the anti-Treaty side in the Civil War and was always to be found on the radical wing of the republican and labour movements of her day, supporting workers' soviets and advocating the syndicalist policies espoused by her political mentor James Connolly. It was from this perspective that she opposed the decision of the Irish Labour Party and the Irish Trade Union Congress to split in 1930. She became a founding member of Saor Éire and the Friends of the Soviet Union.

She was a firm advocate of equal pay for women and the positions she took on this and other social issues became increasingly unpopular at a time of increasing reaction in Irish society. The role of women in public life was discouraged, especially when they held radical opinions. She also found herself fighting a losing battle against legislation that facilitated the displacement of women workers by men in many occupations and underpinned pay differentials between the sexes.

Years of struggle took a severe toll on her health and, although she was elected President of the Irish Trade Union Congress in 1936, in recognition of her services to the labour movement, she was too unwell to deliver her presidential address the following year. She retired on health grounds in 1941.

Molony never abandoned her revolutionary ideals and suffered from bouts of depression and alcoholism, partly due to the stresses of adjusting to an increasingly conservative and conformist society intolerant of dissent. During the 1940s she met Dr Eveleen O'Brien of Grangegorman Hospital who cared for her and they subsequently lived together until Molony's death in 1967. She was buried in the republican plot at Glasnevin.

She was deeply disappointed at the failure of the new Irish State to advance the cause of women or eradicate the inequality that had underlain Irish society from the British era. She believed that this represented a betrayal of the

Irish Republic, the objectives of which were laid out in the 1916 Proclamation and in the Democratic Programme of the First Dáil; and of the vision of her mentor James Connolly.

It is fitting that the first full scale biography of Helena Molony should be written by Nell Regan, who helped revive interest in this forgotten labour leader with her 2001 pioneering biographical essay on Molony in *Female Activists: Irish Women and Change*, and earlier research. Regan has rescued Helena Molony's career from unwarranted obscurity. In doing so she has provided us all with an exemplar who can inspire a new generation of trade union and political activists committed to securing justice at work and fairness in society.

Jack O'Connor	Gene Mealy	Joe O'Flynn
General President	Vice-President	General Secretary
SIPTU	SIPTU	SIPTU

PREFACE

Helena Molony is one of those intriguing historical figures who seems to have been everywhere. She was a feminist, a republican, a socialist, a trade union activist and an actor. Although not as celebrated a writer as some of her contemporaries, she also left a sizeable number of important writings, preserved through her journalism, her involvement with the Bureau of Military History and her long battles with bureaucrats to secure financial justice and recognition for her part in the foundation of the modern Irish state. She has, in many ways, come to represent the intersectional nature of Irish radicalism in the early twentieth century.

Of all the many figures whose political and personal lives have been re-assessed during the decade of commemorations, Molony stands out as one of the most compelling and worthy of further research. Not only was she a remarkable activist whose career had been unjustly overlooked by generations of scholars, she represented the wider omission of women from the historical record. Nell Regan's pioneering 2001 biographical essay on Molony paved the way for this research. Since its publication, the release of important documents and further digging by a number of historians have contributed to a growing historiography, but the publication of this full biography adds enormously to what we know about Molony. It represents a welcome and important development in our understanding of Molony's life and times, as well as deepening our knowledge of the revolution and the Ireland that emerged from it.

This is a book about Molony's political life, but it is also a book about friendships and about the endurance of networks of love and support across the decades. Many of us who work on the history of modern Ireland feel that we know Molony, not least because aspects of her work and her character have been preserved in the memoirs of many of her friends. Many of the people Molony met in her youth remained devoted friends until they were separated by death, and many of these people, most of them women, supported Molony through extremely difficult periods of her life. She in turn was a devoted friend who, for example, firmly and publicly rejected the misrepresentation of Constance Markievicz in Seán Ó Faoláin's biography of one of her closest comrades. In this way, and in many others which are outlined in this book, Molony served as an advocate of women's activism and a defender of its accurate inclusion in the national narrative. Her close friendships with women nourished and sustained her at times, and they provided safe spaces in which she could continue to promote socialism, feminism and republicanism in the context of an increasingly conservative and confessional Irish state.

This biography fills many gaps in our knowledge of Molony's life. It chronicles a life lived against the background of war, revolution, emigration, confessionalism and radicalism – the great social and political facts of modern Ireland. It shows how these forces shaped her life and how she in turn shaped her own society in important ways. The account presented in these pages is not always flattering, but it is an honest and enlightening depiction of a remarkable – and radical – Irish life.

Senia Pašeta
Professor of Modern History
University of Oxford

In memory of my Dad,
Tom O'Regan
1939–1996

HELENA MOLONY
A RADICAL LIFE,
1883–1967

INTRODUCTION

In the early 1980s, Hugh O'Connor, a local historian, was walking near his home in Palmerston when he spotted a bulging folder, stamped with the insignia of 'International Labour Organisation', in a pile of rubbish. He pulled it out and brought it home to discover that it was the remains of someone's papers. In amongst the documents was a Christmas card from Maud Gonne MacBride, a handwritten reference for activities in the Irish Citizen Army between 1916 and 1923, acknowledgements from the Bureau of Military History, typescript articles about James Connolly and a women's clothing co-op, as well as an undated, untitled newspaper clipping headed, 'Someday someone will write the story of Helena Molony'.[1]

Much of the process of the writing of that story has been about sources. If, as Kierkegaard writes, 'A life is understood backwards but lived forwards', then an understanding of the public life of Helena Molony might begin when she first gave her account of the day that she encountered Maud Gonne MacBride and joined Inghinidhe na hÉireann. It was a story that entered her own mythology and that of others. The 'living forward' gathered pace from the day that she joined, and she hurtled through an extraordinary life of activism. Her own process of understanding her life backwards, at least as it is recorded, centred on the events leading up to 1916 and the Rising itself. Periodically interviews with her were published; particularly leading up to the 50th anniversary in 1966 and the following year when her death was front page news. However, in the mid-1970s, Maura Breslin, General Secretary of the Irish Women Workers' Union, attempted to write a history of the IWWU and wanted to look more closely at the role and life of Helena Molony, a central figure in that organisation. She was forced to conclude that,

> It is extremely difficult to adequately assess the contribution made by the late Helena Molony to the shaping of modern Ireland, mainly because no documents remain to my knowledge relating to that early period in her life. From discussions from time to time Miss Molony has referred to those early days but since she never seemed to seek publicity and was generally happy to work in the background, little has been recorded about her.[2]

In the 1980s two groundbreaking books appeared that drew on rich stores of previously disregarded source material. Margaret Ward's *Unmanageable Revolutionaries* (1983) was a history of Irish nationalist women's organisations from the Ladies Land League to Inghinidhe na hÉireann and Cumann na mBan, while Mary Jones' *These Obstreperous Lassies* (1988) was a history of the Irish Women Workers' Union. Between these two books, the structure of Molony's life of activism was discernible. By 1991, the 75th anniversary of the Rising, small biographical pieces were written, but much of the chronology and detail were sketchy.[3]

I began my own research on Helena Molony that same year as a history undergraduate in Dr Margaret Mac

Curtain's 'Women in History' course in UCD. It was exciting; there seemed to be a job to be done to fill in some of the gaps. The 75th anniversary itself was muted and there was little official marking of the event. In terms of historical writing a particular form of revisionism was dominant, perhaps inevitable, given the situation in the North. All of this seemed at odds with what I was reading about the type of nationalism that Molony and her contemporaries were developing in the years leading to the Rising. It felt almost clandestine to be sitting in the National Library reading copies of *Bean na hÉireann* as parts of Molony's editorials literally bounced off the pages, modern and funny.

Alongside the Ward and Jones books was Molony's own interview in R.M. Fox's *Rebel Irishwomen* and two other memoirs of the period, Sidney Gifford Czira's *The Years Flew By* and *The Splendid Years* by Máire Nic Shiubhlaigh. There were fleeting glimpses of Molony in biographies of Markievicz, Gonne MacBride and Connolly, as well as in labour histories such as *The Parliament of Labour*.[4]

Primary sources were limited, as was the available amount of Molony's correspondence. But between intelligence records from British and Irish authorities and other official administrative documents, the skeletal structure was fleshed out. Dublin Trades Council and Irish Trades Union Congress minutes and printed reports were invaluable as were the IWWU minutes, albeit with their frustrating gaps, i.e. 'a discussion followed'. Molony's regular absences were noted, often at crucial stages. Access to the Bureau of Military History records was impossible, but I was lucky enough to be doing my initial research at a time when there were still people alive who had known her. These included Francis Stuart, Louie Coghlan O'Brien, Finian Czira, John de Courcy Ireland, Séamus Scully and Jenny Murray. Their substantial memories of Molony fed into the picture. Others kindly sourced material including Nora Harkin, Proinsias Mac Aonghusa, Tomas Mac Ánna, Michael Ó Riordáin, Peter Beresford Ellis and Donal Nevin.

Margaret Ward and Mary Jones were remarkably generous with their own notes and source materials. I swapped manuscripts with Penny Duggan, a researcher based in Paris, who had also completed substantial work on Molony. We were relieved to find that we had reached similar conclusions and confirmed each other's findings.[5] Convinced that there must be a body of papers out there, I met up with Hugh O'Connor who had found the folder by the Liffey, but it appeared there were no other caches. It seems that her papers had been thrown out and her library sold to a bookseller in the George's Street Arcade in the early 1980s. This would make sense as Dr Eveleen O'Brien died then and her house in Sutton, which she shared with Molony, was sold. At one point a friend gently, but firmly, lent me a copy of *Possession* by AS Byatt. I knew what she meant.

It was exciting to see a portion of that work published as an article in *Female Activists: Irish Women and Change* edited by Mary Cullen and Maria Luddy, and in the *Field Day Anthology of Irish Writing: Volume V*, and to watch from a distance as it began to feed (flaws and all) into the historical narrative and on into secondary texts, while I worked in other areas. However, substantive new primary material has come on stream since then and at the start of the Decade of Centenaries the material began to draw me in again.[6]

This source material includes most notably and obviously, the Bureau of Military History and Military Service Pension Board collections, both now available online. Intelligence records from the Emergency revealed significant new details about Molony's role hiding the Nazi spy Goertz but also laid bare her personal life at a very difficult time. There has been a meticulous cataloguing of the Abbey archive and online playlist, and this led me to revise my original conclusion about when she had retired from the Abbey, as well as providing a significant perspective on her career as an actor. There were also further accessions in the NLI and one of the most astonishing sources, which has fed in to a range of histories, was the diary of Rosamond Jacob. Reading it for the first time was like meeting Molony at 28 and stepping into that world. Thanks are due to Clara Conway for generously allowing me access to her notes.

This full length biography draws on my research done in the 1990s and on new primary source material but also on the substantive scholarship and survey histories published in the interim. Several publications at the time of writing were key and included (though were not limited to), Eve Morrison's work on the Bureau of Military History; Senia Pašeta's *Irish Nationalist Women*; Rosemary Cullen Owens, *A Social History of Women in Ireland*; Ann Matthews' *Irish Citizen Army* and Roy Foster's *Vivid Faces*. As the Military Archives were closed for a period of renovation, I was fortunate to have access to Mary Elliott's research in an unpublished MA thesis on Dr Eveleen O'Brien as well as Fearghal McGarry's *The Abbey Rebels of 1916*. The latter contains a substantive consideration of Molony and reproduces temporarily unavailable documents as well as valuable new records from national archives in the UK. In the field of labour history, further work has been done on Delia Larkin by Therese Moriarty and Louie Bennett by Rosemary Cullen Owens. All of these works shed light on Molony's life and activity and continue to flesh out, enrich and complicate the story of her actions and our understanding of the time.

Several key points are worth mentioning in relation to the literature that has been published since *Female Activists* appeared in 2001. That book contained the first rigorous biographical articles on Rosamond Jacob, Kathleen Lynn, Louie Bennett, Margaret Cousins, Mary Galway as well as Molony. As the editors intended, these have fed into an overall narrative and allowed for greater consideration of broader questions; in particular how the roles of these women, their feminism and their thought developed in the context of their time, how they viewed what they did, as well as how they saw themselves and how others saw them. Setting down an initial structure allowed for revision and refining of aspects of each biography in particular as new material has come on stream, as well as the synthesis of these biographies into wider narratives that consider and include the role of women.

So for example, in Molony's case the equal role of women in the Irish Citizen Army was crucial to her own narrative and an important section in the original biographical article. Jones had already tracked down Hugh O'Connor and the rescued ILO folder, which contained one of the few supporting documents (aside from published interviews) regarding Molony's work with the ICA. Quotes were also taken from Molony's own unpublished typescript in the collection, 'Years of Tension'. Subsequent research and the release of a wealth of primary sources in the form of the Bureau of Military History and the Military Service Pension Board collections, as well as papers in Kilmainham Gaol have challenged the extent to which this was actually the case. It has also prompted a valuable and rigorous debate, both about what active military service and equality meant at that time but also subsequently in the context of the Free State years. Equally Molony's own support of and cooperation with suffrage women, despite their intensely fought debates about competing priorities, have fed into considerations about the interactions between the forces of feminism and nationalism.[7] These are particularly live issues at the time of writing because of the centenary of the Rising but other aspects will also be of interest in the development of a wider historiography.

It took some time to decide on a biographical structure that would highlight the different, overlapping areas of Molony's life, but that would also make for what is hopefully an accessible and interesting read. The chapter headings of radical, actor, soldier, publicist, trade unionist and memoirist seemed to fit and allowed me to look more closely at each of these roles that she played. They also reflect key decisions that she made about her priorities at different times.

In terms of Molony's personal life, three aspects in particular warrant comment. For someone who was initially fascinated with the process of writing history and how a historical 'fact' is 'made', it has been an education revisiting the impact that certain aspects of my original article had. I interviewed Louie Coghlan O'Brien in the ealy 1990s, and based on this, used the phrase 'rumours of a broken love affair' between Molony and Bulmer Hobson. It was not as nuanced as it could have been and has spawned some interesting side narratives.[8] Hopefully the space afforded to the original interview will clarify some of this, while leaving the integrity of Molony's own understanding as relayed to me by Coghlan O'Brien.

The second is in relation to her drinking, which was mentioned by many who knew her. The intelligence records from the Emergency, which are now in the public domain, are stark and leave no room for question about the impact that this had on her life. Certainly in the 1940s it was as catastrophic for her work as it was for her health. The toll that years of revolution, of civil war, of poverty and of defensive battles in a conservative climate took on many of her generation also provides a certain context for this and has been documented by Foster, MacGarry and others.[9]

Finally, my original evidence for the partnership between Molony and Eveleen O'Brien was based on several pieces of information. These included the fact that they shared a home for over twenty-five years, that O'Brien was both executor and sole beneficiary of Molony's will, and an interview with Finian Czira, son of her lifelong friend, Sidney Gifford Czira. Mary Elliot's research and intelligence records provide deeper evidence of a shared life.[10] The affection between them was evident when Molony submitted her rewritten witness statement to the Bureau of Military History. She told Jane Kissane, the investigating officer, that O'Brien had been teasing her about her reticence to tell her story and quoted her as saying,

> It is Miss Kissane who ought to get a special medal as decoration for dragging information out of a lot of unwilling clams like you all. I doubt if any of you were out in the rebellion at all.[11]

It also spoke to the fact that Molony and her friends tended to downplay their contributions.

Finally two quotes guided this full-length biography as they did my early research. The first was a comment made by Francis Stuart, that Molony was a 'practical not an abstract politician'[12] and the second was her own phrase, 'I was always on the side of the underdog'.[13]

SOURCES

1   Accession Number 4660 (uncatalogued, formerly Hugh O'Connor private collection), National Library of Ireland. Hereafter Hugh O'Connor Collection, NLI.

2   Maura Breslin, 'Notes towards a History', File 25, IWWU Archive, Irish Labour History Archive. Hereafter IWWUA, ILHA.

3   For example her birth date was given as 1884 in Henry
        Boylan's *Dictionary of Irish Biography* (Dublin, Gill and
        Macmillan, 1988).

4   Details of these appear throughout the notes. See also, Nell
        Regan, 'Helena Molony: The Formative Years', BA in Pure
        History dissertation, Faculty of Arts, UCD, May 1991.

5   Penny Duggan, *Helena Molony: Actress, Feminist, Nationalist,
        Socialist and Trade Unionist.* Working Paper No 14 (Amsterdam,
        International Institute for Research and Education, 1990).

6   Nell Regan, 'A tigress in kitten's fur', *The Irish Times*, 23 May
        2013; Nell Regan, 'Striking Bravery: Women and the Lockout',
        The Irish Times, 11 September 2014.

7   See in particular Senia Pašeta, *Irish Nationalist Women, 1900–
        1918* (Cambridge, Cambridge University Press, 2013) and Lucy
        McDiarmid, *At Home in the Revolution* (Dublin, RIA, 2015).

8   Nell Regan, 'Helena Molony', in Mary Cullen and Maria
        Luddy (eds), *Female Activists: Irish Women and Change* (Dublin,
        Woodfield Press, 2001), pp 141–168.

9   Roy Foster, *Vivid Faces: The Revolutionary Generation in Ireland,
        1890–1923* (London, Penguin, 2014); Fearghal McGarry, *The
        Abbey Rebels of 1916: A Lost Revolution* (Dublin, Gill and
        Macmillan, 2015).

10   Mary Elliott, 'Inheriting New Opportunities: Eveleen O'Brien
        (1901–1981)', MA in Women's Studies Thesis, Faculty of Arts,
        University College, Dublin, August 2003. See also Katherine
        O'Donnell, 'Lesbianism', in Brian Lalor (ed.), *The Encyclopedia
        of Ireland* (Dublin, Gill and Macmillan, 2003), p. 624 and
        McGarry, *Abbey Rebels*, p. 260 for the historiographical debates
        that followed the publication of the first biographies of
        Molony, Kathleen Lynn and others.

11   Helena Molony to Jane Kissane, 29 September 1949, Bureau of
        Military History, quoted in McGarry, *Abbey Rebels*, p. 328.

12   Francis Stuart, interview with author, 1991.

13   R.M. Fox, *Rebel Irishwomen* (Dublin, Progress House, 1967), p.
        67.

Beginnings

Little is known about Helena Molony's early life which is why this biography opens in the summer of 1903 when she first saw Maud Gonne MacBride speak. However, all surviving accounts indicate that her childhood was not a happy one. Helena Mary Moloney [sic] was born on 15 January 1883 to Catherine and Michael Moloney of Coles Lane, off Henry Street, Dublin. Although various spellings of her surname are used in different sources, and the Moloney version was recorded on her birth certificate, 'Molony' was the spelling that she herself used throughout her life. In 1934 she sternly reprimanded Seán Ó Faoláin for getting her name wrong and in correspondence she spelt MOLONY out in capitals to avoid further confusion. It is also the version used in official documents, including her death certificate.[1]

The family moved to Rathgar when Molony was two years of age and her only sibling, an older brother Frank, was about seven. The Molony's retained a grocer's shop on Coles Lane but moved again soon after. Molony was raised a Catholic and intelligence records noted that her father had been a publican who ran a business at Georges Quay.[2] Judging by her early writing, it was likely that she received a secondary school education.

In 1911 Rosamond Jacob met Molony, then a 28-year-old activist and recorded in her diary that she,

> told me a lot about her early life, how her mother died when she was young and her father when she was six and she and her brother were brought up by an odious drinking stepmother.[3]

Other friends recalled similar stories and Máire Comerford noted that Molony's father was also an alcoholic and apparently used to give her drink as a baby.[4]

Molony was very close to her brother Frank and in 1899 they left their stepmother and 'ran away when he was 21 and she was 16 and the next year he married'.[5] Molony lived with her brother and sister-in-law on Sherrard Street until the couple emigrated to America sometime around 1910. They remained active in Irish-American circles and she must have stayed in close contact, as Finian Czira recalled that Frank's death, possibly in the early 1960s, 'devastated her'.[6] There is also one remaining piece of correspondence to a cousin Madge in May 1916, but aside from this it seems references to her family do not survive.[7] Molony was in receipt of a small bequest from her mother's estate in her twenties but apart from this, she lived on what she earned as an actor and a trade union official.

SOURCES

1   See also Nell Regan, *Female Activists: Irish Women and Change* (Dublin, Woodfield Press, 2001). Helena Molony, Bureau of Military History Witness Statement 391; Hereafter Helena Molony: BMH 391.

2   1918 intelligence record PRO, reproduced in MacGarry, *Abbey Rebels*, p. 250.

3   Rosamond Jacob Diary (hereafter RJD), 20 May 1911, MS 32582, NLI.

4   Margaret Ward, 6 September 1992, letter to author.
5   RJD, 2 August 1911.
6   Finian Czira, interview with author, 1992. The first name of Molony's sister-in-law remains a mystery.
7   Helena Molony correspondence to her cousin Madge, June 1916, MS 49163, NLI.

RADICAL
1903–1911

I was a young girl dreaming of Ireland, when I saw and heard
Maud Gonne ... one evening in 1903 ... To me she epitomised
Ireland – the Ireland of the poets and dreamers. She gathered
all this up and made it real for me. She electrified me and
filled me with some of her spirit ... She made me want to
help.[1]

Helena Molony's long life of activism began that same day.
The twenty-year-old was inspired by the charismatic
nationalist Maud Gonne MacBride, who spoke outside
Dublin's Custom House in protest at the royal visit of
Edward VII. Molony walked home to Sherrard Street,
where she lived with her brother Frank and his wife. It
was Frank whom she 'pestered about politics' and one
night he encouraged her to go and join Gonne MacBride's
organisation for women, Inghinidhe na hÉireann
(Daughters of Ireland).[2] She set off in the morning but
found the Inghinidhe offices at 106 Brunswick Street (now
Pearse Street) locked. A note was pinned to the closed
door directing members to Gonne MacBride's home in

Rathgar. Molony duly arrived and found the 'Battle of Coulson Avenue' underway.

That July Dublin was festooned with Union Jacks to mark the royal visit and Gonne MacBride had hung a black petticoat from her upstairs window, ostensibly to mourn the death of Pope Leo XIII. The police arrived to remove it, but were prevented by the large number of Inghinidhe na hÉireann members and their supporters, including the awed, but determined, Molony. She described to a journalist how, when asked if she was a member, 'I answered boldly: "Yes!" I could not bring myself to deny it, though I had not yet joined. I felt I was claiming too great an honour'.[3]

After this, her 'baptism of fire' as she called it, Molony threw herself into the Inghinidhe.[4] For the next eight years, her life revolved around its activities, as she was immersed in the vibrant cultural and political life of Dublin. She rapidly became a leading member and developed the radical politics, personal outlook and modus operandi that would be the hallmarks of her life's work and activism.[5] Maud Gonne MacBride later described her as, 'the most gallant and bravest of my Inghinidhe girls'.[6] The two women became lifelong friends and Molony described the organisation as the place 'where I was fostered'.[7] She adopted the Irish name 'Emer', which she kept among this circle for the rest of her life.

Inghinidhe na hÉireann was, says historian Senia Pašeta, one of the most important political organisations founded in early twentieth century Ireland.[8] They were formed in 1900 by Maud Gonne and 28 other women, including Jennie Wyse Power, Máire Nic Shiubhlaigh, Maire Quinn, Sara Allgood and Ella Young, partly as a response to their exclusion from existing cultural nationalist organisations. The Inghinidhe members were drawn from a new generation of young, working women who had scant regard for parliamentary Home Rule politics and were a central part of the growing movement of cultural nationalism. As Nic Shiubhlaigh recalled, it was the only organisation 'of its kind to offer young women an opportunity of taking part in national work' and had 'a wide following amongst young girls all over the city'.[9]

Inghinidhe na hÉireann members. President Maud Gonne MacBride is seated behind a banner wearing a hat. It has been suggested that Molony is to her left
courtesy Kilmainham Gaol Museum

When Molony joined in 1903, the Inghinidhe were working to 'combat in every way English influence, which is doing so much injury to the artistic taste and refinement of the Irish people'.[10] They dropped what Molony termed the 'seonín' fashion of using Miss before their names and sought to popularise Irish names.[11] Their activities included the support of Irish manufacturers, classes in

Gaelic language, history and culture for children and adults, monthly ceilis, *tableaux vivants* and theatrical productions as well as a vigorous anti-enlisting campaign.

Many of their activities challenged the limited roles assigned to women. Molony was keenly aware and proud of this. Writing later, she pointed out that, 'At that time the military [sic] "suffragette" movement had not been heard of and women and girls were still living in a semi-sheltered Victorianism'.[12] The tactics they employed, in particular for their anti-enlisting campaign, were very public and often risky, making them the subject of considerable controversy. Leaflets were handed out to young women 'walking' with British soldiers on Sackville Street (now O'Connell Street). Molony described a typical evening,

> A group of us would set out about eight o'clock in the evening and start from the Rotunda Hospital, walking rapidly as far as the Bank of Ireland. We walked in twos, some twenty or thirty yards apart, and managed to 'paper' the whole promenade, before these young people had time to grasp the contents of their hand-bill ... The soldiers when they became aware of this campaign against them, were, of course offensive and threatening. The leaflets had to be concealed in hand-bags or hand-muffs and delivered surreptitiously ... Any hesitation or delay would lead to mobbing [but] we managed to avoid any real unpleasantness.[13]

They did however have a narrow escape on one occasion when,

> Misses E. O'Farrell and Sighle Grenan and myself were spotted by the police. We took to our heels, and were chased through Henry St., Mary St. and right up to the Markets in Capel Street. We got away clear, as we were young and swift ...[14]

She concluded by saying that, even more than the police, they feared the soldiers, who had canes. Their campaign attracted media attention and a resulting, prolonged newspaper controversy ... [that] showered us with abuse and called us all sorts of names and we individually got a constant supply of anonymous letters of the foulest nature. It was not pleasant but it did raise a volume of opinion and we had our defenders too.[15]

ınʒınıðe na héıReann.

IRISH GIRLS!

Ireland has need of the loving service of all her children. Irishwomen do not sufficiently realize the power they have to help or hinder the cause of Ireland's freedom.

If they did we should not see the sad sight of Irish girls walking through the streets with men wearing the uniform of Ireland's oppressor.

No man can serve two masters; no man can honestly serve Ireland and serve England. The Irishman who has chosen to wear the English uniform has chosen to serve the enemy of Ireland,

Anti-Enlistment leaflet, Inghinidhe na hÉireann

Arthur Griffith was one of those who disapproved of their activity and his sister resigned from the Inghinidhe after she had received such a letter. In later years Molony would reflect on the scope to operate that the Inghinidhe gave its members,

> It was a lucky thing that we had our own organisation, because we were independent and not a branch of anything. We were able to do what we liked with the result that we did things in advance of other movements.[16]

Molony also claimed that, 'Anything of an active nature from 1900 to 1914 – those quiet years – was done, not by the IRB, but by the Inghinidhe na hÉireann'.[17] It was, perhaps, not that much of an exaggeration.

Molony's own 'baptism of fire' on Coulson Avenue contained all the elements that would be characteristic of her activities. Here was a form of public protest that was risky and theatrical, a form of direct and practical action.

Here were the tight, supportive networks of female activists and friends, networks that would sustain her throughout her life. Here was the 'making it real', the 'wanting to help' as she began to develop a radical vision of Ireland with gender and social equality at its heart. Here too was the emphasis on realising a poetic vision in concrete terms. All of these elements introduced Molony to, and informed her life's work as a radical nationalist, a 1916 combatant, a publicist, trade unionist and left republican. In fact a good portion of the 'anything of an active nature' undertaken by the Inghinidhe was initiated by Molony herself. It was another feature of her later career that while an organisation radicalised her, she also radicalised it.

Drama was at the heart of the Inghinidhe's activities as well as being central to their modus operandi, and unsurprisingly, the seeds of her acting career were laid here. *Tableau vivants*, often in open spaces around the city and even on Ireland's Eye, as well as lantern shows and productions of plays were staged, both as fundraisers and as vehicles for propaganda. Just before Molony joined, the Inghinidhe played a central role in the formation of what would become the National Theatre. Under their auspices, the Fay brothers produced and trained Irish actors. This was an innovation in itself and many of the women were Inghinidhe members. It is likely that the Inghinidhe were responsible for one of the most pivotal moments in Irish theatre which took place in April 1902, when two new plays, *Deirdre* by George Russell and W.B. Yeats' *Cathleen Ní Houlihan,* were premiered. The Inghinidhe banner hung beside the stage and although the performance was followed by splits and contested versions as to its genesis, their members were central to the resulting development, the Irish National Theatre Society.[18]

Molony received her first taste for theatre from the

Inghinidhe acting classes run by Dudley Digges and perhaps aptly, her first role was in a production of *Cathleen Ní Houlihan,* also directed by Digges, in which she was cast as Delia Cahill. In the debates about art and nation that followed, Molony and her colleagues were clear that the primary role of theatre was to raise national consciousness.

Molony rapidly became central to the organisation. She was elected Honorary Secretary of the Inghinidhe in 1904 when Maire Quinn resigned her position and left for the US, with her new husband Dudley Digges and the National Players. Soon after, Gonne MacBride moved more permanently to Paris. In her absence Molony became largely responsible for the running of Inghinidhe na hÉireann. She dispatched weekly reports and visited Paris regularly to keep Gonne MacBride up to date on their activities. A bitter separation and custody dispute between the Inghinidhe President and her estranged husband Major John MacBride caused huge controversy in nationalist circles as both were major figures. The Inghinidhe stood by their leader and resolved not to speak of it, in public at any rate. Molony explained that they had decided 'there will be no back biting; it is not worthy of Irishwomen; we will talk about neither', but her assessment was that the case had 'horrible repercussions on Ireland'.[19] Gonne MacBride did not return to Ireland full time until 1918 and never regained the same public standing after this.

After she had joined the Inghinidhe, Molony discovered that her brother Frank was in fact involved with the IRB. The Molony home in Sherrard Street became an informal gathering place for friends and like-minded contemporaries. 'Every Sunday evening we had a few friends in. A great deal of things were hatched there – not official at all'.[20] These things would go on to have significant national impact as well as personal implications for Molony. The personal and political really were one at this stage. However, this stable, supportive home life was not to last.

The Inghinidhe moved from their Brunswick Street office to extended premises on North Great George's Street. They rented a whole house and Molony recalled that Gonne MacBride paid the rent for the first year, but after that revenue was generated by sub-letting rooms to societies such as the Gaelic League. They increased the number of classes for children and, as was consistent with the Inghinidhe approach, Molony framed the work that they undertook with children in the broader context of anti-recruiting and the development of Irish national spirit,

> This extra room gave us more scope for our work with the children. We had more classes and oftener … [for the] work of teaching children … from [the] poorest quarters of the city where, at that time the British army got its most valuable recruits.[21]

Molony continued to use inventive publicity methods for the anti-enlistment campaign. Sidney Gifford, a leading member of the Inghinidhe from 1908 and lifelong friend of Molony, who wrote under the pseudonym 'John Brennan', recalled one such occasion. In a quiet suburb Molony was approached by a police sergeant, concerned about the posters appearing on lampposts,

> Helena, pretending to sympathise with his difficulties, clapped him on the back as she was leaving him, at the same time sticking on a notice which appealed to young Irishmen not to join the British Armed Forces or Police. On another occasion she saw Lord Aberdeen's car – he was Lord Lieutenant at the time – standing outside a shop in Grafton St. and she placarded it with the same notices, so that the car, covered with the placards, was going round Dublin all day.[22]

Amidst the flamboyant and sometimes comedic activities of those early years, Molony developed as an effective organiser and an astute tactician. Her ingenuity was evident during a buy Irish campaign conducted by the Inghinidhe. Campaigners were encouraging shops to stock Irish-made items, by requesting them when shopping but,

> Helena Molony said one day that we were going the wrong way about this whole thing ... and suggested this new approach. We were to go into the shop and ask for some article we knew was manufactured in Ireland, without specifying that it was to be Irish, allow the assistant to take down a large number of specimens and then, having ascertained that they were not Irish, say 'Have you not the Irish made one', and if they had not, say 'I only buy the Irish manufactured article' and walk out.[23]

Apparently the new approach was much more successful and Irish-made goods were increasingly stocked. It was made clear to the traders just how much purchasing power women had. Gifford also described how the young women were all very fond of smoking and their favoured method of transport was by bicycle. She christened Dublin a 'city of wobbling wheels'.[24]

The Inghinidhe were viewed with a mixture of affection and respect by many of their nationalist colleagues. They were also derided and Molony remembered that they were dismissed as 'Maud Gonne's unwashed'.[25] Although Gonne MacBride was still the presiding spirit of the organisation, directing operations from France and funding both activities and premises, she was fortunate to have a group of dynamic women in the organisation who initiated and carried on the work.[26] Molony was one of the most central of these.

BEAN NA HÉIREANN

> ... we decided to start a woman's journal. I think we Irish women, in common with the women of the rest of the civilized world, felt that the time had come when the point of view of women on the many aspects of Social and National life, had to be expressed definitely.[27]

First *Bean na hÉireann* header
courtesy Kilmainham Gaol Museum

Molony's most significant venture in these years was her editorship of *Bean na hÉireann,* Inghinidhe's monthly journal. She ran the paper on a shoestring between 1908 and 1911 and it put her at the forefront of the radical nationalist movement and at the centre of debates about the role of women in Irish society. The conversations and arguments that went on in the Inghinidhe offices and the Molony's sitting room, in coffee shops, meeting halls and at theatre performances all over the city, were now articulated in print.

Molony wanted the journal to be 'a woman's paper, advocating militancy, separatism and feminism'.[28] It was also established to counteract Arthur Griffith's *Sinn Féin* newspaper which she said, 'started as a physical force separatist journal but had gradually changed its policy to one of reactionary social and dual-kingdom ideas'.[29] On these grounds Molony and several other Inghinidhe women had refused to join Sinn Féin, the organisation founded by Griffith. She was opposed to the policy of passive resistance and found their policies, 'dull and a little bit vulgar'.[30]

Friends and supporters were asked to subscribe a shilling a month to fund *Bean na hÉireann* in an early form of crowdfunding. Bulmer Hobson suggested this, probably at one of the Sunday night gatherings at the Molony's house, as he had previously run a paper in Belfast in this way. Molony ran with it and set to work. On 9 September 1908, Liam de Róiste of The Cork Celtic Literary Society recorded that 'Helena Molony, Hon. Secretary of Inghinidhe na hÉireann in Dublin writes to say the Inghinidhe are starting an Irish nationalist woman's paper. She asks help in pushing it'.[31] With enough funding in place to pay for printing (contributors would be unpaid), she and members of the Inghinidhe began to make plans for the launch of *Bean na hÉireann*. Mrs N.F. Dryhurst, a Dublin-born, London-based journalist and activist, suggested that they form an editorial committee.[32]

The first meeting of the editorial committee was the occasion of both Sidney Gifford and Constance Markievicz's introduction to the Inghinidhe and the start of two close friendships and working relationships for Molony. It was Molony who had spotted Markievicz as a potential recruit, when she saw her at a Gaelic League meeting. She invited her to the editorial meeting at North Great George's Street. Markievicz arrived straight from a Dublin Castle function, dressed in a ball gown. She received a cool reception from the serious group of young women dressed in Irish tweed. Markievicz told Molony that it was 'the first time she had not been kowtowed to and that this had persuaded her to join them'.[33] Molony later said that she became 'more or less political mentor to the Countess at that time. She was groping at first ...' Under Molony's tutelage, and through her involvement with the Inghinidhe, Markievicz rapidly dispensed with any vestiges of a 'sentimental dreamy love for Ireland', that Molony disapprovingly identified in her sister, Eva Gore-Booth.[34]

Bean na hÉireann first appeared in November 1908 but immediately after Dryhurst returned to London and

Molony took over as editor for the remainder of its two and a half year existence. She was not initially happy about this,

> I was pitchforked into the Editorship, much against my will as I had no experience and no desire for such a responsible post ... I remember sitting up the whole of Christmas night writing a leading article.[35]

Molony persevered and *Bean na hÉireann* was an eclectic and fascinating mixture. Political articles dealt with a wide range of national and international issues. There were notes on the activities of the Inghinidhe and other nationalist organisations; gardening, cooking, fashion and theatre columns; as well as short stories and poems written for the paper by leading writers of the day who included George Russell (AE), James Stephens, Susan Mitchell, Patrick Pearse and Joseph Mary Plunkett. Molony's own favourite contribution was Stephens' poem, 'The Red Haired Man's Wife', which she described as 'perhaps the most complete expression of feminism in poetry ... nearly all of it applying to the Nation as well',

> I am separate still,
> I am I and not you,
> And my mind and my will,
> As in secret they grew,
> Still are secret, unreached and untouched,
> And not subject to you.[36]

The paper was the epitome of the Irish-Ireland movement. It had a Celtic masthead designed by Constance Markievicz and ran advertisements for 'Irish Fern costume tweeds, available in smart colours' as well as for St Enda's school run by Patrick Pearse.[37] Gifford recalled the dilemma they found themselves over a serialised story by Katharine Tynan. The story, a romance set in 1798, ran for several months but it came to the editor episode by episode. Confident that the hero, a wounded insurgent, would recover and marry the rebel heroine, the editor and her committee were horrified to receive a last instalment in which he died. Worse still,

> A gallant (but misguided) English officer led the blushing rebel maid to the altar. This was a bomb-shell dropped on *Bean na hÉireann*. We spent hours arguing over a way out of the difficulty.[38]

Their solution was to rewrite the last chapter, so that the miraculously-recovered insurgent claimed back his bride. History does not reveal what the author thought of the altered ending.

Bean na hÉireann soon became the primary (and only) paper for militant nationalists, male and female. Despite a small circulation, it reached as far afield as England, France and America giving the Inghinidhe and Molony an important voice in the nationalist and women's movement. Gifford claimed that friendly newsagents would say, '*Bean na hÉireann*? That's the women's paper that all the young men buy'.[39]

THE EVER BRIGHT BURNING FIRE[40]

Bean na hÉireann editorials are the only significant body of Molony's writing (published or private) extant from the pre-independence period. Her thought developed over the next two and a half years. Of particular significance is the early date at which she articulated a separatist physical force position, as well as debates which she had with the suffragists and her growing interest in and identification with the labour movement.

Her impatience with her nationalist contemporaries and her desire for action were palpable. She wrestled with issues of the day, nationalist politics and the emerging women's and labour movements. Nationalism informed her view on these as it did on most issues. She argued that the study of Irish, economics and history were all useless,

VOL. I. No. 3.   €ánáιn — JANUARY, 1909.   PRICE—ONE PENNY.

MADE IN IRELAND.

THE KILKENNY WOODWORKERS

MANUFACTURERS OF

Bedroom Suites,
    Diningroom Chairs,
Chesterfield Couches,
Comfortable Easy Chairs,
  In many shapes and sizes.
Writing Tables,
    Roll Top Desks,
    Bookcases,
    AND
Cabinet Making in all
    Departments.

NEW DEPARTMENT—
BASKET AND WICKER WORK,
PERAMBULATORS.

SHOWROOMS—
**6, 7 & 9 Nassau St.,
DUBLIN.**

Cuala Industries
Churchtown,
Dundrum,
Co. Dublin.

(12 minutes walk from Dundrum Station, 20 under in from Nassau Tram.)

Workrooms open to Visitors any day from 10 to 5 o'clock. Saturdays close at 12.

Embroidery - - LILY YEATS
Hand Press - ELIZABETH C. YEATS

Artistic Embroideries, Embroidery for Dresses, Collars, &c., Church Vestments, Banners.

MAUNSEL'S NEW BOOKS.

CONTEMPORARY IRELAND, a translation of M. L. Paul-Dubois' great book, with an Introduction by T. M. Kettle, M.P. Demy 8vo, 456 and XXX pages, cloth, gilt. 7s. 6d. net.

BALLYGULLION. By Lynn Doyle. Crown 8vo, cloth, gilt, 6s. A humorous novel of North of Ireland life.

A PRISONER OF HIS WORD. By Louie Bennett. A new novel of '98. Crown 8vo, cloth, gilt, 6s.

SONGS OF ORIEL. A book of patriotic poems. By Shane Leslie. 1s. net.

**MAUNSEL & CO., Ltd.,
96 Middle Abbey Street, Dublin.**

To Our Sisters.

The new year is the time for good resolutions and editorial sermons, and a good many pious sentiments and meaningless platitudes are preached from editorial arm chairs at this season. The Bean na h-Eireann does not like sermons. We believe there is in Ireland too much preaching and too little practice. The chief fault we find with men is that they talk very big and do very little, and we would like to foster amongst Irishwomen a desire to work, rather than talk about it in the columns of newspapers.

But because we are at the beginning of another year, it is well that we should consider what opportunities the coming year will afford us, and how we can make use of them for the **advancement of Ireland.**

In the beginning some of our critics—who were women, we are glad to say—complained that we had not taken a brave enough position. Well, the Bean na h-Eireann wants to make in this first month of the new year a **Proclamation,** that she never intends to shirk any difficult problem, or public issue, and will always be at least brave enough to speak on the **side of Ireland and Ireland's Women** against the whole world, if need be. We are glad to know such fearless Irishwomen still exist, small though their numbers be in proportion to the great unthinking majority. Our *raison d'être* is to awaken Irishwomen to their responsibilities and long neglected duties. An article by Larguenona appearing in this issue deals exhaustively with this subject. There is little use in as women starting to abuse men and their methods of thought and action. We must remember the humiliating fact that they are largely what their women-folk have made them. Neither must we waste time bewailing our past disabilities. We must set about raising the present position of women in the social and political life of the country, and we must labour to make their present environment compatible with their moral and intellectual advancement, which incidentally means the development of the nation and of the race. Our desire to have a voice in directing the affairs of Ireland is not based on the **failure of men** to do so properly, but is the inherent right of women as loyal citizens and intelligent human souls. It is not our intention to countenance any sex antagonism between Irish women and Irish men. There are too few Irish hearts aflame with pure and **conscious love** of Mother Eire to have them divided by such an unnatural barrier; but we think that men would be the better for a little of women's unselfishness and spirituality, and we look for the advent of women into public life for a loftier idealism

and a purer atmosphere. We, Irishwomen, must learn to throw off our present diffidence, and assume our natural position in Irish life, and men will soon have to frankly admit that it is only by working hand in hand that we can hope to **make Ireland free.**

A great many, if not all, the various pressing social problems could be much more effectively dealt with by women than by men. The squalor and misery of the towns, with the poverty and dulness of the rural parts of Ireland, surely need some attention, and we believe women could relieve much of this distressing state of affairs without legislation or any kind of outside help. The grinding poverty of the rural population, and the town-dwellers alike, which is the result of lack of constant employment, superinduces drink with all its attendant horrors. To relieve unemployment every woman has in her own hands one simple and swift remedy, the **support of Irish manufacture.** We cannot do better than go a step further and reiterate the advice given in our first number: to give preference to those Irish firms who pay their workers honestly for their labour and give them opportunities to live decent healthy lives. Much might be said of the disgraceful conditions under which women work, and we hope to deal with this matter in the near future. If well-to-do Irishwomen interested themselves a little more in their less fortunate sisters, we believe women workers would have many of their grievances redressed. There are many other questions that could be peacefully settled if women only took some real interest in their own country.

In this Number articles appear in Irish and English by Caoilte na Gabana and Larguenona, each treating this all-important subject of women's place in society from slightly different standpoints. Both writers are well-known to Irish-Irelanders. We hope our readers will take their message seriously to heart, and make it the foundation of a new year resolution—unique in this respect that it shall be **faithfully kept.**

The most pleasing memory of the old year was the Christmas Aonac, held in the Rotunda Buildings, Dublin. Owing to its great success we understand the Aonac of 1909 will be on a much larger scale. It will soon be looked forward to by Dubliners as the event of the winter. The Samain Festival, which, up to a few years ago, was such a pleasant busy week, has unhappily been allowed to die out; we hope to see it revived again in all its glory, and we hope the Christmas Aonac will grow until it becomes as important to the trade of Ireland as its great prototype of Leipsic is to that of Germany, and that it will rival the splendour of its forerunners, the great gatherings at Tara and Loc Garmain.

If there is not behind the great driving force, the ever bright burning fire that is the National Faith, love of Ireland and of everything great and small that belongs to Ireland because it belongs to Ireland and for no other reason.[41]

Molony defined the Inghinidhe's first principle as 'the re-establishment of the complete independence of Ireland'.[42] This was to be achieved by fostering a sense of national pride through cultural activities, propaganda and by force of arms if necessary. Other accounts suggest that the rather more vague formula, 'accept the principal of independent nationality for Ireland' was used initially.[43] This highlights Molony's pivotal influence, both on the organisation and in the subsequent writing of its history. Through her editorship of the paper and later statements for the Bureau of Military History, she helped formulate its policy and its legacy.[44]

Her editorials were designed to inspire Irish women to involve themselves in the nationalist cause and encourage armed resistance to British rule. In a fiery start to 1909, Molony wrote that,

The *Bean na hÉireann* does not believe in sermons. We believe in Ireland there is too much preaching and too little practice. The chief fault we find with men is that they talk very big and do very little and we would like to foster among Irish women a desire to work rather than talk about it in the columns of newspapers.[45]

That year Molony was involved in the establishment of Fianna Éireann, a new venture which would put some of this talk into practice. She recalled that the Inghinidhe 'had abandoned the boy's classes. We found them hard to manage. We were hard pressed to cope with everything and we let the boys' classes go'.[46] However, Markievicz wanted to set up something specifically for boys as working with girls frustrated her. Molony remembered her saying 'They always confuse me – those dreadful girls'.[47] At the Sunday evening gatherings at the Molonys, she, Markievicz and Bulmer Hobson discussed and planned a new national boy scouts' movement, initially called the Red Branch Knights.[48] Hobson had tried such a venture previously in Belfast and Markievicz enthusiastically took up the idea announcing 'Let us begin'.[49] She approached a local school and rented a hall on Camden Street. In the July 1909 edition of *Bean na hÉireann*, Molony announced that the first branch of the National Boy Scouts had been formed. They were to be the first step towards the formation of an Irish army and the nationalist equivalent of the Baden Powell scouts, which was a recruiting ground for the British army. Molony was on the committee and Markievicz taught Molony how to shoot. The two women brought recruits on camping trips to Markievicz's rented cottage in Sandyford where the countryside was 'really wild'. Molony recalled, 'I helped to the extent of making jam sandwiches, and helped to feed the youngsters who forgot their lunch'.[50] She also mentioned that Seán McGarry gave a good deal of help, but that he was not as encouraging about the next venture that Markievicz, Molony and Hobson embarked upon. Molony reported monthly on the activities of Fianna Éireann (as they were now called) and on the formation of new branches all over Dublin and the rest of the country. Many of their recruits went on to join the Irish Volunteers and fought in the 1916 Rising.

Things were about to change in Molony's personal life as her brother Frank and his wife made plans to move to America. Molony's almost full-time work for the Inghinidhe was largely unpaid and she lived on a bequest of £30 a year from her mother. Molony's role in the Inghinidhe was so crucial to the organisation, that Gonne MacBride repeatedly used her influence to secure employment for her, so she could remain in Ireland and carry on this important, unpaid work.

In June 1909, a part-time but salaried position of secretary at the United Arts Club came up. Gonne

MacBride wrote to W.B. Yeats and asked him to use his influence on behalf of,

> Miss Moloney [sic] the editoress of *Bean na hÉireann* for it ... this would make it possible for her to live in Ireland, and I *want her there very much.* She is a very intelligent girl, will scrupulously do any work she undertakes. Please do this for me.[51]

Meanwhile, Molony's editorials were urging nationalists to take note of international developments. For several months Molony wrote about the case of Madar Lal Dinghra, the Indian nationalist condemned to death for the assassination of Sir Curzon Wylie in July 1909. Molony refused to enter into a debate about the morality of political assassination, but wrote that the Irish, instead of condemning him ought to 'aspire to the honour of laying down their lives for the cause of their country'.[52] When sentenced, Lal Dhingra had declared 'I am proud to lay down my life for my country' and the Inghinidhe machine swung into action.

> We got posters printed immediately, and fly-posted through the City, stating, 'Ireland honours Madar Lal Dhingra, who was proud to lay down his life for his country.' There was nothing insular about Inghinidhe's political outlook. We reproduced this poster in *Bean na hÉireann,* and it resulted in the loss of some advertisements and subscriptions.[53]

In her New Year editorial for 1910 she expressed disappointment that no steps had been taken to organise armed resistance to British rule as tensions between Britain and Germany increased. The formation of the Fianna was the only hopeful sign. She wrote that,

> There are many who constantly state that they are working to free Ireland. Now, we would like to ask them a straight question. Do they mean what they say, or do they not mean what they say? If the German invasion so dreaded by England actually took place, have we anything to offer to Germany in return for her help? Have we one thousand trained men who can shoot straight or walk thirty miles? At any moment

England may be in difficulties, and is Ireland making any attempt to be ready to seize her opportunity? If the men mean what they say let them act. If not let them give up talking of still holding the principles of Tone and Emmet.[54]

Molony concluded that there was little hope of change until, 'women come into the nationalist movement … and imbue with fresh enthusiasm and vigour the tired warriors who will be glad to share some of the fighting at least with their women folk'.[55]

THE FEMINIST CAUSE IN IRELAND IS BEST SERVED BY IGNORING ENGLAND[56]

Molony and the women of Inghinidhe na hÉireann had little patience with those who sought to deny women equality. Their activities were radical and on the tenth anniversary of its founding, she wrote that the Inghinidhe's early work had 'exploded for ever that silly "women's sphere" idea'.[57] Much of that work focused on the education and welfare of children but she differentiated between the,

'rámeis' of the early Victorian male mind which prates much of the sphere of women, the influence of the mother etc. etc. when he wants to oppose her claim to equal civic rights … [and] the undeniable fact that women have the children in their own hands, to mould their minds as they will.[58]

She wrote that,

our desire to have a voice in directing affairs of Ireland … is not based on men's failure to do so but is the inherent right of women as loyal citizens and intelligent human souls.[59]

Given that Molony asserted that the feminist cause was in fact part of the nationalist cause, she was rapidly involved in disagreement with suffragists.[60] The debate between suffragists sympathetic to nationalism and women involved in the nationalist cause was first articulated in the pages of *Bean na hÉireann*. In 1908 a militant suffrage society was founded in Dublin. The Irish Women's Franchise League (IWFL), politically non-aligned but nationalist in sympathy, took issue with Molony's stance. In her third editorial, Molony responded to 'some of our critics who are women we are glad to say, [who] complained that we had not taken a brave enough position ... [on suffrage]', and said that, '*Bean na hÉireann* ... will always be at least brave enough to speak on the side of Ireland and Ireland's women against the whole world if need be'.[61]

Bean na hÉireann had suggested it should be possible to elect a woman to the civic chair of Dublin. Hanna Sheehy Skeffington, leading member of the IWFL, wrote in to point out that women were prohibited from holding this office and that this could not change until there was a widespread suffrage movement in Ireland. Molony replied that she did not think that winning the Irish public to female suffrage would be a 'colossal' task and if the case were put,

> logically and forcibly before our country men, their love of freedom and sense of justice would compel them to give to women a voice and a place in the government of their common country.[62]

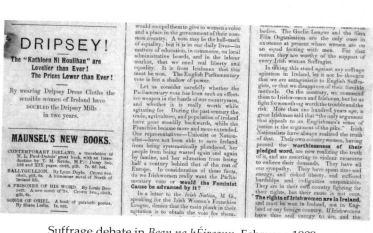

Suffrage debate in *Bean na hÉireann*, February 1909, with editorial by Helena Molony
courtesy Kilmainham Gaol Museum

ɠean na h-ɠipeann

(THE WOMAN OF IRELAND)

VOL. I. No. 4.   Feadra — FEBRUARY, 1909.   PRICE—ONE PENNY.

Editorial Notes.

ALAS, our statements on Women's Suffrage have got us into serious trouble. We carelessly stated in our December issue that there was nothing illegal in electing a woman to the Civic Chair of Dublin. This, it seems, is not so. Mrs. Sheehy-Skeffington has kindly written to us, pointing out our mistake. Such an election would be against the English Law, and so we cry *peccavi* to those more learned in it than ourselves. We ought to have remembered that when England happens to pass a really good law, it seldom applies to Ireland. We still maintain that it would be an excellent propagandist policy for a woman to stand for election to the Municipal Council. If the Town Clerk could be induced to accept her nomination, and the Corporation and the ratepayers were prepared to stand by him, we fail to see how the illegality would matter. **When a law is obviously unjust and iniquitous it should be unhesitatingly broken or ignored** by all right-thinking people. The task of winning over the Irish public and the members of our elected bodies to the cause of Woman Suffrage does not appear to be a colossal one. We feel sure that if the case were put logically and forcibly before our countrymen their love of freedom and sense of justice would compel them to give to women a voice and a place in the government of their common country. A vote may be the hall-mark of equality, but it is in our daily lives—in matters of education, in commerce, on local administrative boards, and in the labour market, that we need real liberty and equality. It is from Irishmen that this must be won. The English Parliamentary vote is but a shadow of power.

Let us consider carefully whether the Parliamentary vote has been such an effective weapon in the hands of our countrymen, and whether it is really worth while agitating for. During the past century the trade, agriculture, and population of Ireland have gone steadily backwards, while the Franchise became more and more extended. Our representatives—Unionist or Nationalist—have not been able to save Ireland from being systematically plundered, her people from being wasted again and again by famine, and her education from being half a century behind that of the rest of Europe. In consideration of these facts, do we Irishwomen really want the Parliamentary vote or **would the Feminist Cause be advanced by it?**

In a letter to the *Irish Nation*, M. G., speaking for the Irish Women's Franchise League, denies that the main plank in their agitation is to obtain the vote for themselves, but states that their object is to obtain the vote on the same terms as it is, or may be granted to men. That is to say, they are not agitating for the Parliamentary vote because it is a desirable thing to have, but simply because men have it. We respectfully submit to the Irish Women's Franchise League that this is an unworthy and humiliating position for them to take up. If the English Parliamentary vote is not, in itself, a source of power, then we should not stultify ourselves by wasting time and energy agitating for it. **It is disappointing to find women** simply wanting to follow blindly in men's footsteps, instead of profiting by their experience and avoiding their mistakes. **Dean na h-Eireann** is, and will always be, as keen and enthusiastic an advocate for the Cause of Women as the most extreme "Suffragette" could wish. It is not a question of putting Nationality before sex, or sex before Nationality. The two questions do not clash at all, although at first sight they appear to. The Feminist Cause in Ireland **is best served by ignoring England** and English politicians, just as it is best served in England by keeping aloof from Party politics. At all events, women should first set their own house in order. Women are denied a place in some of the most important political organisations in Ireland. The United Irish League (with the exception of one branch, we believe), the Loyal Orange Association, the Liberal Home Rule Association, are exclusively masculine bodies. The Gaelic League and the Sinn Fein Organisation are the only ones in existence at present where women are on an equal footing with men. For that reason they are not worthy of the support of every Irish woman Suffragist.

In taking this stand against any suffrage agitation in Ireland, let it not be thought that we are antagonistic to English Suffragists, or that we disapprove of their forcible methods. On the contrary, we commend them to Irishwomen and Irishmen, but let us fight for something worth the trouble and the risk. More than one hundred years ago, a great Irishman said that "the only argument that appeals to an Englishman's sense of justice is the argument of the pike." Irish Nationalists have always realized the truth of that. Their own countrywomen, having proved the **worthlessness of their pledged word**, are now realizing the truth of it, and are resorting to violent measures to enforce their demands. They have all our sympathy. They have spent time and energy, and risked liberty, and suffered hardships and indignities unspeakable. They are in their own country fighting for their rights, but their cause is not ours. **The rights of Irish women are in Ireland**, and must be won in Ireland, not in England or any foreign country. If Irishwomen have time and energy to use, and the will to make sacrifices and risk liberty, let it be for a nobler and greater end than the right to send hostages to England.

Front page of *Bean na hÉireann*, February 1909
courtesy Kilmainham Gaol Museum

Further, it was 'unworthy and humiliating' to seek the English parliamentary vote. Men's votes had not saved Ireland from the ravages of the famine or even achieved Home Rule. 'Do we Irishwomen really want the Parliamentary vote or would the Feminist Cause be advanced by it?' she continued. It was not,

a question of putting Nationality before sex or sex before Nationality. The two questions do not clash at all although at first sight they appear to ... the feminist cause in Ireland is best served by ignoring England.[63]

The Gaelic League and Sinn Féin were the only Irish organisations that allowed women in on an equal footing and so,

are worthy of the support of every Irish women suffragist. The rights of Irishwomen are in Ireland and must be won in Ireland, not England or any foreign country. Freedom for our nation and the complete removal of all disabilities to our sex will be our battle cry.[64]

This was more than slightly ironic given Molony's stated reasons for the establishment of *Bean na hÉireann* and Hanna Sheehy Skeffington was quick to point out the practical inconsistencies inherent in the stance. However, Molony was crystal clear on the policy and its importance. This was underscored by the work she put in to bring her political 'apprentice', Markievicz, around to this point of view. It was also another indication of Molony's role and influence in the Inghinidhe. She wrote that Markievicz,

supported the Women's Movement, but did not join their organisation in Ireland, because she was a member of Inghinidhe na hÉireann, and adopted their attitude on this very vital point. We held that an agitation for votes for women in Ireland, inferred claiming British citizenship, and consequently was inconsistent with Irish Republicanism and Separatism. I remember having some difficulty in bringing her to this point of view.[65]

Despite these tactical differences, Molony supported the suffrage movement over the following years, politically and personally.[66] As she herself said, 'Of course on the principle of Equal Rights we were all united, and we, worked in the most friendly way with the Irish 'Suffragettes'.[67] Sheehy Skeffington and Molony knew each other and went on to work together on many different causes. She had actually written to Sheehy Skeffington while *Bean na hÉireann* was being planned to look for contributions. Molony worked closely with other suffrage women on various causes, performed in suffrage plays, spoke on platforms and reported with approval the militant actions taking place in England. Their rigorous debates were also a mark of the time as positions, policy and views were constantly being hashed out and formulated. These debates would become more fraught as political developments in Westminster meant that Home Rule was pitted against female suffrage.[68]

The Inghinidhe also worked hard to establish a genealogy of strong Irish women and just as James Connolly sowed socialism into a Gaelic past in order to radicalise the present, so Molony and the Inghinidhe were finding (and sometimes creating) radical antecedents and constructing an Irish feminist lineage which would inform their struggle for an equal Ireland.[69] To this end their fortnightly lecture series often featured talks on historical figures as well as 'on subjects of National interest'. However, Molony's work in the Inghinidhe and editorship of *Bean na hÉireann,* linked her even more directly to an earlier generation of women activists.[70]

Molony found out that Anna Parnell, leader of the Ladies' Land League in the early 1880s, and sister of Charles Stewart Parnell, was staying in Bray. She invited her to give one of the Inghinidhe's fortnightly talks and called her 'one of the most notable of our lecturers'.[71]

Molony's later vivid description of the evening brings alive the atmosphere and Anna Parnell who,

> consented and came one cold rainy November evening although suffering from a bad attack of tonsillitis, of which disaster she informed me by two telegrams, and ordered a succession of blackcurrant drinks to be made ready. We were all terribly excited and we had a very large audience, as the name of Parnell still had some magic although it had been in the shadow for nearly twenty years. She was a frail elderly figure of a woman. She had an intense quietness – an impassive steeliness about her that was almost repellent, but on the other hand queerly attractive. She spoke for three hours, but no one grew impatient, her story and method of telling it were so fascinating.[72]

Francis Sheehy Skeffington asked Parnell about her brother and the Kilmainham Treaty, and she shocked them all when she said coldly,

> Oh, I think my brother found himself in an uncomfortable position and he did what *men* usually do – got out of it in the easiest way possible for himself, regardless of the consequences to others.[73]

Parnell was very interested in the work of the Inghinidhe and Molony subsequently visited her several times in her rooms in Bray. She asked Molony to publish her account of the time, *Tale of a Great Sham*. Molony wanted to print extracts, but Parnell insisted it be published in its entirety,

> She left Ireland and left me this manuscript. If ever I could publish it, I was to do so. I said I would, but I had no money and the Inghinidhe were unlikely to make much. 'Well', she said, 'we will leave it at that. I will give it to you. If you can see your way, will you promise to publish it?' I gave her my promise.[74]

It appears Molony did begin work on the manuscript for serialisation in *Bean na hÉireann* as their correspondence revealed Anna Parnell moving from lodging house to lodging house in England, determined to get the story into the public arena.[75] She explained that she had 'avoided personalities as much as possible' and concentrated on the more important 'actions of groups (and) classes of persons'. She told Molony that she might write a preface to any extracts that would appear.[76] The manuscript never made it on to the pages of *Bean na hÉireann* as it was seized in one of the many raids on Molony's belongings.[77] Anna Parnell died from drowning in September 1911. Molony later recounted in a witness statement to the Bureau of Military History that 'She was always a good swimmer. She was of the determined type and, if she made up her mind to commit suicide, she would'.[78] However Molony decided to remove this opinion from her final official statement.[79] In the weeks before Anna Parnell drowned, she would play a curious role in relation to Molony's own story and first imprisonment.

LABOUR MATTERS

> My attention was turned to Labour matters, when I discovered that one of the best and most intelligent girl members we had was getting 5/- a week as a shirt maker.[80]

In 1910 Molony decided to introduce a regular column of 'Labour Notes' in *Bean na hÉireann* to discuss labour questions, especially as they affected women. Their author, 'A Worker', was a collaboration between Molony and Carl O'Knapton of the Dublin Trades Council. This was the start of Molony's long career as a trade unionist and socialist as she later recalled: 'I went to the Trades Hall for my labour notes ... and I knew little of labour ideas. But I was always on the side of the underdog'.[81] The Inghinidhe had already shown themselves to be socially radical but from this point her knowledge of labour matters and socialist outlook quickly developed and within three years she would identify herself completely with that movement.

'A Worker' dealt with a wide range of contemporary issues. The trade union movement was described as 'a living corpse', and the need for a strong independent Irish labour party and trade union movement stressed. The impact of James Larkin and his newly-formed Irish Transport and General Workers' Union, which organised unskilled workers, was welcomed and praised. When Larkin was jailed in 1910, readers were urged to join the campaign for his release. The 'Labour Notes' paid particular attention to the plight of women workers. Their conditions and lack of organisation were frequently referred to, as was the ambivalence of prominent male trade unionists to these issues.

> While admitting the needs of the unorganised female worker, the male members of the wage earners look with suspicion on their sisters and are seemingly loath to offer any help.[82]

This was a problem that Molony would continue to encounter, and oppose, right through to the 1940s when she retired from public life.

Her views on labour and property were developing from a variety of sources and books such as Standish O'Grady's *History of Ireland* and PW Joyce's *A Social History of Ireland* were influential at this time in forming a concept of 'Gaelic communism',

> I had been studying Irish land tenure and found that up to the sixteenth century no chief had an absolute right to the land and that he could not surrender it without the consent of his people. This Irish view of property seemed to me to be right, and it helped to form my Labour views. I also found much support in the Christian moral code of justice and righteousness.[83]

Molony made a sharp distinction between the nostalgic form of nationalism prevalent in the Celtic Revival and the squalid realties of contemporary Irish life. An article appeared in the newspaper of the co-operative movement,

The Irish Homestead, which 'timidly suggested' that Irish women should wear a national costume for its picturesque value and also to encourage native industry. Molony agreed that foreign clothes were undesirable, but was scathing about the suggestion, writing that 'all that about red petticoated barefooted *cailíní* is most pernicious nonsense'.[84] The *cailíní* went barefoot because they could not afford boots and petticoats provided little protection from the wind. While the *Homestead* bemoaned the numbers of women emigrating, Molony countered that young women would continue to leave rural Ireland while it could only offer 'squalid poverty and certain horror commonly called a women's sphere which included the dullest work and lowest pay'.[85] Until Ireland had an equitable economic base, the 'rural civilisation' of which the *Homestead* dreamt, could not exist.

Her thought was developing along these lines when she came into contact with James Connolly. Connolly had a huge impact on Molony, both politically and personally;

> At this period I was fumbling at the idea of a junction between labour and nationality – which Connolly worked out clearly. The connection was always there though at first we did not perceive it. Labour and nationality were one.[86]

Connolly argued that the national and the social causes were two sides to one struggle. English colonisation had destroyed the Gaelic communal system and imposed an alien social as well as political system on the Irish people. Consequently the 'reconquest of Ireland' would have to involve both social and political transformation. It was a position enthusiastically embraced by Molony and one which informed her life.

At this point Connolly was living and working in America where he also published *The Harp*. Molony wrote to him in June 1909, 'I only wish it was in Ireland you were publishing *The Harp* … There is a *very very* great need for a worker's journal in Ireland'.[87] The letter had a significant impact and Connolly wrote to William O'Brien, 'Like her I wish I was in Ireland' and asked O'Brien, several times, to make contact with Molony.[88] He was impressed by *Bean na hÉireann,* which had already come to his notice. In the *Harp* he welcomed the first edition and said that until women made their influence felt in Ireland, men would continue to,

Rave about the beauties of the daughters of Erin and continue telling those same daughters to stay at home and mend socks or plant potatoes, whilst their lords and masters are settling their fates over a pint of Guinness.[89]

When Connolly did return to Ireland in 1910, he and Molony became good friends and colleagues.

In 1910, a vigorous debate occurred on the pages of *Bean na hÉireann* about a school meals scheme that the Inghinidhe were involved in. The driving force behind it was Gonne MacBride and as well as the Inghinidhe women, she involved women from the IWFL who formed a Ladies' Dinner Committee. The aim was to have the 1906 School Meals Act extended to Ireland. Dublin Corporation was lobbied to effect this and school dinners were then provided in several schools in Dublin, in order to provide a practical demonstration of how such a scheme might actually be run. Molony and Gifford recalled how the meals of Irish stew with desserts of rice pudding and jam were made up by the Penny Dinners Ladies' Committee on Meath Street and served by the Inghinidhe volunteers. Molony, Gonne MacBride, Markievicz, Helen Laird, Madeleine ffrench-Mullen as well as Grace, Muriel and Sidney Gifford served up the dinners in national schools on High Street, St Audoen's and John's Lane.[90]

In *Bean na hÉireann,* 'A Worker' argued that the scheme smacked of charity rather than social justice and as such would be counterproductive. An editorial defended the rationale behind the scheme and pointed out that, following necessary Parliamentary reform, rate payers money would be used to run the scheme (this reform was never quite squared with Inghinidhe policy on other matters, including suffrage).[91] Ward has identified the argument as being between Gonne MacBride and Helena Molony but it is probable that it was between Gonne MacBride and O'Knapton, who collaborated with Molony on the Labour Notes.[92] Molony, herself involved in serving the meals, later wrote about it, adamant that it was not a charitable scheme. The schools worked it in such a way that some children paid, but no one knew who had or had not.[93] In any event the scheme was successful, both at this local level and (as a result of the lobbying) the Act was later extended nationally. The work was also a prelude to cooperation and the relief work many of these women would undertake during the Lockout.

However, the appearance in *Bean na hÉireann* of criticism of the Inghinidhe (or more specifically, Gonne MacBride's) school meals policy through the 'A Worker' column was interesting in terms of the development of Molony's own thought. Regardless of whether she penned it, as editor she had allowed its publication and it was the case that Molony's thinking was progressing in a more socialist direction, one that was more radical than that of her first mentor, Gonne MacBride.

Due to financial difficulties, *Bean na hÉireann* did not appear between March and August 1910. On its reappearance, Molony explained to readers that the paper was, 'run by a band of amateurs, all painfully aware of their inefficiency' but nonetheless proud at producing the first women's political and nationalist journal.[94] The gap may also have been a reflection of the flux in Molony's own life, as her brother Frank and his wife were about to leave for America. Their move would mark the start of Molony's precarious living arrangements. Over the next 30 years, she would spend long spells staying with friends as well as in lodgings and short term rentals, with little security.[95]

Constance Markievicz, c 1914
private collection

Molony's first move was up to Raheny where Constance Markievicz had already relocated. Along with Bulmer Hobson and Donald Hannigan (an agricultural expect and later in the IRA), they planned to establish a rural co-operative and a Fianna camp. Molony offered 'the portion of money she was expecting to get from the sale of a small estate of her mother's through the Land Court'.[96] She explained how Markievicz,

> gave up her house, 59 Frankfort Avenue, and moved her furniture out to Belcamp Park in Raheny. As my family shortly after went to America, I moved out there too. Our idea was to provide a camp for the Fianna and to try an experiment on the same lines as the Ralahine experiment in Tipperary, in the early 19th century. We both thought we could make the place self-supporting by market-gardening. Some of our young men friends, such as Bulmer Hobson, encouraged us in the project. Others, especially Seán McGarry, were very much against it and branded us as 'idiots'.[97]

Gifford wrote later that,

> the police of the neighbourhood were perturbed for a few months by the sight of the Fianna boys in the grounds of the Markievicz house practicing shooting at a row of dummy English soldiers.[98]

On an early encampment, one of the boys went foraging and returned triumphantly with a dead hen that belonged to one of Markievicz's neighbours. Constance Markievicz's stepson stayed with them on holidays but was very happy to return to boarding school. He described how they were 'installed there like gypsies with only a few of the rooms furnished and one servant and a gardener' and that,

> Miss Helena Molony first came to live with us at Belcamp and helped mother with the housekeeping. Bulmer Hobson also lived there for months, and his room I recall, was one mass of printing material papers and the like.[99]

The co-operative, perhaps inevitably, ended in failure. Gifford put this down to the Fianna boys as 'They were all town bred and they could not endure the limitations of country life'.[100] Molony was more positive,

> Financially it was not a success, but the Fianna enjoyed it thoroughly and put a lot of work into developing the grounds. When we decided to wind up the experiment we succeeded in getting a buyer, and the losses which we shared were not very great.[101]

Na Fianna with Constance Markievicz.
Image donated, described and signed by Bulmer Hobson
courtesy Military Archives, Ireland

Apparently Hobson returned to Dublin before it was wound up and left the two women to split the losses between them. In the 1930s, Molony told Louie Coghlan-O'Brien, then a young woman living in Frankfort House, Rathmines where Molony lodged, that it had been 'understood' that she and Hobson were to get married. She said that he had made promises to marry her but had broken her heart.[102] There is no other confirmation of this. They were obviously close; he had spent time in her brother's house, had made important contributions to the establishment of *Bean na hÉireann* and the Fianna and was involved with the co-operative. Whatever occurred or didn't occur between them, Molony evidently felt the betrayal for many years. This must have been magnified by the fact that their 'understanding', as she saw it, was reached at around the same time as her brother and sister-in-law emigrated. In another context she wrote, 'Bulmer Hobson was a very convincing man – a spellbinder'.[103] She would be deeply critical of his cautious approach and political influence on organisations in the years that followed.

Bean na hÉireann had ceased publication by March 1911 and Molony wrote that,

> by that time there were other national journals and the need for our paper was not so urgent and the strain of getting it out was too much in the midst of other activities.[104]

She pointed out that *Bean na hÉireann* was the only paper that articulated a separatist physical force position until the 1910 launch of *Irish Freedom*, edited by Seán MacDermott. It was not just Molony who identified that continuity; when *Bean na hÉireann* ceased publication, *Irish Freedom* announced that as a consequence, it would publish at the start of the month (*Bean na hÉireann*'s usual slot) instead of the middle. In 1912 the IWFL launched a new feminist paper, *The Irish Citizen*.

Years later Molony reflected on how proud she was that the paper ran for over two years and repaid all of its debts. She assessed her own role, and rightly commented that given the 'list of contributors … I cannot have been quite a failure, as Editor'. She also said of *Bean na hÉireann* that,

> one cannot help thinking that it was an odd kind of woman's paper … It was a mixture of guns and chiffon … a funny hotchpotch of blood and thunder, high thinking and home-made bread.[105]

The paper remains one of the most significant and fascinating sources for the period.

The appearance of the last edition of *Bean na hÉireann* also seemed to herald a quieter phase for Inghinidhe na hÉireann. Marie Perolz had taken on the role of Honorary Secretary while Molony and other members became more involved in other activities. Following the collapse of the Belcamp experiment Markievicz and Molony moved back to Dublin to a rented flat on Mount Street and a new chapter in Molony's life began.

Later Molony would say that her 'brightest memories' were of the Inghinidhe days and perhaps this is not surprising. Running through all of the accounts is an extraordinary sense of *joie de vivre*, of purpose and enthusiasm, of camaraderie and of the 'political religion' (as Molony termed it) that they were swept up in.[106] Her immersion into the Inghinidhe, and the political life of Dublin, developed in Molony a style of politics which suited her and stayed with her. She developed a brand of nationalism which was radical and incorporated a feminist and socialist outlook. This would determine much of the rest of her life's work as she sought to 'reconcile in the most practical ways possible the causes of Ireland, women and labour'.[107] She always saw direct action, if necessary outside existing organisations, as the preferred means of effecting change. She continued to use the flamboyant and often melodramatic publicity methods adopted by the Inghinidhe. Importantly, the cause she was involved in during this, her political apprenticeship, was successful in that it culminated in a national revolution. Later she saw no reason why this could not again be the case, if sufficient willpower was exerted.

Molony had also developed as an astute organiser, editor, publicist and tactician. She was personally very influential as she drew into the movement, and mentored, some of the leading women activists of the time. These included Constance Markievicz and later Kathleen Lynn. She would do the same for the Irish Women Workers' Union when she drew in Louie Bennett and Helen Chenevix, who would lead the union with her. In this early period she founded deep friendships that would sustain her throughout her life, politically and personally. She developed a personal life that was radical for the time with unorthodox views on religion, love and relationships. In common with many of her contemporaries she had a lack of personal ambition or desire for financial stability when there was so much work to be done for Ireland. This would remain consistent and evident throughout her life.

In 1911 and 1912 Molony began a career as a successful professional actor. However, these years were also the prelude to a turbulent decade in Ireland. Her acting career would be the bridge between the end of her secretaryship of the Inghinidhe and the start of her active service with the Irish Citizen Army and her life's work with the IWWU.

SOURCES

1   R.M. Fox, 'Helena Molony', *Rebel Irishwomen* (Dublin, Progress House, 1967), p. 66.

2   Helena Molony, Draft Witness Statement, 1949, KMGLM 2011.0283.01, Kilmainham Gaol Museum. Hereafter Helena Molony, Draft WS Kilmainham.

3   Fox, *Rebel Irishwomen*, p. 66.

4   *Ibid*.

5   Regan, 'Helena Molony', p. 142.

6   Séamus Scully, interview with author, 1992.

7   Helena Molony: BMH WS 391.

8   Senia Pašeta, *Irish Nationalist Women, 1900–1918* (Cambridge, Cambridge University Press, 2013), p. 33.

9   *Ibid*.

10   Helena Molony, Draft WS Kilmainham.

11   *Ibid*.

12   Helena Molony: BMH WS 391.

13   *Ibid*.

14   *Ibid.*

15   *Ibid.*

16   *Ibid.*

17   Helena Molony, Draft WS Kilmainham.

18   Pašeta, *Irish Nationalist Women*; Roy Foster, *Vivid Faces: The Revolutionary Generation in Ireland, 1890–1923* (London, Penguin, 2014).

19   Pašeta, *Irish Nationalist Women*, p. 93.

20   Helena Molony: BMH WS 391.

21   *Ibid.*

22   Sidney Gifford Czira, *The Years Flew By* (Galway, Arlen House, 2000), p. 11.

23   Sidney Czira, Bureau of Military History Witness Statement 909; Hereafter, Sidney Czira: BMH WS 909.

24   Czira, *The Years Flew By*, p. 8.

25   Helena Molony: BMH WS 391.

26   Pašeta, *Irish Nationalist Women*, p. 39.

27   Helena Molony: BMH WS 391.

28   *Ibid.*

29   Quoted in Regan, 'Helena Molony', p. 143.

30   Helena Molony: BMH WS 391.

31   Liam Roche, Bureau of Military History Witness Statement 1698.

32   Helena Molony: BMH WS 391.

33   'The Green Jacket', broadcast 13 May 1960, RTÉ Sound Archives.

34   Helena Molony: BMH WS 391.

35   Fox, *Rebel Irishwomen*, p. 66; Helena Molony: BMH WS 391.

36   Quoted in Regan, 'Helena Molony', p. 143.

37   *Bean na hÉireann*, November 1909. As the paper was produced intermittently, all issues are noted by month of publication.

38   Czira, *Years Flew By*, p. 44.

39   Helena Molony: BMH WS 391.

40   *Bean na hÉireann*, July 1909.

41   *Ibid.*

42   Margaret Ward, *Unmanageable Revolutionaries, Women and Irish Nationalism* (Dingle, Brandon Books, 1983), p. 51.

43   Pašeta, *Irish Nationalist Women*, p. 38.

44   Helena Molony: BMH WS 391; Helena Molony, Draft WS Kilmainham.

45   *Bean na hÉireann*, January 1909.

46   Helena Molony: BMH WS 391.

47   *Ibid.*

48   Bulmer Hobson, Bureau of Military History Witness Statement 1365.

49   Helena Molony: BMH WS 391.

50   *Ibid.*

51   Anna MacBride White and A. Norman Jeffares (eds), *The Gonne-Yeats Letters, 1893–1936: Always Your Friend* (London, Pimlico, 1992), p. 274.

52   *Bean na hÉireann*, July 1909.

53   Helena Molony: BMH WS 391.

54   *Bean na hÉireann*, January 1910.

55   *Ibid.*

56   *Ibid.*

57   *Bean na hÉireann*, April 1910.

58   *Bean na hÉireann*, June 1909.

59   *Ibid.*

60   *Bean na hÉireann*, January 1909.

61   *Ibid.*

62   *Bean na hÉireann*, February 1909.

63   *Ibid.*

64   *Ibid.*

65   Helena Molony: BMH WS 391.

66   Regan, 'Helena Molony', p. 145.

67   Helena Molony: BMH WS 391.

68   Pašeta, *Irish Nationalist Women*, p. 15.

69   Declan Kiberd, 'Inventing Ireland', *The Crane Bag*, Vol. 2, 1984.

70   Helena Molony: BMH WS 391.

71   *Ibid.*

72   *Ibid.*

73   *Ibid.*

74   Helena Molony: BMH WS 391.

75   'The Tale of a Great Sham', a history of the Land League by Anna Parnell, with some associated letters from Miss Parnell to Miss H. Molony, 1909–1911, MS 12144, NLI.

76   *Ibid*, Anna Parnell to Molony, 7 July 1910.

77   Helena Molony: BMH WS 391.

78   Helena Molony, Draft WS Kilmainham.

79   Helena Molony: BMH WS 391.

80   Fox, *Rebel Irishwomen*, p. 63.

81   *Ibid.*, p. 67; see also Helena Molony, 'James Connolly', typescript article, Hugh O'Connor Collection, where she mentions Carl O'Knapton.

82   *Bean na hÉireann*, March 1910.

83   Fox, *Rebel Irishwomen*, p. 67.

84   *Bean na hÉireann*, February 1910.

85   *Ibid.*

86   Fox, *Rebel Irishwomen*, p. 67.

87   William O'Brien Papers, MS 13940 (ii), NLI.

88   *Ibid.*

89   *Bean na hÉireann*, April 1909.

90   Czira, *Years Flew By*, p. 46.

91   Ward, *Unmanageable Revolutionaries*, p. 82.

92   *Ibid.*

93   Helena Molony: BMH WS 391.

94   *Bean na hÉireann*, August 1910.

95   Regan, 'Helena Molony', p. 142.

96   Anne Marreco, *Rebel Countess* (London, Weidenfeld and Nicolson, 1967), p. 131.

97   Helena Molony: BMH WS 391.

98   Czira, *Years Flew By*, p. 101.

99   Pašeta, *Irish Nationalist Women*, p. 213.

100   Czira, *Years Flew By*, p. 101.

101   Helena Molony: BMH WS 391.

102   Louie Coghlan O'Brien, interview with author, 1991.

103   Helena Molony, Draft WS Kilmainham.

104   *Ibid.*

105   *Ibid.*

106   *Ibid.*

107   Regan, 'Helena Molony', p. 141.

ACTOR
1911–1915

I am so glad to hear you think Helen Moloney [sic] has the makings of an actress ... She has great power of throwing herself completely into different parts ... she is also, which is very rare in characters of her type, without jealousy and has a great power of working with others.

– Maud Gonne MacBride to W.B. Yeats.[1]

Theatre was inseparable from the political and social life Molony had been living since 1903.[2] Plays, *tableau vivants*, the social life around performances and even flamboyance were integral parts of the political movement and a form of national consciousness-raising. Padraic Colum, the poet and playwright wrote that,

Poets wrote treatises on wireless telegraphy and wireless telegraphists produced drama. Every organisation produced plays: some produced propaganda plays, others produced non propaganda plays, that they might raise funds to carry on their propaganda. It was rather like taking in each other's washing. Those who were not interested in any particular propaganda produced plays to revenge themselves on the propagandists.[3]

The cast of *The Devil's Disciple*, George Bernard Shaw. Count
Markievicz's Independent Repertory Company, 1913
private collection

Detail of *The Devil's Disciple* showing Sidney Gifford and Helena
Molony above Constance and Casimir Markievicz
private collection

Molony was to prove herself among a cast of activists
talented enough to become professional actors and would
earn her living as such. After engagements and tours with
the Theatre of Ireland, the Independent Theatre Company,
the National Players and the Irish Repertory Company,
Helena Molony became one of the Abbey Theatre's
upcoming stars. She rose rapidly from the ranks of the
Abbey School of Acting to the Second and then the First
Company during 1912. She toured with both in Ireland
and Britain, and appeared in Synge's *Playboy of the Western
World* on the stage of the Royal Court, London with the
First Company. As was usual in a repertory company, she
performed a wide range of roles, both lead and
supporting, from the ingénue to the old woman
(sometimes on the same night) and everything in-between.
Critics praised and singled out many of her performances
in glowing terms such as 'notable success', 'finest piece of

work she has ever done', 'best acting was from Miss Molony' and 'Miss M was best of all'.[4]

Before she became a member of the Abbey Theatre Company, Molony's life was at a crossroads. *Bean na hÉireann* had closed by March 1911, and for the next year she was pulled in different directions as she made decisions about where to live and how to earn her living. Her brother Frank and his wife urged her to join them in America and Gonne MacBride, who still 'very much want(ed) her in Ireland' wrote to Yeats to encourage him to take her on in the Abbey, but on contract, as 'she cannot live on air'.[5] Meanwhile, it was clear that she increasingly identified and involved herself with the labour movement. She was a member of the Socialist Party of Ireland and James Connolly offered her a position as a union organiser in Belfast. However, before she made her decision about which route to take, Molony was catapulted onto a very public stage and became the first female political prisoner of her generation. She was arrested twice, in the space of a month, for her part in the protests against the visit of newly-crowned George V to Ireland.[6] As befitted the actor she was becoming, this was as a result of a single, irresistible gesture.

MISS MOLONY … IS A ROCK OF SENSE[7]

Opposition to the royal visit of 1903 had been the occasion of Molony's introduction into the movement and by now she was at the heart of that movement, and organised resistance to a visit planned for July 1911. At a joint Inghinidhe na hÉireann and Socialist Party of Ireland meeting in March, Molony and James Connolly called on workers to oppose the adoption of a loyal address. In April, Molony was invited to Waterford by Rosamond Jacob to address a meeting about the anti-loyal address.

Jacob's diaries, written with a novelist's eye, provide us with the first and best contemporary impression of the 28-year-old Molony. They vividly introduce her through a growing friendship and reveal Molony's radical views on religion, relationships and politics. On Saturday 20 May, Jacob met Molony off the train and wrote: 'She is small and rather plain, very unimposing altogether and rather shy I think but has a nice voice and plenty worth saying to say'.[8] They spent Sunday morning in conversation and,

> Miss Molony who is a rock of sense in every direction ... did not go to Mass at all, only for a stroll around the town. She says she is not a very good Catholic.[9]

Later, Molony reiterated that she was 'far from an Orthodox Catholic' and impressed Jacob as '[she] did not seem at all shocked when I said I had no religion'.[10] The meeting Molony addressed was well reported in the papers and Jacob recorded in her diary that Molony,

> got a tremendous reception when she stood up ... why I don't exactly know for I don't think people can have heard of her ... she seemed to have no difficulty in making herself heard though she did not speak loud.[11]

Given that Molony had published extensively in *Bean na hÉireann* and the national press on the royal visit, Jacob's comments revealed as much about her own judgement as they did about her subject. The meeting was evidence of Molony's skills as an actor as well as her talent and public profile as an agitator. The two women continued their conversation after the meeting and Molony repeated views that she had been articulating on the pages of *Bean na hÉireann* over the past three years, about men and the future of Ireland,

> Miss Molony was complaining of the hopelessness of men and how they never think anything can be done whereas a woman would simply go and do it ... her idea is you can do

practically nothing for this country until the English are cleared out.[12]

She concluded the visit by giving Jacob a standing invitation to come and stay with her and the Markieviczes in Mount Street.

Molony's frustration with the inaction of her male counterparts reached boiling point during the royal visit in July. Much to her disgust, and that of her colleagues, restrained opposition was planned by a broad alliance of nationalists. Constance Markievicz recalled that the United National Societies Committee organised a quiet protest out to Bodenstown, in honour of Wolfe Tone, to remove from the centre all the 'turbulent young men who might possibly make a disturbance'.[13] Molony, Markievicz and Jennie Wyse Power, all of the Nationalist Women's Committee, and others sought to force the pace and organise public dissension. They even adopted tactics from Russia, as Sidney Gifford recounted,

> It was suggested to us by Conrad Peterson who was a student in the College of Science and who had some experience of shock tactics in Czarist Russia, he was from Riga – that we should adopt the methods used by demonstrators in Russia, i.e. fold all the leaflets in two and catching them by the corner, fling them into the air if we saw the police approaching. They would then fan out among the crowd and be picked up. We sat up until a late hour the night before the procession, engaged in the work of folding the leaflets.[14]

Molony's brother Frank had filled her in on his activity during an earlier royal visit and 'told [her] about previous stone throwing'.[15] Providence even seemed to provide these when en route to a large all-Party meeting they discovered that,

> the streets were being repaired, and in neat heaps were conveniently sized broken stones. We thought it a splendid idea to collect quantities of these and distribute them amongst

the more ardent of our young men sympathisers. This was duly done.[16]

As crowds gathered along the route, a small group of women, and members of the Fianna began to hand out fliers. Interestingly, the crowds were more used to feminist than anti-loyal opposition and Gifford commented,

> Fortunately for us, the people along the route thought we were suffragettes, as the leaflets were folded and they had not time to open and read them before we disappeared. Smiling indulgently they said, 'Votes for Women'.[17]

Constance Markievicz attempted to burn a flag but in the event only James McArdle, who had aided her, was arrested for this. No one threw any stones. After the large protest meeting, Molony returned in a wagonette with Wyse Power and Markievicz, her bag still full of the stones. As they passed the corner of Grafton Street, she caught sight of illuminated portraits of the king and queen in a chemist's window, looking 'smug and benign … [which] was too much for me'.[18] She let fly with a stone, in a gesture of defiance and frustration. The police gave chase and Molony, already well known to the authorities (as copies of *Bean na hÉireann* were in their files) was arrested. There were wild scenes in court when she refused to pay a fine of 40/- and was sentenced to a month in prison.

Molony was released before the month was out when an anonymous donor paid her fine. She was furious, and thought that it had been paid by the Lord Mayor of Dublin wishing to avoid negative publicity during the royal visit. 'I am extremely sorry his kindness took this form which is most distasteful and irritating to me and was done against the wishes of myself and friends'.[19] Rosamond Jacob wrote in her diary that 'some fool' paid the fine.[20] Ironically, the donor was Anna Parnell, herself a political prisoner of a previous generation. She wanted Molony to continue work on her Ladies' Land League book, *The Tale of a Great Sham*, a fact Molony only found out later.[21]

A few days after Molony's release from prison, Jacob took her up on her invitation. Molony cycled to the station to meet her and brought her to Mount Street. Jacob's diary entries for the visit record Molony's daily life, her views, the overlapping networks of Dublin at the time as well as the home that she shared with the Markieviczes,

> 15 Lwr Mount Street is a big house but they only have 3 or 4 rooms in it I think. They are leaving it as soon as they can. Countess is out rehearsing for the Oireachtas pageant, the Feis of Tara tomorrow evening. Miss Molony and I went out a little after tea and she showed me the optician's place at the corner of Nassau St where the big ... portrait of George was that she threw a stone at.[22]

The next day was fine and the two women spent the morning looking for and bumping into friends. They called into, 'Mrs. Wyse Powers on Henry St. We dined at the vegetarian and afterwards ... we overtook John Brennan and her sister Nellie I think ...'[23] They went on to the Oireachtas and on the way home, now joined by Markievicz, they stopped off to buy cigarettes at Tom Clarke's tobacconist. Molony taught Jacob how to smoke, and she wrote proudly, 'I can do it all right. She and JB ["John Brennan"/Sidney Gifford] are very fond of smoking and so is Madeleine [ffrench Mullen]'. Jacob provided an extraordinary insight into the relationship between Molony and Markievicz, who discussed the Bodenstown picnic, Sinn Féin and the Fianna over breakfast the next morning: 'The Countess in particular had a lot to say and she and Miss Molony contradict and criticise each other almost in the manner of Beechgrovians'.[24]

By Monday, Jacob was comfortable enough to call Molony 'Emer', her name amongst the Inghinidhe circle and close friends.

Over the next few days, in between visits to the Oireachtas and the Inghinidhe offices on Harcourt Street, as well as dinners in the vegetarian restaurant on Westland Row, the pair spent much of their time in Mount Street, talking and smoking. In a series of candid and revealing conversations, Molony told Jacob about her unhappy early life, her attitude to men, women and love and she also aired her views on theatrical staging and the political issues of the day. Molony was unwell and preoccupied for much of the week, perhaps nervous about the monster demonstration planned for the following Sunday to mark her imprisonment and McArdle's release.

They called into 6 Harcourt Street where they found a noisy crowd including Sidney Gifford and 'a man called Larkin in the Inghinidhe room doing nothing in particular'.[25] They went to the Oireachtas pageant at eight that evening where, in a *tableau vivant*, the provincial queens of Ireland were played by among others, Dorothy Macardle, Muriel Gifford and Markievicz. For Jacob, the latter was the finest of the queens. However, 'Emer found great fault with the whole thing and most of what she said was true, especially her strictures on the lack of music such as harps or pipes'.[26] Molony retired early and left the others to go on to the dance. She was still unwell for the next two days, uninterested in food or activity and 'doesn't even feel like smoking' which amazed Jacob, who had had another busy morning at the Oireachtas. They spent the rest of that day and evening at home, while Jacob practiced 'a little smoking'.[27]

> She is extremely good company and very hard to shock. She seems to regard men, as men, more as the relaxation of an idle hour than in any more serious light, does not appear to believe much in the one love of a lifetime, but rather in one minor flame after another. She prefers women and Madam prefers men.[28]

little smoking ... quite well, or she would have smoked too. She is extremely good company and very hard to shock. She seems to regard men, as men, more as the relaxation of an idle hour than in any more serious light, does not appear to believe much in the one love of a lifetime, but rather in one minor flame after another. She prefers women and Madame prefers men. She was telling me ...

Rosamond Jacob records Molony's views on love and men
in her diary on 4 August 1911
courtesy Jacob Estate and National Library of Ireland

It is intriguing to consider whether Molony was referring at this stage to working with and being in the company of women, or romantic involvement, or both.

The following morning they rose at 6am and went to Mountjoy to accompany James McArdle out on his release. On the way back to Mount Street, Jacob found a stray kitten which she picked up and brought with her, much to the amusement and derision of Larkin and the Gifford sisters. However, Molony reassured her and, 'was the only decent person there'.[29] Molony retired to bed when they got home and stayed there all morning.

Throughout her life Molony would continue to suffer bouts of depression and exhaustion, which were also exacerbated (and presumably partly caused) by drinking. However, a potent mixture of public bravado and private insecurity also marked her reactions in this period, not evident in Jacob's diaries, except perhaps through references to her feeling unwell.

Rosamond Jacob records in her diary on 5 August 1911
how Molony, 'Emer', was ill
courtesy Jacob Estate and National Library of Ireland

ATTACK ON THE KING: TWO SPEAKERS ARRESTED[30]

On Sunday 6 August, the 'monster demonstration' was held under the auspices of Inghinidhe na hÉireann and the Socialist Party of Ireland to welcome Molony and McArdle. Jacob recorded 'violent rain in the morning but it cleared up and in time for me to go to the meeting in Beresford Place'.[31] According to the *Irish Worker*, large crowds attended and Constance Markievicz presided over the meeting. She read letters of support from Bulmer Hobson, James Connolly, Seán MacDermott among others and Francis Sheehy Skeffington spoke about the inspirational example of the two released prisoners. Towards the end of the meeting, Molony (by now clearly recovered) took the platform,

> I am very thankful to see this meeting to welcome us. When I think of the people who have been in prison for 10 or 15 or 20 years for what they did, [previous generations of political prisoners] I feel humbled and proud to be associated with the people that the citizens of Dublin would like us to honour. There is one man not with us – that is Walter Carpenter (*cheers*). That man was sent to prison for saying that King George was the Descendant of the worst scoundrel in Europe.[32]

The police were alert, nervous that she was about to refer to a bigamy scandal that was being written about in the English radical press and which had been mentioned on the pages of *Bean na hÉireann*. The *Irish Worker* reported her speech as it was interrupted, and the dramatic events that followed,

> Well, I ask this meeting to endorse and agree with everything he said. I don't believe in making personal attacks on any man or woman, king or queen. But it is not – (Miss Maloney was here taken into custody).[33]

The platform was stormed, she and Markievicz were 'dragged with some violence ... and taken to Store Street Station',[34] while the police baton-charged the remaining crowd. James Larkin, disgusted, got up on the platform and said that, 'a young lassie has been taken away from amongst you; but if you had only half the spirit she has, she would not have been taken'.[35] The case attracted considerable media attention; Monday's edition of *The Irish Times* provided a detailed account and outlined how Miss Molony 'then proceeded to use words insulting to the King' and the police tried to arrest her but, were 'repelled by Countess Markievicz by means of her foot'.[36] Molony was initially charged with high treason which she recalled,

> was marvellous. I felt myself in the same company as Wolfe Tone. Then they reduced it to 'using language derogatory to His Majesty'. In my secret heart of hearts I felt degraded by such a miserable accusation.[37]

Molony was denounced in an open letter in the English paper *John Bull*, and compared to the suffragettes in England, only on a lower level. Even some of her friends thought her conduct 'reprehensible and rowdy'.[38] Molony later recalled feeling,

> crushed about this ... for I was still young and inexperienced ... when I received a telegram from Maud Gonne (still in Paris), it read, 'Splendid. You have kept up the reputation of Ingheannana h-Eireann'. I cannot describe how elated I felt when I received this. My heart was lifted up.[39]

In any event, the case against her was dropped, as the authorities gauged its explosive potential. Molony returned to the platform on Sunday 26 August, at a meeting organised by the SPI, to welcome Walter Carpenter out of prison. James Connolly came down from Belfast to preside and opened the meeting by saying that, 'They had their comrade, Carpenter again with them and next to him, but perhaps higher in the degree of criminality they had Miss Molony'.[40] The announcement was greeted with applause and it was an indication of Molony's identification at this point that she was introduced as a member of the Socialist Party of Ireland. She got up to speak and was cheered enthusiastically as she seconded the resolution of welcome. She went on,

> I also take this opportunity of thanking those who at the last meeting came to welcome myself and continue *to say what I was prevented from saying by the police* in a summary manner and that is that the Irish National Cause is not based on the virtues or vices of any English Monarch; it is based on Ireland's inherent right to freedom; just as the Socialist cause is not based on the vices or virtues of the capitalists or the aristocracy. It was based on the Christian solution – that labour was the only order of society.

She also stated that, 'In spite of misrepresentation this [socialist outlook] was the point of view of all Irish nationalists that I have been acquainted with'.[41] Just as with the issue of suffrage, she projected the progressive and radical views that she and her close colleagues held onto the wider nationalist movement. Time would prove her overly optimistic.

Another important event took place that autumn when on 5 September 1911, the Irish Women Workers' Union was founded. James Larkin became the union's first President with his sister, Delia, its first Secretary. The union went on to play a crucial role in the 1913 Lockout, and subsequently Molony went on to play a crucial role in the union.

Molony was still not settled on whether or not to join her brother and sister-in-law in the US. Gonne MacBride was concerned that she might as, 'she is constantly being urged by her family who are in America to go out to them'.[42] The bequest from her mother, which she survived on, began to run out and she had to find a way to earn her living. That winter, theatre began to figure even more centrally in Molony's life.

UNEXPECTED JOY

> It was a liberal education to act in a play, produced by Dudley Digges, and it was an entirely unexpected joy to me to be introduced to the stage and literary drama under such auspices.[43]

Like many of her generation Molony received her first taste of theatre through Inghinidhe na hÉireann. Molony, Seán Connolly, Marie Perolz as well as Sara and Molly Allgood and Máire Nic Shiubhlaigh, all received their early training as actors through the drama classes run by the Fay brothers and then Dudley Digges, in the York Street Workman's Club. Soon after joining, Molony was cast in her first performance and she played Delia Cahill in a production of *Cathleen Ní Houlihan* by Yeats. She continued to play small roles over the next five years and was a member of the National Players Society whose, 'avowed object ... was to give dramatic expression to national political propaganda, as distinct from the "Art for Art's sake" school' as she put it.[44] This debate about the purpose of theatre, which had led to the formation of the Abbey Theatre and subsequent breakaway groups, or 'dissident congregations', as Foster terms them, continued to occupy her on the pages of *Bean na hÉireann*.[45] In 1908 she praised Máire Nic Shiubhlaigh's performance in the

Cluithcheóirí na hÉireann production of *The Shuilers' Child* at the Rotunda which she said was,

> not of merely local or dramatic interest. It must give great pleasure to every Irishwoman to know we have a young artiste like Máire Nic Shiubhlaigh capable of such really great work, and generously using her wonderful talent in Ireland and portray Irish life.[46]

Molony's readers would have been aware that Nic Shiubhlaigh, a founder member of the Inghinidhe, had left the Abbey on just such grounds and that the Cluithcheóirí were in fact, the reconstituted Theatre of Ireland. Molony's awareness of the craft of acting and its status (or lack thereof) developed and this was also evident on the pages of *Bean na hÉireann*. She took theatre critics to task for not crediting actors, on whom, she pointed out, the success or otherwise of a play depended,

> I have noticed that when a new play is produced our Dublin critics are so engrossed in retelling the plot and criticising the literary merits of the production that often little attention is given to the artists who interpret for us.[47]

She went some way to rebalance this, in her own review of the Abbey production of Lennox Robinson's play *The Cross Roads*, when she declared, 'We would like to lay our tribute at the feet of the actors who gave Mr Robinson's play to the public in such an absolutely artistic as well as true form'.[48] She even picked out the nuanced performance given by Máire O'Neill who,

> produced a new old Irish woman. Subtle and studied to the last detail, no business, no gesture was twice repeated and the little, rather insignificant part was in her hands worked into a little gem of great artistic merit.[49]

In the summer of 1910, Molony was a member of Casimir Markievicz's Irish Repertory Company who produced his play *The Memory of the Dead* at the Gaiety Theatre. The play was set during the 1798 rebellion and she played the part of the 'patriot girl' who saved the 'young rebel leader', played by Seán Connolly. Life would imitate art six years later, as the two took their positions on the roof of City Hall during the Easter Rising. The play is notable for its gender roles and was reviewed positively on the pages of *Bean na hÉireann* by one Delia Cahill, surely a reference to the character in *Cathleen Ní Houlihan*. The reviewer wrote of her relief at seeing,

> a man shouldering a pike, to go out to fight the English, and to see a woman send him. We want more plays of that style in Ireland of today – rousing, Nationalist plays. Art, not for art's sake, but for Ireland's.[50]

In 1911, Casimir Markievicz decided to produce novelist George Birmingham's first play, *Eleanor's Enterprise*. Eleanor, who apparently resembled Constance Markievicz, was the idealistic daughter of aristocracy and the play concerned her misadventures trying to better the lives of the Finnegan's, a poor family on her father's estate. However, it required considerable work to make it stage worthy and, after restructuring it, he gave it to Molony who rewrote the dialogue. She recalled that, 'It was very stage-Irish when we got it first, but I deleted a good deal of it. It made a good hit'.[51] It was not the only time Molony's dialogue was used. Sidney Gifford recalled that she,

> had such a wonderful talent improvising dialogue ... that at least three playwrights, Count Markievicz, George Birmingham and Lennox Robinson decided that the lines she had introduced were so good that they must be kept in their plays.[52]

Eleanor's Enterprise became a highly-successful comedy and played to packed houses in Dublin. Molony was cast as Mrs Finnegan, again opposite Seán Connolly as Mr Finnegan. In December 1911, both the play and actors received excellent reviews; one noted that 'best of all was the Mrs Finnegan of Helena Molony'.[53] Her largely unacknowledged contribution also came in for much praise. One critic wrote that the play's 'dialogue is directly fresh and natural. It is its chief feature and charm'.[54]

Molony now lived and worked with the Markieviczes, which was not always easy. Sidney Gifford described how, on entering their house, you could not be sure 'as to whether you were going to walk in on a rehearsal for a play, a piece of real life drama, a political discussion, or a placid domestic scene'.[55] Over Christmas and in the early spring of 1912, Molony took refuge in the quiet of Balally Cottage in Sandyford, the one-roomed cottage rented by Constance Markievicz where she often went out to stay.[56]

On 11 January 1912, Molony appeared in her first production on the Abbey stage. It was in the Abbey School of Acting's production of *Mac Daragh's Wife* by Augusta Gregory. Critics picked out her performance and commented that 'she is full of admirable dignity and character though curiously enough she had seemed no good in the other rehearsals'.[57] In February as she appeared in another Abbey School of Acting production, James Connolly wrote to offer her the position of Belfast organiser for the newly-formed Irish Women Workers' Union. Molony declined with regret in a long and self-deprecating letter which began,

> I am not competent to fill a position like that. I am singularly lacking in the power of organisation even in small things like my own affairs but I have the saving virtue of being able to realise it. An organiser such as you need should I know, have the organising ability, business-like mind, be a good speaker and be able to inspire people with confidence. In most of these things I am afraid I would fail.[58]

She was also, she wrote, thinking of going over to help her brother Frank in America for a few months (as her sister-in-law was seriously ill) and was committed to a nine week tour of *Eleanor's Enterprise*. It was clear that behind the confidence of the orator, the stage craft of the actor and the certainty of the editorial writer, Molony was a woman at sea and painfully insecure about her own abilities. Her letter continued,

> It is a great opportunity and if I had the ability there is nothing I would like better, I hope when I have straightened out my own affairs, to do something to help Miss Larkin in Dublin and after serving an apprenticeship like that I might be useful on some future occasion.[59]

Connolly evidently did not agree with her self-assessment and did not give up his efforts to persuade her to become a union organiser, until she agreed in 1915. Molony did not go to America and although her sister-in-law recovered, few references to her or to Frank survive after this.

A NOTABLE SUCCESS[60]

In March 1912, Molony appeared in a third production with the Abbey School of Acting. The School was a prelude to the formation of a Second Abbey Company. It was intended that this new company would perform on the Dublin stage while the First Company was on tour. Molony's acting impressed Yeats and Gonne MacBride wrote to him about her talent as an actor and power of working with others. Gonne MacBride had, she continued in her letter, 'been rather unhappy about her. She was not fitted for the life she was leading ... and was getting wretched and unsettled'.[61] The planned Second Company would be semi-professional, but Gonne MacBride illuminated the fragility of Molony's financial position, albeit in a rather patronizing manner,

> Of course though, if she stays with you she must get enough money to live on, for though she has simple tastes and no exaggerated idea of life, and cares little for money, she can't live on air.[62]

That month Molony was among the first intake of actors to the Abbey Second Company and on 19 March 1912 the company made its debut with *The Mineral Workers* by William Boyle. Molony played Mary Mulroy, a role she would play many more times in her career. The press warmly welcomed the establishment of this 'reserve corps'.[63] Seán Connolly and Michael Conniffe were among the other actors in the new company. *The Mineral Workers* ran once more that month and over the summer Molony returned to perform as Mrs Finnegan with Casimir Markievicz's Irish Repertory Company.

Even allowing for the fact that she was working nights, Molony's living arrangements were unorthodox at this point. Rosamond Jacob called in one day in late July and found,

> Emer and her friend finishing what they called their breakfast at a quarter to two. They thought it was much earlier and of course none of the clocks in the house were right.[64]

In September, Molony and the company set off for a nine week tour of Ireland and Britain with *Eleanor's Enterprise*.

There is an hilarious account of the tour in *The Years Flew By*, which also highlighted Molony's personal warmth and generosity. Following successful runs in Cork and Belfast, the company arrived in Liverpool only to discover that it was illegal to employ child actors. In their place, several adults of restricted growth were hired,

> Unknown to Helena Molony, one such little man was hired and, dressed as a small boy, acted the part of one of the pestiferous young Finnegan's. When she arrived in the theatre every night, the kind-hearted actress gave the 'little lad' a few sweets, and at the close of the performance she would put her arms around him in a motherly fashion and calling him by endearing names, advise him to run home and get a good night's rest after a hard day. Then one night, hearing him talking outside her dressing room long after she had banished him to home and bed, she went out to admonish him. She found the 'child prodigy' dressed as a man, smoking a pipe,

and recounting to some of the stage hands how 'the Hirish lady 'as fallen 'ead hover 'eels in love with 'im.[65]

When Molony returned to Dublin after the tour, Connolly made another effort, 'to invite her to come to Belfast to help him organise the mill girls'.[66] Ina Connolly travelled down to Dublin with the Belfast Fianna and her father asked her to call in on Molony at the Abbey. Connolly recalled that,

As a leading feminist she was anxious to do so, but was afraid it would cut her off too much from the theatre, and once she had left she might find it very difficult to get started again.[67]

The next time that Connolly asked her to become involved in the Irish Women Workers' Union, she would agree.

Throughout 1912 Irish suffragists became increasingly militant in the face of the Irish Parliamentary Party's refusal to support female suffrage bills at Westminster, where they held the balance of power. As Molony's acting career was taking off, another group of Irish women began to take centre stage in public life. The Irish Parliamentary Party had also refused to include female suffrage in the proposed Home Rule Bill. Women of all shades of opinion, nationalist and unionist, came together for a mass meeting in Dublin in June 1912. They called for the exclusively male franchise proposed in the Bill to be extended to women. Molony was unable to attend but was one of those who sent a message of support. There was no response from MPs and the Irish Women's Franchise League initiated militant action in Ireland.

One of the most celebrated acts was in July 1912 when an axe was flung at visiting Prime Minister Asquith, which grazed John Redmond's ear. Mary Leigh, an English suffragette, was convicted for this. In 1972 Marie Johnson, who had been a member of the Irish Women's Suffrage Society, claimed that it was Molony who had thrown it.[68] There is no other evidence of this (she would have claimed it proudly) and intelligence records noted that she was not very active in the suffragette movement, although she attended and spoke at meetings of the IWFL and WSPU. It was interesting though that she was associated with the most militant act of 1912. Later, one can detect a note of annoyance from Molony that any women active at this point were assumed to be suffragettes and that 'Any phase of the Suffragettes' activity was front page news, whereas the "extreme" Nationalist movement was not news at all'.[69]

On 7 November 1912 Molony appeared in the First Company's production of *Patriots* by Lennox Robinson, alongside Sara Allgood and Kathleen Drago. Critics noted that Helena Molony as Mrs Sullivan was, 'very successful'.[70] This rapid promotion from the Abbey School of Acting to the Second Company and then to the First, over the course of six productions, was a clear indication of her talent as well as a powerful mentor. The following month, when the First Company departed to tour the US on a six month tour, Molony was taken on by the Abbey on a full-time paid contract. Over the next year, she appeared in almost 50 productions with the First and Second Companies. She regularly played in seven different productions a month and often in two a night. On 26 December 1912, she again played Mary Mulroy in *The Mineral Workers*, in what a critic called an 'exceptionally good' performance.[71]

The Second Company developed quickly and from the spring of 1913 onwards they began to premiere new Abbey plays. Molony's ninth role of the year was as Aunt Nancy in the premiere of *The Cuckoo's Nest* by John Guinan, directed by Lennox Robinson. The *Evening Herald* called it the 'finest bit of work she has ever done', and added with relief, that 'Miss Moloney [sic] at last got an opportunity of showing how undoubtedly clever she can be'.[72] *The Irish Times* called her, 'a notable success' in the role, while the

Daily Express praised the ensemble saying, 'The Second Company had indeed never done better'.[73] After the interval, she changed costume to play Nora in Synge's *Riders to the Sea*. In April 1913, Molony performed in the premiere of Gertrude Robin's *The Homecoming*. However, the Dublin critics were left unimpressed, both by the play and by the acting. The *Evening Telegraph* commented, 'We do not thus criticise Miss Molony's acting because it is bad but because we know she can do much better', while the *Independent* sniped 'Even Miss Molony could make little of the Mother Loweski. For a lowly ill-fed peasant she looked decidedly robust and had a nice taste in brown boots'.[74]

Despite the occasional sour note, the Second Company was going from strength to strength. On 18 April, *The Mineral Workers* followed *The Homecoming* and she again played Mary Mulroy. A critic commented that 'she has filled few parts with such happy discernment'.[75] She performed in seven productions that month and then toured to Mallow and Tralee, where she reprised her very first role, that of Delia Cahill in *Cathleen Ní Houlihan*. She also played Nora in *Riders to the Sea* and Mrs Donoghue in Lady Gregory's *The Workhouse Ward*.

As the spring of 1913 turned to summer, Molony's star rose in the Abbey. The First Company had returned from America and she joined them on their British tour in late May. They performed in Oxford and Birmingham and then went on to London. In June, on the stage of the Royal Court London, the First Company of the Abbey Theatre, Helena Molony among them, presented a double bill of J.M. Synge's *Playboy of the Western World* and *The Magnanimous Lover* by St. John Greer Ervine. In *Playboy*, alongside Kathleen Drago, Molony played Honor Blake, the teenage girl smitten by Christy Mahon. Toni Desmond, J.M. Kerrigan, Eithne Magee, Fred O'Donovan and Arthur Sinclair were among the rest of the cast. She then played Mrs Cather in Ervine's play, with Sara Allgood leading a much smaller cast. The play was only performed six times in all and Molony was in four of those productions. Molony looked to be on course to become one of the leading names in Irish theatre.

ROYAL COURT THEATRE.

Proprietor   - - - Mr. J. H. LEIGH

Under the Joint Management of Mr. J. H. LEIGH & Mr. R. T. E. NEEVES

MONDAY, TUESDAY and WEDNESDAY EVENINGS,

JUNE 2nd, 3rd and 4th, at 8.30

And MATINEE WEDNESDAY, at 2.30

First Production in London of

The Magnanimous Lover

A PLAY IN ONE ACT

BY

ST. JOHN G ERVINE

Produced by LENNOX ROBINSON

Sam Hinde	J. A. O'ROURKE
Mrs. Cather	HELENA MOLONY
William Cather	SYDNEY J. MORGAN
Henry Hinde	J. M. KERRIGAN
Maggie Cather	SARA ALLGOOD

First Abbey Company production of *The Magnanimous Lover*,
Royal Court, London, June 1913
courtesy Abbey Theatre Archive

As the actors took a well-earned break over the summer, Dublin's fraught industrial relations began to boil over. In the middle of August, when William Martin Murphy sacked members of the ITGWU in the *Irish Independent*, sympathetic action and pickets resulted and further sackings followed. The dispute would rapidly become one of the biggest industrial disputes in Europe at the time, with employers and police ranged against workers led by James Larkin of the ITGWU. Over 20,000 workers in the city were locked out which impacted on many more workers and their families. On 25 August, Molony returned to the Abbey stage after the summer break, and appeared as Mrs Tarpey in Lady Gregory's *Spreading the News*. The following morning ITGWU employees of the Dublin Tramway Company (also owned by Martin Murphy) withdrew their labour in a move that coincided with the first day of the Dublin Horse Show. Violence followed in clashes with police, the strike spread and workers all over the city were attacked. That night, Molony was on stage as Mary Mulroy in *The Mineral Workers* while her husband was played by Michael Conniffe, also a labour supporter. They had a scene together where they sat backstage by the fireplace but the 'old couple' on stage were actually discussing the far more dramatic events taking place on the streets.

Events moved rapidly. Larkin was arrested then released on 28 August. Two days later a warrant was put out for his arrest and a mass meeting on Sackville Street planned for 31 August was prohibited. Molony who now lived with the Markieviczes in their new home, Surrey House, Rathmines, played a key role in that evening's events. That night, partly to help Larkin evade the police, a party was hosted at Surrey House, ostensibly to welcome Casimir back to Dublin. As violent riots took place all over the city, with police baton-charging workers, Larkin slipped into the busy house unnoticed. When Molony discovered that Larkin was considering obeying the ban the following day, she and Markievicz persuaded him to change his mind. Early the next morning, Molony took out her stage makeup and made Larkin up as a clergyman.[76] Accompanied by Nellie Gifford, the disguise enabled Larkin to pass through police cordons and into the Imperial Hotel on Sackville Street. From the balcony of the hotel, owned by William Martin Murphy, he threw off his disguise and addressed the crowds below. The day became known as 'Bloody Sunday' as the police rushed to arrest Larkin and dispersed the meeting in a violent and indiscriminate manner.

Saturday Night
August 30th, 1913, at 8.15

THE SHADOW OF THE GLEN, A PLAY IN ONE ACT, BY J. M. SYNGE

DAN BURKE, farmer and herd	
NORA BURKE, his wife	Sydney J. Morgan
	Ann Coppinger
MICHAEL DARA, herd	J. A. O'Rourke
A TRAMP	
	J. M. Kerrigan

SCENE—The last cottage at the head of a long glen in County Wicklow

THE MINERAL WORKERS, A PLAY IN THREE ACTS, BY WM. BOYLE

MARY MULROY	
	Helen Molony
UNCLE BARTLE	J. A. O'Rourke
NED MULROY	
	Michael Conniffe
PATRICK, his son	H. E. Hutchinson
KITTY, his daughter	Eithne Magee
DAN FOGARTY, a farmer	J. M. Kerrigan

Second Abbey Company production of *The Mineral Workers*
at the start of the 1913 Lockout
courtesy Abbey Theatre Archive

For Molony, the Lockout also marked the effective end of her association with Inghinidhe na hÉireann and she later said, 'I was not out of the Inghinidhe, but apart from it ... I had also got into the Labour movement a good deal and it was absorbing me'.[77] The Lockout was the apprenticeship of sorts she had told Connolly she needed. Her public profile was substantial and she was recorded as being one of the 'prominent citizens' who followed the coffin of James Nolan, killed by police at the weekend.[78] In what time she had spare in between rehearsals and performances, Molony was involved in relief work and also addressed strike meetings.

Food kitchens were set up in Liberty Hall for the large numbers of families affected and were run by Delia Larkin. Many other nationalist women and feminists, including Hanna Sheehy Skeffington and Louie Bennett, were drawn into the labour movement at this point. Seamus Kavanagh, an early recruit to the Fianna, recalled that,

> The Countess Markievicz, Inghinina hÉireann [sic], Dr. Kathleen Lynn, Mrs. Darrell Figgis, Miss French-Mullen, Miss Molony and other women connected with the National movement assisted in preparing and serving meals to the wives and children of the men on strike.[79]

Molony's own view of the Lockout and of 'Larkinism' was informed by her nationalism and her relationship with Connolly. She later wrote that while,

> All of the sympathy of the Irish Ireland movement was with the strikers ... not all of us were in sympathy with James Larkin or his outlook which was that of a British socialist. He attacked the 'nationalist' outlook which he dubbed 'Capitalist'. There was some foundation for this.[80]

It was an interesting admission and perhaps only made with the benefit of thirty-five-years hindsight. She was less nuanced in December 1913, when in conversation with a friend she referred to 'The revolting unwholesome

Englishness of Larkin and the strike and all'.[81] Between the two great figures of the Irish labour movement, she was in no doubt as to where her loyalties lay. Larkin had,

> dragged the unskilled workers up off their knees and did a great work but between himself and James Connolly, there was a bitter feud. It was only a battle of temperaments, and I was on the side of James Connolly.[82]

Connolly's analysis of Irish history and society as well as the organising experience which he had developed in America meant that he was becoming increasingly influential. His ability to weave together forms of radical nationalism, feminism and socialism, both practically and ideologically, was extraordinary for its time and Molony was one of those who identified with that unity and worked to achieve it.

As the Lockout progressed in September 1913, Molony appeared in six productions with the Abbey Second Company. Her roles included the Sweetheart in *The Dean of St Patrick's* and the Middle-aged Woman in *An Pósadh (The Marriage)* by Douglas Hyde. Her commitment was the same, whether she played a lead or a bit part, regardless of the quality of the play. When she appeared as the Nurse in *My Lord* by Mrs Bart Kennedy, the *Evening Herald* singled out her performance. Molony,

> was always in the picture in the trifling part of the nurse and by her delicate by-play lent sound illusion to the scene but even the soundest of acting could not disguise the blemishes [of the play] ...[83]

After the interval she took the more central role of Mrs Sullivan in *Patriots* by Lennox Robinson, in which she again played opposite Seán Connolly. In the middle of all of this, Molony found time to appear in a suffrage play, written by Susan Day of the Munster Women's Franchise League.[84]

Molony did not appear on the Abbey stage for nearly six weeks, between the end of October and into December.

This was perhaps a forewarning of what was about to occur. In November 1913 she visited Gonne MacBride in Paris, who wrote to Yeats that she, Iseult, Helena Molony and Miss Gifford [probably Sidney] had all played planchette one evening and 'A spirit called Teig O'Driscoll of Bantry who lived in 1691 communicated'.[85] Apparently Teig 'talked a good deal about ships and the sea' and became very exercised after telling them to open the bible.[86] On 9 December, Molony was back on the Abbey stage as Mrs Sullivan in *The Patriots* and the following week she played Mary Mulroy in *The Mineral Workers*.

The Lockout took its toll on the city and later, in a vivid description of the time, Molony wrote about the long winter where strikers drifted back to work, 'This social battle had been fought with blood and tears. Houses were bare of furniture; pawnshops were full of the poor treasures of the workers. Hunger was rife'.[87] However, it also took its toll on Molony. The frantic round of rehearsing, performing, political activity and appearances, and possibly other factors too, seriously impacted on her health. Rosamond Jacob was back in Dublin and recorded on 13 December that she 'went to Aonach with Emer [who was] very listless and unwell'. Two days later, Dr Kathleen Lynn informed her that she was looking after Molony who had had a nervous breakdown.[88]

I WAS GOING OFF THE BOIL THROUGH ILL-HEALTH[89]
It was clearly a very serious breakdown as it took her over six months to recover. It would be a year before she worked in Dublin again. True to form however, Molony did not waste time and even while she was recovering she was busy and converted Lynn to the cause. Lynn takes up the narrative with her own account,

It was quite in a casual way I first got in touch with the national movement. Helena Molony was ill and Mme. Markievicz came and asked me to go & see her. I did not know Mme. Markievicz although she was a distant cousin of mine through the Wynnes, my mother's people. After Miss Molony got better she came and stayed with me in Belgrave Road where I have always lived since I left the hospital. We used to have long talks and she converted me to the National movement. She was a very clever and attractive girl with a tremendous power of making friends.[90]

Markievicz later said that she had introduced Lynn to the movement, but Lynn herself credited Molony with it. Like Markievicz, Lynn became increasingly radical and socialist in outlook under Molony's influence.

Molony then continued her recuperation in France and in the spring of 1914, she went to stay with Gonne MacBride and her family in Paris. The break had the desired effect and in July, Gonne MacBride wrote to Yeats and told him that Molony was,

looking ever so much stronger and better and from what the Doctor writes I believe the cure is complete … I hope I will be able to tell you that she is really quite recovered and able for steady work again in the Autumn.[91]

Later that month she again wrote about Molony's recovery and expressed hope that she would be able to join the Abbey again. 'She seems *perfectly well and strong again*. She is a charming companion. We are all fond of her'.[92] In August, to escape the Parisian heat, Molony went with Gonne MacBride and her children, Iseult Gonne and Seán MacBride to Arrens in the Pyrenees. There Molony took long walks and practised her voice projection 'on the edge of a mountain torrent'.[93] She was anxious to get back to Dublin and, over the next five months, Gonne MacBride regularly wrote to Yeats about this,

She is very well, in good spirits and *quite strong* again. I think you will be quite safe in taking her back to the Abbey – She will not break down again – Let me know *when* she ought to be back in Dublin.[94]

They were still in Arrens when World War One broke out in September 1914. The war changed everything. Immediately they moved to Argelès,

> to help nurse the wounded soldiers of whom the numbers are simply appalling. Every hospital is overcrowded and every public building throughout France is turned into a hospital.[95]

Gonne MacBride was taken on as a regular Red Cross nurse, with Molony and Iseult as helpers. Molony was still nursing in November 1914 but 'without enthusiasm' as she wanted to get home. Yeats' lack of response to Gonne MacBride's letters may have been due to the poor financial state of the Abbey, as well as management concern about Molony's health.[96] Gonne MacBride suggested that Molony could even go back without salary,

> while things are so bad, it would keep her working and learning parts and prevent her from getting rusty. She is quite well and strong and is longing to get back to work,

and 'She is very serious about it' she wrote in November.[97]

Finally, the letters produced the desired result and at the end of the year, the Abbey manager wrote to Yeats saying that he would use Molony as much as possible. Helena Molony returned to Dublin just before Christmas, 1914.[98]

IRELAND'S OPPORTUNITY

> I still had a contract with the Abbey Theatre, but the political situation had a bigger attraction for me than a theatrical career.[99]

Initially, Molony moved into 10 North Great George's Street and stayed with Marie Perolz. She threw herself back into acting and appeared regularly in Abbey productions. In February 1915, she again played Mrs Cather in *The Magnanimous Lover* by St. John Greer Ervine,

Ellie Clohessy in *The Country Dressmaker* by George Fitzmaurice and Mrs Palmer in Lennox Robinson's *The Dreamers*. In April, she stepped in to play the part of Mrs Simpson in *The Bargain* by William Crone, two days before it opened. Reviewers, unimpressed with the acting as a whole, singled out Molony saying that,

Cover of Abbey Theatre Programmes
courtesy Abbey Theatre Archive

The best acting came from a wholly unexpected quarter. Every allowance could have been made for Miss Helena Molony had she failed in her portrayal of the shrewd, strong minded Mrs. Simpson, as she only took up the part a day or so before the production. As a matter of fact however, she succeeded in extracting every ounce of effect out of the part, getting all her lines home with telling effect and humorous acerbity.[100]

While Molony recovered and nursed in France during 1914, developments at home had been uppermost in her mind. Her guiding principle had always been that England's difficulty was Ireland's opportunity. As early as 1910, when war between Britain and Germany looked likely, she decried the lack of a trained army that could secure Irish independence and asked; 'have we anything to offer Germany in return for her help?'[101] The situation was very different in 1914 and from her point of view, much more hopeful. Even before the outbreak of war, Ireland had become an increasingly militarised and militant place. Since Edward Carson had formed the Ulster Volunteers in 1913, the Irish Volunteers, Cumann na mBan and the Irish Citizen Army had all been founded in Dublin.

Molony kept a close eye on and participated in crucial debates from France. In May 1914 a storm erupted on the pages of the *Irish Citizen* after the IWFL criticised the role and outlook of the newly-formed Cumann na mBan. This echoed the debates first published on the pages of *Bean na hÉireann* five years previously and as Pašeta points out, it was Molony who 'set out the most eloquent objection to the *Citizen*'s position'.[102] There was much more at stake now; a Home Rule Bill seemed imminent and Redmond's Irish Parliamentary Party held the balance of power at Westminster, which they had used to defeat suffrage bills. Cumann na mBan came under sustained criticism from the IWFL on the pages of the *Irish Citizen* for being nothing more than an 'animated collecting box' and setting back the cause of Irish women.[103] Mary MacSwiney responded to their initial criticism and accused the paper of alienating nationalists from the suffrage cause. On 9 May 1914 Molony's letter from France in defence of Cumann na mBan was published. She argued that the 'slavish spirit' that the *Irish Citizen* identified in Agnes O'Farrelly's inaugural speech was in fact 'an expression of allegiance to anti-English militancy',

It is with great regret I see the *Citizen* ranging itself on the side of those who are against women taking part in the armed defence of their country – because they may, incidentally be a source of strength to Mr Redmond. This is an attitude which, as Miss Mac Swiney says, will do much to injure Suffrage in Ireland. The Volunteers, men and women, have been called into being to defend the liberties of all Irish Citizens ... every Nationalist knows this to be true. You do not alter the facts of a case by dubbing other people's principles 'party' and calling your own 'freedom'. It is possible and may be desirable to support the Parliamentary party without necessarily supporting Mr Redmond's anti-suffrage opinions; and personally I have great confidence in the ability of Irish suffragists to deal with Mr Redmond and the other antis on the subject of women when we get them away from the protection of the English Parliament. It is also possible for some women, without being what you call 'camp followers', to imagine that the freedom – even the partial freedom – of a nation to be of more importance that the partial freedom of the feminist portion of it. You say truly, 'there can be no free nation without free women', but neither can there be free women in an enslaved nation, and it seems to me sound citizenship to put the welfare of the whole nation before any section of it.[104]

This had been the kernel of Molony's argument in 1909: 'freedom for our nation and the complete removal of disabilities to our sex'.[105] Molony had already mentored and brought to this point of view Markievicz and Lynn. The latter came to the movement from suffrage while the former took much persuading. Molony continued,

Of course these views are opposed to the policy of 'Suffrage first' for which you stand, but I do not think that the fact of our holding different views justifies your accusing us of being 'reactionary', 'camp followers', 'patient thralls', and 'false to our sex and the highest ideals of Nationalism'. Such an article is designed to make the *Irish Citizen*, and what it stands for, unpopular with many Nationalists; and that is a thing, I am sure, most of the Volunteers would be very sorry to see.[106]

Slightly curious, however, given all her previous stands, was her line that it was possible and might even be desirable to support the Irish Parliamentary Party. She also seemed to be making positive noises about the partial freedom promised in the form of Home Rule. As with many of those involved in the movement for independence, it is fascinating to speculate where her life might have gone had national and international developments not heightened her militant tendencies.[107] It was also the first time that Molony had spent considerable time with Gonne MacBride since she was a very young woman and it is possible that this was a factor. Gonne MacBride was very involved in seeking to affiliate Cumann na mBan with the International Red Cross at this point.

However Molony's closest association was not with Cumann na mBan but with the Irish Citizen Army which had been formed to defend workers against police intimidation. When James Larkin left for America in October 1914, James Connolly took over the ITGWU and the ICA, seeing World War One as the opportunity for a national and social revolution all over Europe. He was transforming the ICA into a viable, if small, military force. Molony described how Markievicz,

Had taken a very active part in the Strike and with her flair for military organisation she naturally was absorbed into the Citizen Army and given high rank. Her knowledge of firearms was an invaluable asset ... Connolly – staunch Feminist that he was – was more than anxious to welcome women into the ranks on equal terms with men, and to promote them to such rank and position as they were suited for.[108]

All of this increased Molony's longing and determination to return home from France. When she did, anti-recruiting and anti-conscription agitation took up much of her time. Molony regularly addressed meetings in between performances and sometimes even during them. This caused serious tension between herself and the Abbey manager (and author of *The Magnanimous Lover*), St. John Greer Ervine. Molony was playing a part in which she appeared in the first act but not again until the last act,

> In the interval, one night, I went and spoke at an open-air anti-recruiting meeting at Beresford Place – a stone's throw away. When Irvine [sic] heard of it he flew into a violent rage. He was a real Britisher. He ordered Kathleen Drago to dress up in my attire. She was very reluctant to do it. When I came back, half an hour before I was due to appear on stage, he said to me 'Kathleen Drago will take your part'. I said: 'What about it? I am here half an hour before the time'. He said: 'You have no right to address a meeting. This is not a tea party or a Sunday School party'. I said: 'I have no experience of Sunday Schools. I have experience of the stage'. He was very cross. He was not in a position to dismiss me as I was Yeats' protégé and had a contract. I got an endless ragging about that. The fact that I was addressing an anti-recruiting meeting amused the Company.[109]

When the 1916 Conscription Act was introduced and the spectre of Irishmen being conscripted was raised, it was one of Molony's practical suggestions and her characteristic move to immediate action which had very far-reaching consequences. As Ireland was explicitly exempted from the Act, activists debated whether this meant that Irishmen in Britain were also exempted. Nellie Gifford recalled that,

> We discussed the matter. Miss Molony suggested that the only method, in the time at hand, would be to have a question asked in Parliament, as to whether 'Ireland' or 'Irishmen' were to be exempt. The only M.P., who had not already gone over to London, was Alfie Byrne. After some delay, we located Alfie Byrne, and asked him if he would put the question,

which he did. In consequence, numerous Volunteers from England and Scotland came to Ireland …[110]

The subsequent letter from Byrne, along with a copy of the question from the Westminster Order Book, had pride of place in Molony's papers until she donated them to the Bureau of Military History. Nellie Gifford also recalled that one of these returned Volunteers was the young Michael Collins.[111] Molony was then asked by James Connolly to become registered proprietor for his new paper, *The Workers' Republic*, successor to the suppressed *Irish Worker*. She agreed and was thus responsible for any treasonable material published.

In the midst of all of this activity, Molony's living arrangements were erratic. Rosamond Jacob went to visit her at North Great George's Street on 21 May, and recorded that, 'Miss Parroles [sic] says that she only goes there for her letters and sleeps God knows where'.[112]

THE IRISH WOMEN WORKERS' UNION

The Co-op – … gave employment to 8–10 girls, none of whom could get employment as they were 'marked men' on account of their strike activities.[113]

In July 1915, Delia Larkin, first General Secretary of the Irish Women Workers' Union left for England amidst bad feeling. The nearly moribund union and a clothing co-operative were left in the hands of James Connolly. That August he approached Molony, for the third time, to become involved in the IWWU and this time she accepted.

The young union was in serious difficulty. It had been virtually devastated by the Lockout with large numbers of its 1,000 members left unemployed. The Irish Women Workers' Co-operative Society was set up by Delia Larkin to provide employment for some of these, with funds that had been raised on a drama tour. Its members produced and sold clothing and soft goods.[114] That autumn Molony's introduction to the business of running a union began, as she and Connolly recruited new members. She later recalled,

> I had no experience or idea of any kind of organising and it was really he [Connolly] who did the work, coming with me to the various factory gates to try and enlist girls into the union.[115]

Initially Molony's position was a voluntary one, which suited her as it gave her the evenings to perform in the Abbey. However, the ITGWU were unwilling, under trade union rules, to allow unwaged officials. In November the Co-operative was reopened on Eden Quay, as the Irish Workers' Co-operative Society (still referred to as the Co-op). Jane (Jinny) Shanahan was appointed manager, the shop assistant was Rosie Hackett and Helena Molony was Secretary of the Co-op workroom and shop, on a weekly wage of between 10–15 shillings.[116] They sold items of women's and men's wear made in the workshop and, following Molony's suggestion that they manufacture a 'Red Hand' shirt, it became their bestselling item. Radical papers were also on sale while *The Workers' Republic* had been printed from the backroom of the premises since May. The Co-op would play an important role during preparations for the Rising.

On 15 November, the new Secretary of the IWWU gave a lecture on 'Women's Wages and Trade Unionism' to the Women's Industrial Conference in the Mansion House. She spoke of the benefits of the newly-reformed Co-op and 'showed that cooperation secured to workers the product of their labour and was thoroughly in harmony with the Irish instinct for communal life' and pointed out women were receiving wages as low as three shillings a week.[117]

For Molony, August 1915 was the beginning of a high profile trade union career that spanned over a quarter of a century and she remained with the IWWU until 1941. Her professional acting career was by no means over and she continued as a member of the Abbey Company until 1927. However, she appeared on stage sporadically and only once again, in 1922, did her career look like reaching the heights it had in 1913. From now on, theatre played a supporting role in her life's work. In *Bean na hÉireann* in 1910, perhaps in premonition of decisions she would go on to make, she wrote that, 'By true lovers of Ireland many sacrifices must be made and many high ambitions surrendered, but for all that they will think they are well paid'.[118]

The actor had become a trade unionist and was about to become a soldier and these roles would merge over the next nine months. Foster comments that, 'the climactic performance [of the Easter Rising] was in some ways the result of intense rehearsals conducted since the turn of the century'.[119] Molony, who had been centre stage for these rehearsals, would now play her part in the main performance.

SOURCES

1   MacBride White and Jeffares, *Gonne-Yeats Letters*, March 1912, p. 308.
2   See also Regan, 'Helena Molony', pp 147–8.
3   Diane Norman, *Terrible Beauty: A Life of Constance Markievicz, 1868–1927* (Dublin, Poolbeg Press, 1988), p. 45.
4   Abbey Theatre Scrapbooks, Vols. 7–9, 1911–16, MS 25495–500, NLI; Hereafter Abbey Theatre Scrapbooks, NLI.
5   MacBride White and Jeffares, *Gonne-Yeats Letters*, March 1912, p. 308.
6   Regan, 'Helena Molony', p. 147.
7   RJD, 20–22 May 1911.
8   *Ibid.*
9   *Ibid.*
10   *Ibid.*
11   *Ibid.*
12   *Ibid.*
13   Ward, *Unmanageable Revolutionaries*, p. 86.
14   Sidney Czira: BMH WS 909.

15 Helena Molony: BMH WS 391.
16 *Ibid.*
17 Sidney Czira: BMH WS 909.
18 'The Green Jacket', RTÉ Sound Archives.
19 Ward, *Unmanageable Revolutionaries*, p. 79.
20 RJD, 10 July 1911.
21 Molony transcribed the manuscript in the mid 1950s and it was finally published by Arlen House in 1986, edited by Dana Hearne.
22 RJD, 28 July–5 August 1911.
23 *Ibid.*
24 It has proven impossible to understand what they mean by this reference.
25 RJD, 28 July–5 August 1911.
26 *Ibid.*
27 *Ibid.*
28 *Ibid.*
29 *Ibid.*
30 *The Irish Times*, 7 August 1911.
31 RJD, 6 August 1911.
32 *The Irish Worker*, 5 August 1911.
33 *Ibid.*
34 *Ibid.*
35 *The Irish Worker*, 12 August 1911.
36 *The Irish Times*, 7 August 1911.
37 Undated newspaper clipping, Hugh O'Connor Collection, NLI.
38 Fox, *Rebel Irishwomen*, p. 68.
39 *Ibid.*
40 *The Irish Worker*, 2 September 1911.
41 *Ibid.*
42 MacBride White and Jeffares, *Gonne-Yeats Letters*, March 1912, p. 308.
43 Helena Molony: BMH WS 391.
44 *Ibid.*
45 Foster, *Vivid Faces*, p. 87.
46 *Bean na hÉireann*, June 1909.
47 *Ibid.*
48 *Ibid.*
49 *Ibid.*
50 *Bean na hÉireann*, August 1910.
51 Helena Molony, Draft WS Kilmainham.
52 Czira, *Years Flew By*, p. 36.

53   R. Hogan, R. Burnham and D. Poteet (eds), *The Rise of the Realists* (Dublin, Dolmen Press, 1979), p. 153.

54   *The Evening Herald*, December 1911.

55   Pašeta, *Irish Nationalist Women*, p. 213; Czira, *Years Flew By*, p. 56.

56   Helena Molony: BMH WS 391.

57   Hogan *et al*, *Rise of the Realists*, p. 173.

58   William O'Brien Papers, MS 13940 (ii), 9 January 1912, NLI.

59   *Ibid*.

60   *The Irish Times*, 14 March 1913.

61   MacBride White and Jeffares, *Gonne-Yeats Letters*, March 1912, p. 308.

62   *Ibid*.

63   Abbey Theatre Scrapbooks, Vol. 7, NLI.

64   RJD, 26 July 1912.

65   Czira, *Years Flew By*, p. 37.

66   Ina Connolly Heron, Bureau of Military History Witness Statement 919.

67   *Ibid*.

68   Rosemary Cullen Owens, *A Social History of Women in Ireland, 1870–1970* (Dublin, Gill and Macmillan, 2005), p. 338.

69   Helena Molony: BMH WS 391.

70   Abbey Theatre Scrapbooks, Vol. 7, NLI.

71   *Ibid*.

72   *Evening Telegraph*, 14 March 1913.

73   *Daily Express* and *The Irish Times*, 14 March 1913.

74   *Irish Independent*, 11 April 1913.

75   *Irish Independent*, 18 April 1913.

76   Helena Molony interview with Prionsias Mac Aonghusa, August 1963, private collection. See also Padraig Yeates, *Lockout: Dublin 1913* (Dublin, Gill and Macmillan, 2000).

77   Helena Molony: BMH WS 391.

78   Jacqueline Van Voris, *Constance de Markievicz in the Cause of Ireland* (Cambridge, MA, University of Massachusetts Press, 1967), p. 108.

79   Seamus Kavanagh, Bureau of Military History Witness Statement 1670.

80   Helena Molony: BMH WS 391.

81   RJD, 11 December 1913.

82   Helena Molony: BMH WS 391.

83   Abbey Theatre Scrapbooks, Vol. 8, NLI.

84   *Ibid*.

85 MacBride White and Jeffares, *Gonne-Yeats Letters*, p. 328.

86 *Ibid.*

87 Helena Molony, 'Years of Tension', Typescript article, Hugh O'Connor Collection, NLI; Hereafter, Molony, 'Years of Tension'.

88 RJD, 13–15 December 1913.

89 Helena Molony, Draft WS Kilmainham.

90 Kathleen Lynn, Bureau of Military History Witness Statement 357; Hereafter, Kathleen Lynn: BMH WS 357.

91 MacBride White and Jeffares, *Gonne-Yeats Letters*, July 1914, pp 343–352.

92 *Ibid.*

93 *Ibid.*

94 *Ibid.*

95 *Ibid.*

96 *Ibid.*

97 *Ibid.*

98 Helena Molony: BMH WS 391.

99 Helena Molony: BMH WS 391.

100 Abbey Theatre Scrapbooks, Vol. 9, NLI.

101 *Bean na hÉireann*, January 1910.

102 Pašeta, *Irish Nationalist Women*, p. 143.

103 Cullen Owens, *A Social History of Women in Ireland*, p. 114.

104 *The Irish Citizen*, 9 May 1914.

105 *Bean na hÉireann*, April 1909.

106 *The Irish Citizen*, 9 May 1914.

107 Nell Regan, 'A tigress in kitten's fur', *The Irish Times*, 23 May 2013.

108 Helena Molony: BMH WS 391.

109 Molony in her BMH statement dates this during the War of Independence and she did appear in *The Mineral Workers* at a time that would tally. However Ervine was manager of the Abbey in 1915–16 and it is more likely that she got the play wrong on this particular occasion than the manager.

110 Nellie Donnelly (nee Gifford), Bureau of Military History Witness Statement 256.

111 *Ibid.*

112 RJD, 21 May 1915.

113 Helena Molony: BMH WS 391.

114 Therese Moriarty, 'Larkin and the Women's Movement', in Donal Levin (ed), *James Larkin: Lion of the Fold* (Dublin, Gill and Macmillan, 2006), p. 100.

115 Molony, 'Years of Tension'.
116 Helena Molony, Draft WS Kilmainham.
117 *The Irish Citizen*, 20 November 1915.
118 *Bean na hÉireann*, August 1910.
119 Foster, *Vivid Faces*, p. 112.

SOLDIER
1916

It is part of our military duty to knit and darn but also to march and shoot, to obey orders with our brothers in arms.[1]

Helena Molony did not just run the Workers' Co-op and revive the union – she was also partly responsible for the organisation of women in the Irish Citizen Army. One of these, Rosie Hackett, recollected that,

When Miss Larkin left Liberty Hall, Miss Helena Molony came to take charge, and that is when the work of the women's section of the Irish Citizen Army started in earnest.[2]

Molony and the women of the Co-op were involved in the concrete preparations for the military challenge to British rule in Ireland that she had urged for so many years. They played an active part in the Rising and would all be imprisoned for their role, along with many members of Cumann na mBan. However, only three women, Constance Markievicz, Helena Molony and Winnie Carney, were incarcerated for a substantial length of time following Easter week. They were all members of the ICA.

The same week that she was announced as IWWU Secretary, the formation of a new 'Girls' Ambulance Corps' was announced under ICA news in *The Workers' Republic* of 21 August 1915,

> All members of the Irish Women Workers' Union are cordially invited to attend. A competent doctor is in attendance, and the lessons are bright and interesting. Names of intending members should be handed in to Miss Molony, Sec., Liberty Hall or at 31 Eden Quay.[3]

Just as Molony worked to bring in activists on the union end, it is likely that she was responsible for helping to draw in other prominent women to the ICA, many from the Inghinidhe days. Dr Kathleen Lynn, with Madeleine ffrench-Mullen as her assistant, ran the first aid classes, while Nellie Gifford ran cookery classes.

Molony was later adamant that women were admitted into the Citizen Army on equal terms and 'were an integral part of the Army and not in any sense a "Ladies Auxiliary"'.[4] It was a statement she continued to make throughout her life and was crucial for her to clarify, both in the context of the debates that happened at the time about the status of the self-identified ladies auxiliary, Cumann na mBan, but also later, with regard to the recognition of women's work as soldiers and the legacy that this left. Although the Inghinidhe as an organisation became a branch of Cumann na mBan (and was re-energised by this), several of its prominent members, including Molony, Markievicz, Perolz and ffrench-Mullen were in the ICA. It was a clear indication of their labour affiliations by this point. Molony did not join Cumann na mBan as a member at any point after 1916, and strongly reiterated this fact. Although ICA women often undertook what we might perceive as gendered roles, for Molony this was done in the spirit of equality,

> Women were recruited into the Citizen Army on the same

terms as men. They were appointed to the duties most suitable to them – as were men – and these duties fell naturally into dealing with Commissariat, Intelligence, First Aid and advanced Medical Aid, but their duties were not confined to these.[5]

Historians have debated the actual extent to which women were equally admitted and organised in the ICA.[6] Ann Matthews has shown that it was less than had been assessed previously and that Connolly initially conceived a Women's Section as an auxiliary or ambulance corps.[7] As the Women's Section was being organised throughout late 1915, Connolly was tightening up ICA membership and a new roll book showed 339 names with just one woman in full membership.[8]

However what was most significant was the degree to which Molony articulated this equality, believed that she lived it and recorded it as such over the next half century.[9] The role of Markievicz was one obvious marker. Because the ICA was considerably smaller than the Irish Volunteers and Cumann na mBan combined, and activities were undertaken together, the day to day contact and scope for involvement was greater. Records do not always show the developing nature of organisations and just as the Inghinidhe had officially become a branch of Cumann na mBan, some of its previously most prominent members were dynamic within the ICA. Having already run their own organisation, it was unlikely that any of these women would play, or see themselves playing, a subordinate role. Certainly Molony herself continued to expand her role and that of the women she organised. For others, such as Maeve Cavanagh, who had never been involved in the Inghinidhe but was initially a branch secretary in Cumann na mBan, the ICA certainly offered the prospect of playing a much more active part,

I got tired of that, as they were only collecting money and suchlike activities. I went to Liberty Hall for good and took part in all the activities of the Citizen Army. We had route marches through the city and suburbs.[10]

Molony had spent nearly ten years arguing that the best way to gain equality for Irish women was through the struggle for Irish freedom. Given the active and militant role she had played up to that point, it was both likely and critical for her that she participated (and was seen to participate) on equal terms.

In October 1915 it was reported that the First Aid classes were going well and a more specialised medical corps would be formed under the command of Dr Kathleen Lynn. From this point onwards in reports, the descriptor 'girls' was dropped in favour of the Citizen Army Women's Ambulance Corps, referred to as the Women's Section. Molony later testified that she worked to organise the women of the Co-op into a military unit rather than a medical corps,

> In the Citizen Army I was in actual charge of the girls on the military side. Dr Lynn was chief officer on the medical side. I hold I was given the title of captain on the military side, anything that was not medical service was done by the girls … under me, Jane Shanahan and Mrs. Barrett who sort of ranked as sergeants.[11]

Matthews has recorded that it was Lynn who appointed Molony. In the 1930s, Molony and the surviving women of the ICA decided not to claim their allocated ranks for the purposes of a military pension. The full significance of this decision has not yet been assessed. Molony gave evidence that, 'Generally speaking there was a small number and these ranks were more nebulous and had not really the same significance as men's ranks'.[12] However, Molony's statement of rank as she surrendered as well as her lengthy internment confirmed her senior status.

In his editorials in *The Workers' Republic*, Connolly was increasingly critical of the Irish Volunteers and its leaders, including Eoin Mac Neill. Molony gave a vivid account of the splits in the separatist movement and how, in the six months before the Rising,

> *The Irish Volunteer* edited by John Mac Neill [sic] and controlled by Bulmer Hobson – had taken on a curious and intangible tone of caution ... This provoked a storm of angry sarcasm, at least from us women.[13]

She described the hard time they gave their 'unfortunate young men friends' with Perolz coining the phrase the 'Fan go Fóills', or 'Wait a whilers' and contrasted 'the silent anger among the Volunteers', with the high morale of the ICA who 'felt very proud and confident in our leadership'.[14]

THE ATMOSPHERE WAS LIKE A SIMMERING POT[15]

Molony was still living with Constance Markievicz at Surrey House in January 1916, when James Connolly disappeared. Fearful that he might have been arrested and 'put ... quietly out of the way' by the authorities, Molony, Markievicz and William O'Brien got hold of a car and spent three days searching frantically. They went 'around the country to various places where Connolly had been seen last'.[16] He returned late one night and Molony enacted the scene,

> 'Where have you been?' I gasped, 'I have been through hell', he said wearily. 'Did they kidnap you?' asked Madame. 'Yes' replied Connolly, 'but I converted my captors'.[17]

Connolly had in fact been co-opted onto the IRB Supreme Council and Easter Sunday set as the date for an armed rebellion by the Irish Volunteers and the ICA. Molony and Markievicz did not push him for further information that night but,

> following on that and my more or less intimate conversations with him I tried to get from Connolly a hint as to the date when we were going 'out'. His answer was, 'I can't tell you that but it won't be long'.[18]

From then, preparation and tension proceeded apace and central to these was the clothing Co-op on Eden Quay. The Co-op, attached to, but with its separate entrance from, Liberty Hall was ideal as a meeting place and private post office for the conspirators. Parcels of arms and ammunitions were dropped off and collected and Patrick Pearse, Tom Clarke and Seán MacDermott were frequent visitors to meet with Connolly. Molony later said that, 'if the simile "a wolf in sheep's clothing" be used then the Worker's Co-op might be described as a "tigress in kitten's fur"'.[19] Behind the innocuous manufacture of men's shirts and children's pinafores, the women of the Co-op churned out ammunition cartridges and belts, uniforms and flags under Molony's management. She recalled that the machine gun belts 'gave us women headaches because of the extreme accuracy of the measurements'.[20]

Molony questioned Connolly one Saturday as he chalked up ICA manoeuvres on the large blackboard outside Liberty Hall,

'Why put up a thing like that and bring the police on us?' He said, 'You know the story of "Wolf! Wolf!", so naturally I saw the wisdom of it. Each week there would be something worse than the last on the board – "Dublin Castle to be attacked at midnight" was put up several times. We often had midnight marches. Therefore it was commonplace to hear that the Citizen Army was showing off.[21]

Molony moved into a flat on Eccles St but spent little time there between her work on Eden Quay and at the Abbey. On Saturday 26 February, she played the part of Mrs Palmer in the matinee and evening performances of *The Dreamers* by Lennox Robinson, changed out of her costume and left the Abbey stage. She intended taking a three month leave of absence to concentrate on her work with the union and the ICA, but it would be much longer before she returned. Also in the cast that evening were Arthur Shields, Peadar Kearney and Seán Connolly. Connolly would never be back.

Tuesday, 22nd February, 1916
and following Four Evenings, at 8.15 p.m.
Saturday Matinee at 2.30 p.m.

THE DREAMERS, A PLAY IN THREE ACTS, BY LENNOX ROBINSON

Characters in the order of their appearance :

JOHN BRADY	Arthur Sinclair
ROBERT BRADY	H. E. Hutchinson
MARTIN BRADY	Arthur Shields
ROBERT EMMET	Fred O'Donovan
LACEY	Eric Gorman
SARAH CURRAN	Beatrice Drury
HENRY HOWLEY	J. M. Kerrigan
THOMAS FREYNE	Fred Harford
McCARTNEY	Sean Connolly
HANNAY	C. McSwiggan
MORRISSEY	J. M. Kerrigan
TRENAGHAN	Robert Coyle
PETER FREYNE	John Murphy
ROCHE	J. A. O'Rourke
MULLIGAN	E. Reardon
JULIA	Kathleen Drago
JERRY	S. J. Barlow
JIM	P. Kearney
PETER FLYNN	Sydney J. Morgan
FELIX ROURKE } LARRY	J. M. Kerrigan
CON	Sean Connolly
MICKEY	J. H. Dunne
KATE	Mona O'Driscoll
MARY	Kathleen Murphy
QUIGLEY	Eric Gorman
PHILLIPS	Fred Harford
MIKE	J. A. O'Rourke
MANGAN	Sean Connolly
MRS. DILLON	Maureen Delaney
MRS. PALMER	Helen Molony
JANE CURRAN	Kathleen Drago
MAJOR SIRR	Eric Gorman
JONES	C. McSwiggan
OTHER MEN :	Frank Lynch, Edward Reardon, James Dunne, etc.

The Dreamers, February 1916 with Helena Molony, Seán Connolly, Arthur Shields all in the cast
courtesy Abbey Theatre Archive

On Friday 24 March the police raided radical presses and seized publications all over the city. As the Co-op shop stocked many of these and *The Workers' Republic* was being produced from behind the shop, they were on alert, Rosie Hackett recalled. The police entered the Co-op and though witness statements vary, at some point in all of them Molony drew her revolver to cover a policeman as James Connolly came out from the back room.[22] Connolly was also armed and told the policeman to drop the papers that he held or he would 'drop him'. Constance Markievicz came out of Liberty Hall and in through the front door of the Co-op shop, also armed, and the police retreated hastily. They said they would return with a warrant.[23] Immediate reprisals and raids were expected, and as Liberty Hall had a considerable stockpile of munitions by this stage, the ICA was rapidly mobilised. From that point on until the Rising there was a constant armed ICA presence outside Liberty Hall and Molony and Jane Shanahan took it in turns to sleep in the Co-op. That same weekend, Molony received a hint from Connolly about the planned date of the Rising. He told her,

> 'If you were arrested now and got the same sentence as you got before, maybe you would be out in time to take part in the rebellion'. I said, 'I got a month's sentence'.[24]

In early April Molony was sent on a mission to England by Seán MacDermott. It was the only mission that she was sent on. She was to arrange the return of Ernest Blythe and help Nora Connolly arrange the return of Liam Mellows, both of whom had been deported to England the previous month. The Irish MP Laurence Ginnell recorded on 14 April that he,

> Had a call from Miss Helena Maloney [sic] asking him to try to find out the whereabouts of some Volunteers who had been brought to England, neither interned nor imprisoned, but under Government supervision – Mellowes, Blythe, etc.[25]

Whether through Ginnell or some other source, she found

out that Blythe was in Abingdon. As her acting background meant that she 'knew the ropes in London', she stayed in her old theatrical lodgings, 'away from the Irish set' and then travelled there.[26] In fact, Ernest Blythe was arrested that morning and recalled that,

> About half an hour later the sergeant told me that a lady had called to see me but that she had not come into the barracks. I heard afterwards that Helena Molony had been sent over with money and to make arrangements for my getting away.[27]

Molony was nervous anyway and,

> rather glad it [his arrest] was the morning I arrived and not the following morning that this happened. I would have been afraid that his arrest might have been due to some indiscretion on my part.[28]

In the event, Ernest Blythe was to remain in prison until the end of the year and miss the Rising. He and Molony would be bitter enemies in the years that followed and she opposed his policies in the Free State. The mission was not a complete waste, however, as she brought back a consignment of guns from London, given to her by Dermot O'Leary (later married to Philomena Plunkett). When she headed for Euston, her landlady's nephew,

> a nice young lad – an Army recruit – carried my suitcase filled with revolvers and gun parts to the boat train. The perfect gentleman! There was no question of any 'G' men spotting it, and in that way I was a safe person for delivering the arms ...[29]

Molony also used her theatre training to help Nora Connolly arrange the return of Liam Mellows in a more successful mission. Molony travelled to Belfast to let Connolly know where Mellows had been deported to. She arrived at nine that night to tell her that 'They had got no word, but it might come later'.[30] In the meantime Molony suggested that Barney Mellows and Nora Connolly set off for Birmingham and that they would get word to them there. Nora was well known in Belfast so to avoid detection, 'Helena, from her stage experience, did me up, and made me old-looking'.[31] Molony also knew which crossing was best suited to a clandestine operation and,

> It was decided that we would go on the boat, on which all the theatrical companies went: it was held over late, for scenery: and there would be a lot of strangers on it: and we would be less likely to be noticed on that boat.[32]

By the time Molony returned to Dublin, the Rising was less than a week away. She later recalled 'I should think I knew it a week beforehand, although I cannot now say how I knew it. But I must have been very sure'.[33] Marie Perolz was sent off on Easter Thursday to deliver the message 'Dublin is to come out'.[34] Although Molony did not specifically know what she was delivering she knew it was significant and recalled 'Our little group of women were on the alert practically the whole time'.[35] From then on she spent all her time at the Co-op. 'From 9 in the morning till 12 at night … I might almost say 20 hours of the day and certainly 24 hours the last week'.[36] She had all of her clothes there, including her 'spare underclothing' which would cause problems for her after arrest.[37]

On Easter Saturday night Molony did leave the Co-op shop for a brief period at about half past six. She dashed out to catch a tram to Rathmines to leave a letter for her close friend Ella Young, in case anything should happen to her. The two knew each other from the early Inghinidhe days when Young, an artist, designed theatre sets. Molony later wrote, 'I was closely associated with her and she was very much with us but was more of an artist than a politician'.[38] Young and another woman, Mairin Fox, were in and she told them that 'she thought there would be trouble over Easter'.[39] She returned and found a furious Connolly was waiting for her. Later she recorded their exchange and her reaction,

> I think he thought I had left for the evening. I was much hurt …

I had never seen him angry before ... I did not tell him where I had been. 'You have no business to go out for even half an hour' ... I replied that I had no instructions not to go out.[40]

Whatever the details of the event (and her versions for the Bureau of Military History vary slightly), it was obviously very important for Molony to get word to Young and the two women were close enough for an absence from the Co-op to be chanced.

Events soon took over and she later described the aftermath of the countermanding orders issued by MacNeill,

That Easter Sunday was a day of confusion, excitement and disappointment in Liberty Hall. I stayed there all day and all night. There was a lot of work to be done preparing food upstairs for the men who came from different parts of the city and had brought no rations. As a result of the calling off of the fight, there was plenty of food. Large joints were cooked and all the Co-operative girls were busy cutting up bread, butter and cooked meat. They were killed working. One of them I remember was Brigid Davis. Dr. Lynn went home, but Jinny Shanahan and I slept again on the overcoats in the room behind the shop.[41]

Later that night, sometime between 12 and 1am, Christopher Brady finished printing up the 1916 Proclamation on the press behind the Co-op. Connolly told him to tie up the 2,500 copies into two parcels and he,

brought them to Miss Helena Molony who was lying on a couch in the Co-op ... She told me to put them under her pillow. She was armed with a revolver.[42]

Molony slept that night with the Proclamation under her head.

WALKING WITH IRELAND INTO THE SUN[43]

At twelve o'clock on Easter Monday, as part of an ICA force that numbered less than 220, Helena Molony mobilised outside Liberty Hall, at the head of a small detachment of nine ICA women,

> The women had no uniform, in the ordinary sense – nor the
> men either. Some of the men had green coats ... I had an Irish
> tweed costume, with a Sam Browne. I had my own revolver
> and ammunition.[44]

Molony and her detachment were posted to Dublin Castle under the command of Seán Connolly, her close friend and colleague in the Irish Citizen Army and the Abbey Theatre. She was very surprised and disappointed not to be going to the GPO with James Connolly. She was even more surprised that Winnie Carney, his secretary, was to accompany him.[45] Seemingly she was the best shot among the women. Just before they were to set off, James Connolly 'gave out revolvers to our girls, saying: "Don't use them except in the last resort"'.[46] Molony later said, 'we felt in a very real sense that we were walking with Ireland into the sun'.[47]

She described how they,

> went out in detachments. Seán Connolly and, I think, about
> twenty men perhaps, walked up Dame Street; and I, walking
> at the head of my nine girls, was, I believe, perhaps two or
> three ranks behind Seán. We simply followed the men.[48]

Her detachment included Emily and Annie Norgrove, Jane Shanahan, Brigid Davis, Molly O'Reilly and Katie Barrett. They turned left up the narrow street to Castle Gate and Constable James O'Brien came out. He assumed that this was a Citizen Army parade and that they would continue up Ship Street; he only reacted when Seán Connolly attempted to go past him into the Castle. O'Brien became the first casualty of the Rising as he was shot dead by Connolly. 'We were all in excitement', Molony said but she reacted quickly,

> When I saw Connolly draw his revolver, I drew my own.
> Across the road, there was a policeman with papers. He got

away, thank God. I did not like to think of the policeman dead.[49]

There followed a crucial hesitation on the part of the men behind Connolly to proceed into the Castle; Molony later speculated that they were unaware that this was the plan. (In fact, it appears that it was not the plan). The gates were secured and 'the sentry began firing before any of them could gain access to the Castle'.[50] Other statements indicate that Molony was mistaken and the sentry did not in fact fire at the rebels.[51] In the midst of all this, the Army's Chief Medical Officer, Dr Kathleen Lynn, pulled up in her car with medical supplies. In Lynn's account, Molony fired at the sentry responsible for closing the gate.[52] It may have been one of the crucial moments of the Rising. Behind Molony's fulsome regret, 'It breaks my heart – and all our hearts – that we did not get in. We would have captured the Under Secretary, who was having lunch in the Castle', there was the very real possibility that they might have taken the position as there were so few troops in the Castle that morning.[53]

City Hall and Dublin Castle where Molony was posted
courtesy Military Archives, Ireland

Seán Connolly ordered them into City Hall and Molony recalled climbing over the railings but having 'no need to smash windows or doors to get in'.[54] Keys had actually been made, and as Molony surmised, probably by

Connolly, who was a clerk in City Hall as well as being an Abbey actor. Once inside they took up various positions,

> My idea was to find out where there was a kitchen, and where there was a suitable place for a hospital. There was a kitchen upstairs ... we discovered a large dish of fruit – oranges and apples. I said: 'Nobody is to touch these, because there will be wounded probably'. We got ready for the wounded.[55]

Emily Norgrove recalled that some of the Women's Section carried on up towards Christ Church and they were met by Markievicz on her way to Stephen's Green. She ordered them back to City Hall as 'Dr Lynn was already there'.[56] Initial firing was heavy and when Molony and Shanahan went up onto the roof to talk to the men they saw,

> one young British soldier killed in Ship Street. I could see him lying wounded. I remember saying to Jinny Shanahan: 'I wonder should we do something for him?' Connolly said: 'No. Some of his own lads will come'. And they did.[57]

With sixteen men and nine women the garrison was not going to be able to hold out for long. In her later witness statement Molony recounted that at this point she was dispatched to the GPO to request reinforcements. She made her way down Dame Street where she met pacifist Francis Sheehy Skeffington, 'looking very white and dispirited' as he tried to stop the looting that had already begun: 'he was really looking distressed. He was standing in the midst of the bullets, as if they were raindrops'.[58] Molony arrived at the GPO where,

> There was great excitement. I simply gave the request of Seán Connolly for reinforcements. I saw James Connolly himself. He said: 'We will send them as soon as we can'.[59]

The first casualty of the rising was the policeman shot by Connolly but later that first afternoon he himself was the first casualty on the rebel side, as he was killed by sniper fire,

Seán Connolly, who was on the roof, was hit by a stray bullet and killed. Dr. Lynn was still there. She came up and attended him. She said: 'I'm afraid he is gone.' He was bleeding very much from the stomach. I said the Act of Contrition into his ear. We had no priest. We were very distressed at Seán Connolly's death, I particularly, as I had known him for so long and acted with him.[60]

Lynn's account was that Shanahan said the prayer. Others recalled that Molony and Molly O'Reilly went to the GPO for reinforcements *after* the death of Seán Connolly and they wore Red Cross VAD nurse uniforms.[61] Jack O'Reilly took over command after Connolly's death, but was also killed. The nature of the later surrender indicated that Lynn was recognised as the most Senior Officer in the garrison.[62]

After Connolly's death, there was nothing to do, only sit. The men in the main positions fired desultory shots all day. They fired at anything they saw. I was busy with food. As things were fairly quiet, the men came up according as they wanted food. There was, apparently, no enemy in sight. We got the shots at odd times. I had noticed the one hitting Connolly fatally, and, I foolishly, watched one taking a chip out of the chimney stack. I said to myself then: 'I'd better not stand looking at the scenery'. I remember that, because later that night a young officer asked me: 'Were you on the roof any time during the day?' I said: 'I was – once or twice'. He said: 'Yes. I thought I got you one time'.[63]

Their position was about to come under sustained attack and they watched as troops poured into Dublin Castle from both directions, up Dame Street and along Ship Street. Emily Norgrove recalled that her father George Norgrove, with seven other ICA members, was sent from the GPO by James Connolly to reinforce and take command of the City Hall garrison in the early evening.[64]

Then as Molony explained,

At about half-past eight or nine o'clock, when nightfall came, there was a sudden bombardment. It came suddenly on us. On the roof level, on which were glass windows, and through the windows on the ground floor of the City Hall, there were machine gun bullets pouring in. From the ceiling the plaster began to fall. It was dangerous ... This bombardment went on and on. By this time it was dark. I had gone upstairs on a couple of occasions to see that the girls were attending to the three or four wounded we had there – perhaps more.[65]

Molony and Lynn were among those on the ground floor and as all this went on, they tended to a wounded eighteen year old,

We put him sitting in one of the porters' chairs, so that he was almost enveloped in it ... We put his chair in to face the wall so as to safeguard him from the falling ceiling. I remember saying to myself I would not mind being shot but I would not like to be crushed. There were big cornices falling. We said to the wounded boy, 'We are all here. It is all right'.[66]

SURRENDER

The surrender took place that night and Molony recalled the moments before they were taken by British forces,

At this time the firing was very intense. A window was smashed at the back, and then we knew they were pouring in – and they did come in at the back. A voice said: 'Surrender, in the name of the King'.[67]

Molony 'felt a pluck on [her] arm' and the youngest member of the Women's Section, Annie Norgrove, said to her,

'Miss Molony, Miss Molony, we are not going to give in? Mr Connolly said we were not to surrender.' She was terrified but there was no surrender about her. The call to surrender was repeated ... There was no reply. I heard Dr. Lynn quite close, over near the window. 'Surrender', was called out again. Then we were taken.[68]

Molony glossed over the moment of actual surrender in later interviews. Consummate publicist that she was, she preferred instead to repeat the moment with Annie Norgrove. Annie Norgrove herself recalled that when the British officer enquired as to who was in charge, Lynn 'spoke to my father George Norgrove, then she stepped forward and surrendered'.[69] 1918 intelligence reports noted that Molony was,

> arrested by the Military in City Hall on 24th April, 1916, having in her possession an auto pistol and ammunition. She then described herself as Secretary of the Women's Union and Commandant of the Women's Section of the Citizen Army.[70]

The insurgents were taken out through the window, one by one, into the Castle grounds and on into Ship Street Barracks. However, the troops who stormed City Hall had no idea of the numbers that remained in the garrison and it took many hours before they cleared the building. Shanahan later told Molony what had happened. The troops came to where the rest of the ICA women were, and assumed that they had been taken prisoner by the rebels, 'never imagining that they were soldiers'.[71] Shanahan used this to their advantage, much to Molony's pride as her superior officer,

> They asked them: 'Did they do anything to you? Were they kind to you? How many are up here?' Jinny Shanahan quick enough – answered: 'No, they did not do anything to us. There are hundreds upstairs – big guns and everything.' She invented such a story that they thought there was a garrison up on the roof, with the result that they did delay, and took precautions. It was not until the girls were brought out for safety and, apparently, when they were bringing down some of the men, that one of the lads said: 'Hullo, Jinny, are you all right?' The officer looked at her, angry at the way he was fooled by this girl. I think that is important, because that may have delayed them, by some hours, from getting to the men on the roof.[72]

Molony concluded, 'I thought that was something for which Napoleon would have decorated her'.[73] After this delay, the remaining women were also brought to Ship Street Barracks where they were all held until after the general surrender.

Conditions for the prisoners were dire and they were kept in a small room, described later by some as a cupboard. Molony said,

> It was a disused room at the back of the building, on the west side. There were old bits of mattresses in it, used by the soldiers. They were covered with vermin; and before a day had passed we were all covered with vermin too ...[74]

The infestation was terrible, to the point that Lynn was unable to rest, but slightly indignant that 'even' Molony seemed able to sleep.[75] Lynn put the women through a daily delousing drill but it was another month before Molony felt finally rid of them. She recalled that 'Of course, all sorts of girls were put in this room – a couple of poor devils out of the streets too'.[76]

In fact, in her diary written at the time, Lynn recorded Molony's instinctive reaction when one of these women, a prostitute, was being brutalised by a soldier. 'Emer jumped up, told him to stop and had a revolver turned on her. They were brutal'.[77] The next day the woman was released and took with her 'notes for E. Young and L.S.'[78] Initially their food was reasonable and 'the soldiers [Dublin Fusiliers] decent enough to us', recollected Molony years later.[79]

However, from mid-week the rest of the city was under sustained bombardment and as the fighting intensified, provisions for the prisoners ran low. By Friday she recalled 'we got nothing except hard biscuits and dry bread'.[80] Lynn remembered that 'when we only had a couple of ship's biscuits, Miss Molony and I used to give our share to the younger girls who were very hungry'.[81] What stuck in Molony's memory was not the hunger, but the implication. The sergeant told them,

'It is bad stuff, but that is what we are getting ourselves'. We were delighted that they were cut off from supplies. They were only getting bully beef. That caused us more joy than anything else.[82]

Liberty Hall after the destruction of the Rising.
Irish Women Workers' Union logo visible
courtesy National Library of Ireland

After the final surrender on Sunday they, along with the other insurgents, were brought to Richmond Barracks and from there the women were brought to a disused wing at Kilmainham. According to Lynn, conditions, even in the disused wing, were better than what had been endured in Ship Street, at least they had access to some washing facilities,

> I remember we were given one basin of water for the three of us to wash in ... I, being the doctor, used it first, Miss ffrench Mullen second and Miss Molony was last ...[83]

However, the emotional impact of that time was seared into their memory,

Madame Markievicz was overhead in the condemned cell and we used to hear reports that she was about to be executed. It was very harrowing.[84]

Kilmainham Gaol main entrance
courtesy Kilmainham Gaol Museum

Molony recalled, 'I heard the shots every morning at dawn, and knew that that meant they were executing our men'.[85] One of the last to be taken out was James Connolly. On 12 May he was executed and the death of the man who had had so much influence on Molony's thought and work devastated her. She wrote that, 'after 1916 the colour went out of life for me'.[86] Apparently Molony tried to tunnel out of her cell with an iron spoon and as a result female prisoners were not allowed to eat with utensils for a time.[87]

The anniversary of Connolly's execution would always be a special day for her and she believed that commemoration of his spirit and work could provide impetus for future change. For Molony, as for others, Easter 1916 was the highpoint of the nationalist struggle; the time of greatest untainted idealism but also of real possibility. Thereafter she would point to the 1916 Proclamation as the basis and inspiration for change in Ireland, incorporating as it did a vision of socio-economic redistribution and sexual equality within Irish nationalism.

WE HARDLY KNOW WHAT TO EXPECT NOW[88]

By the end of May 1916, the majority of the women arrested after the Rising had been released, but the commander of the British forces, General Maxwell, felt that eight of these, Molony among them, were significantly more dangerous. He said, 'had they been male prisoners I would have at least recommended them for internment'.[89] Molony was brought to Mountjoy. Kathleen Lynn recalled that they had cells to themselves and were 'hailed with great joy by the wardresses because [they] were interesting prisoners'.[90] They were also allowed to receive parcels but Molony advised her cousin Madge, 'Don't worry to send me anything. We get more things than we can get through'. The loss of her underclothing was an intimate detail amid this national narrative, but one which remained with her for life, 'I had not a thing to change into, and had to borrow from Nell Ryan and Dr. Lynn who were in prison too'.[91] On 9 June, Molony wrote to her cousin Madge from Mountjoy, in shock at what had just occurred,

> Seven out of our little party have been released as you may know by the papers. Five unconditionally and 2 (Countess Plunkett and Dr Lynn) deported ... Every minute we expect news. So I put off writing letters to anyone. The deportation of the last two was a great surprise to us as we all expected unconditional release. We hardly know what to expect now.[92]

It looked possible that she too might be deported and what Molony was most worried about was the fate of the IWWU, left without either herself or Connolly. In a move that marked the beginning of a productive but fraught working relationship, she sent a message out to Louie Bennett. Molony asked her to try and see if she could get a permit to visit her, which Bennett did. She went to her cell in Mountjoy and later wrote,

> It was the one and only time I have seen a person utterly *devastated* by tragedy. (In her cell [in Kilmainham] she had heard the shots of the 'Executions'.) But her one word to me *was*, help the women workers. Revive their Trade Union.[93]

Bennett had been very active in the suffrage movement and, like many other women, it was through involvement in relief work for the 1913 Lockout that she became interested in the conditions of women workers. Molony had tried to involve her in 1915, but Bennett, an ardent pacifist, distrusted Connolly and asserted that the union should not participate in politics and 'Miss Molony agreed'.[94] It was likely that Molony did not consider plans for the Rising a 'mere' political issue. Beyond the two women's shared concern for women workers, they had little in common politically.

Helena Molony writing to her cousin Madge from Mountjoy Prison
courtesy National Library of Ireland

Maud Gonne MacBride wrote from France to Yeats and asked him to procure legal aid for Molony.[95] However, in the end, five more women were deported to England – Molony, Nell Ryan, Marie Perolz, Brigid Foley and Winnie Carney. They were initially brought to Lewes Jail where, for the first time since Ship Street, Molony felt that she was free of the lice that had plagued her. In a bizarre episode soon after, the five women were brought, by train and under guard, to be arraigned in front of the House of Lords Advisory Committee. The Irish MP Alfie Byrne first brought them to lunch in the members' dining room. After their arraignment Molony recalled that,

> Alfie said that as we had been confined for so long, tea at a restaurant where we could hear some music – would be a change. None of us dreamed it would be allowed, but he talked to the wardresses, and gave our word of honour that there would be no attempt at escape. He led us out to the Corner House (ABC I think) anyhow a crowded sunny afternoon amidst a fashionable London crowd, – we a very draggled-tailed group, – as we still wore the clothes we were arrested in.[96]

They duly returned after their meal and the guards were most impressed with the Irish MP. Following the arraignment Brigid Foley and Marie Perolz were released while Molony, Nell Ryan and Winnie Carney were sent on to Aylesbury.

AYLESBURY

Ryan was released soon after, but intelligence reports from December showed that Molony was among 34 rebels classified as sub-leaders and 'extremists of some importance' and consequently on the police B List.[97] Her occupation was listed as actress and it was noted that she was the registered owner of *The Workers' Republic* and Secretary of the WWU [sic].[98]

During the long months in Aylesbury, Molony kept in contact, as far as prison regulations allowed, with the acting world. A cheerful and humorous letter she wrote on 22 August 1916 to Ellen Bushell, Abbey usher and fellow participant in the Rising, survives and gives a wonderful insight into the 33-year-old woman in prison; soldier, actor, satirist, friend and activist ... and nascent playwright,

> I wish you would write me a long gossipy letter about Abbey affairs. I am lost for inside news. Sometime I shall give way to a temptation I have long resisted – in public anyhow – and take to playwriting. I shall begin with a farce called 'The Passing of the Manager'. [St. John Greer Ervine] It should play to packed houses (entirely composed of past managers and unappreciated Great Actors).[99]

She was only allowed two visits a month and explained the procedure to Bushell,

> I would love you to make this business of visits known to my friends. It is in the nature of an obstacle race or the labour of Hercules ... You may be an Objectionable Person in the eyes of the Home Office and your visit disallowed. There are other difficulties such as your once having a bowing acquaintance with the cousin of a friend of a person suspected of Sinn Fein involvement which would cause grave doubt and long delays.[100]

None of these difficulties or obstacles deterred her friends and colleagues, Maeve Cavanagh and Kathleen Lynn, from visiting her there. Lynn had avoided further internment, on the basis of her position as a doctor in wartime. Influential family representation had also played a part, in fact initially they had argued that Lynn should be put in the care of a family friend as she '... was a sort of a lunatic' because of her involvement in the Rising.[101] Cavanagh recalled,

> I went down to see Dr. Lynn in Bath. She was supposed not to leave the place, but we both went to Aylesbury Prison to see Helena Molony. They did not want to let us in, but we asked them to ring up the Home Office and they gave permission. We said we were relatives of hers.[102]

Helena Molony writing from Aylesbury prison to Ellen Bushell,
eager for Abbey gossip and outlining her playwriting ambitions
courtesy National Library of Ireland

Significant support came from the trade union
movement and in October, the Dublin United Trades
Council and Labour League issued an appeal on behalf of
Molony and Carney.[103] William O'Brien wrote to the Chief
Secretary for Ireland to call for their immediate release. He
queried whether they were still interned because they
were trade union officials. When MP Tim Healy protested
at the internment of the two, he said it seemed 'the offence
of one [was] that she had played at the Abbey Theatre'.[104]
Neither appeal had the desired effect so Molony the actor

and Molony the trade unionist remained in prison. On 8 November William O'Brien wrote to the Home Secretary to apply for permits for himself and Thomas Foran to visit trade union officials interned in England who included Molony, Carney, P.T. Daly, Charles Shannon and John O'Neill.[105] However, Molony would be disappointed at the manner in which many of her trade union colleagues negotiated the turbulent times ahead.

Another visitor was her old friend Alice Ginnell, whose husband was the MP Laurence Ginnell, and the two went to great lengths to smuggle out an article about prison conditions. Molony hid it in her slipper and at one point, under the watchful eye of the warder, she held out her foot and showed it to Ginnell, who 'while talking intimately got it out of my shoe'.[106] The article was taken to Sylvia Pankhurst who published it but also mentioned how it had been smuggled out. This 'spoiled our plan altogether. Mrs. Ginnell was very indignant'.[107]

In fact, Aylesbury proved to be a not unpleasant experience. When Nell Ryan was released, Molony, alert to the propaganda value, warned her not to say how well treated they were. Two days before Christmas 1916, Molony was part of a general release of internees from England. She later told Ryan that given the choice she would have stayed in over Christmas! They had become firm favourite of the warders to the point that,

> They were all so overwrought that we both hated leaving them … you'd think we were their nearest relation. Miss Carney collapsed on the table sobbing and even I felt a bit damp. I was sad, leaving them on Christmas Eve.[108]

They were returned on the 3.55am sailing from Holyhead and found themselves among Christmas revellers, all of whom were supportive. James Kavanagh, released from Frongoch, spoke with Molony and Carney on what was evidently a surreal journey home,

We bore a very disreputable appearance at that time. Our clothes were in tatters, and with standing so long in the snow and sleet we looked even worse than usual. Some of the girls who had been released were going home on the same boat. I remember talking to Miss Helena Moloney [sic] and, I think, also Miss Kearney [sic]. It was a very rough passage. The night was wild. There were no lights showing anywhere on board as this was in the middle of the first Great War, and the ship took a zig-zag course and went at its maximum speed. The jolly crowd of Christmas home goers were singing while we were in port but the singing did not last long when we got out into the open sea. You could hear it gradually getting weaker and weaker until it stopped altogether and was replaced by another and less pleasant sound.[109]

Helena Molony returned to a very different Dublin. Over the next seven years the country would be in turmoil and she was at the heart of public resistance to both the British and pro-Treaty authorities. Molony was arrested briefly in 1917, but was not imprisoned again. Although her return marked the effective end of her role as a military combatant or soldier, she was recorded as being on active service for the Irish Citizen Army for the period to 1923.[110] She was involved in intelligence and publicity work, provision of safe houses, movement of arms, as well as first aid, all of which she argued forcefully was military work, albeit non-combatant, especially given the nature of the guerrilla war that was to transpire.

SOURCES
1   Kilmainham Tales, www.kilmainhamtales.ie/women-prisoners -of-1916.php.
2   Rosie Hackett, Bureau of Military History Witness Statement 546; Hereafter, Rosie Hackett: BMH WS 546.
3   Ann Matthews, *The Irish Citizen Army* (Cork, Mercier Press, 2014), p. 61; hereafter Matthews, *ICA*.
4   Molony, 'Years of Tension'.
5   Helena Molony, Draft WS Kilmainham.

6   Ward, *Unmanageable Revolutionaries*; Regan, 'Helena Molony'; Pašeta, *Irish Nationalist Women*; Matthews, *ICA*; McGarry, *Abbey Rebels*.
7   Matthews, *ICA*, p. 56.
8   *Ibid*.
9   See in particular Pašeta, *Irish Nationalist Women*.
10   Maeve Cavanagh MacDowell, Bureau of Military History Witness Statement 258; Hereafter, Maeve Cavanagh MacDowell: BMH WS 258.
11   Helena Molony: Military Service Pensions Collection, 11739; hereafter, Helena Molony, MSPC 11739.
12   *Ibid*.
13   Helena Molony: BMH WS 391.
14   *Ibid*.
15   *Ibid*.
16   *Ibid*.
17   Molony, 'Years of Tension'.
18   Helena Molony: BMH WS 391.
19   Molony, 'Years of Tension'.
20   *Ibid*.
21   Helena Molony: BMH WS 391.
22   Helena Molony: BMH WS 391; Christopher Brady, Bureau of Military History Witness Statement 705; Rosie Hackett: BMH WS 546.
23   Interview with Christopher Brady, *Portraits of 1916*, RTÉ Sound Archives.
24   Helena Molony: BMH WS 391.
25   Alice Ginnell, Bureau of Military History Witness Statement 982.
26   Helena Molony: BMH WS 391.
27   Ernest Blythe, Bureau of Military History Witness Statement 939.
28   Helena Molony: BMH WS 391.
29   *Ibid*.
30   Nora Connolly O'Brien, Bureau of Military History Witness Statement 286.
31   *Ibid*.
32   *Ibid*.
33   Helena Molony: BMH WS 391.
34   *Ibid*.
35   *Ibid*.

36   Helena Molony, MSPC 11739.

37   Helena Molony: BMH WS 391.

38   *Ibid.*

39   Helena Molony: BMH WS 391; Helena Molony, Draft WS Kilmainham.

40   *Ibid.*

41   Helena Molony: BMH WS 391.

42   Christopher Brady: BMH WS 705.

43   Fox, *Rebel Irishwomen,* p. 121.

44   Helena Molony: BMH WS 391.

45   Helena Molony: BMH WS 391.

46   *Ibid.*

47   Van Voris, *Constance de Markievicz,* p. 199.

48   Helena Molony: BMH WS 391.

49   *Ibid.*

50   *Ibid.*

51   Fearghal McGarry, *The Rising: Ireland, Easter 1916* (Oxford University Press, 2011).

52   Marie Mulholland, *The Politics and Relationships of Kathleen Lynn* (Dublin, Woodfield Press, 2002), p. 43.

53   Helena Molony: BMH WS 391.

54   *Ibid.*

55   *Ibid.*

56   Emily Norgrove quoted in Matthews, *ICA,* p. 90.

57   Helena Molony: BMH WS 391.

58   *Ibid.*

59   *Ibid.*

60   *Ibid.*

61   Kathleen Lynn: BMH WS 357.

62   Mulholland, *Kathleen Lynn,* p. 43.

63   Helena Molony: BMH WS 391.

64   Emily Norgrove quoted in Matthews, *ICA,* p. 90.

65   Helena Molony: BMH WS 391.

66   Helena Molony: BMH WS 391.

67   *Ibid.*

68   Helena Molony: BMH WS 391.

69   Annie Norgrove quoted in Matthews, *ICA,* p. 110.

70   McGarry, *Abbey Rebels,* p. 251.

71   Helena Molony: BMH WS 391.

72   *Ibid.*

73   *Ibid.*

74   *Ibid.*

75   Kathleen Lynn: BMH WS 357.

76   Helena Molony: BMH WS 391.

77   Kathleen Lynn diary, 29–30 April 1916, quoted in McDiarmid, *Home in the Revolution*, p. 134.

78   *Ibid.*

79   Helena Molony: BMH WS 391.

80   *Ibid.*

81   Kathleen Lynn: BMH WS 357.

82   Helena Molony: BMH WS 391.

83   Kathleen Lynn: BMH WS 357.

84   *Ibid.*

85   Helena Molony: BMH WS 391.

86   Fox, *Rebel Irishwomen*, p. 131.

87   Sinead McCoole, *No Ordinary Women: Irish Female Activists in the Revolutionary Years, 1900–1923* (Dublin, O'Brien Press, 2004), p. 50.

88   Helena Molony, letter to her cousin Madge, 9 June 1916, MS 49163, NLI.

89   McGarry, *Abbey Rebels*, p. 181.

90   Kathleen Lynn: BMH WS 357.

91   Helena Molony: BMH WS 391.

92   Helena Molony, MS 49163, NLI.

93   Louis Bennett correspondence, 10 February 1953, private collection.

94   R.M. Fox, *Louie Bennett: Her Life and Times* (Dublin, Talbot Press, 1958), p. 49.

95   Quoted in Regan, 'Helena Molony', p. 153.

96   Helena Molony correspondence, Cathal O'Shannon Collection, ILHA; Hereafter COS, ILHA.

97   Dublin Metropolitan Police Chief Commissioner to Chief Secretary, 8 December, 1916, MS 16627/18, CSO RP, National Archives, Dublin.

98   *Ibid.*

99   Helena Molony, letter to Ellen Bushell, 22 August 1916, Ernest Blythe Papers, MS 49163, NLI.

100   *Ibid.*

101   Mulholland, *Kathleen Lynn*, p. 48; Kathleen Lynn: BMH WS 357.

102   Maeve Cavanagh MacDowell: BMH WS 258.

103   Matthews, *ICA*, p. 33.

104 McGarry, *Abbey Rebels*, p. 188.
105 William O'Brien Papers, MS 13961, NLI.
106 Helena Molony: BMH WS 391.
107 Helena Molony: BMH WS 391.
108 Foster, *Vivid Faces*, p. 369.
109 James Kavanagh: BMH WS 889.
110 Helena Molony, MSPC 11739.

PUBLICIST
1917–23

After our release, our activities were more or less routine. For
us, it was only a matter of taking up the gun again.[1]

Helena Molony stepped off the night crossing from
Holyhead and immediately renewed her activity on all
fronts. Her time in Aylesbury had served to re-energise her
and Máire Comerford recalled that Molony told her she
had received '... so many insults about stabbing them [the
British] in the back, that she came back determined to do it
all again'.[2] Molony juggled a vast array of roles between
1917 and 1923, a period she later dubbed 'the terrible
years'.[3] One of her main priorities was publicity work,
initially for the developing movement for independence,
then the fledgling government and subsequently for the
anti-Treaty side in the Civil War. As a propagandist she
was tactical and persistent, as an orator she was influential
and much in demand and she also campaigned for
candidates in elections all over the country. She was also
one of the first members of and regular speakers with the
Women's Prisoners Defence League (WPDL). As well as

continuing to act on the Abbey stage, work in the IWWU and the wider trade union movement, she was actively engaged in and supported the military work of Irish Citizen Army and republican forces.

Molony initially stayed with the MacGarry family at Upper Fitzwilliam Street who helped herself and Marie Perolz. They were very active in the Irish National Aid Association and Voluntary Dependents Fund or National Aid. This had been established in August 1916 and provided a network of propaganda, support and fund-raising for the large number of families affected by the deportations and executions. During the eight months of Molony's internment, the city had been somewhat rebuilt following the devastation of the Rising. However, there were still chronic food shortages and hardships as a result of bad harvests and World War One. Only one woman, Constance Markievicz, remained in prison following Molony's release, but large numbers of men were still detained. These included the surviving leaders of the movement. The organisations that had taken part in the Rising were in disarray while the authorities continued to monitor them closely. Molony recalled that 'At this time ... we were defeated; nobody thought we would rise up again'.[4]

In February, Molony appeared in the first Irish production of Anton Chekhov's *Uncle Vanya*, at Hardwicke Street presented by the Irish Theatre. She moved into 9 Belgrave Road in Rathmines, Kathleen Lynn's home, where she lived for nearly a decade. She was re-elected General Secretary of the IWWU and was busy with the Co-op on Eden Quay which had been reopened under National Aid and re-named the Connolly Co-op.[5] She was also on the Dublin committee of the National Relief Fund and involved in opening a communal food kitchen in

Liberty Hall. However, the first opportunity of taking 'up the gun again', as she phrased it, came up at Easter 1917.

A Dangerous Woman[6]

1917 commemoration, Irish Citizen Army members outside Liberty Hall, Helena Molony front row, third from lamppost, in black
courtesy Military Archives, Ireland

On 6 April 1917, the authorities prohibited any gatherings to commemorate the Easter Rising under the Defence of the Realm Act. For Molony it was imperative to demonstrate in as visible a manner as possible that 'A Republic has been declared, has been fought for; and is still alive'.[7] She and others ensured that the Rising's first anniversary, and the execution of James Connolly, was marked and brought to the attention of Dublin's citizens and the authorities.

> We had a lot of discussions. There were concerts arranged but what I was concerned with most was our decision to beflag all the positions that had been occupied in the 1916 Rising ... and

to get out the proclamation and proclaim it again.[8]

Molony ordered facsimiles of the 1916 Proclamation from printer Matthew Walker. Walker was the founder of Tower Press, had printed *Bean na hÉireann* and was also the father of fellow actor and republican, Máire Nic Shiubhlaigh. When he found he was short of type, Molony brought him to what was left of the print room at the back of the Co-op. There, amidst the destruction, they found the type that had been used to print the original, 'all smashed up, and thrown about'. Useable letters were retrieved from a corner and she recorded that these were enough to complete and typeset the 1917 Proclamation. In later years Molony was able to clear up the confusion that resulted about the provenance of the two different versions.[9]

Three large tricolours were made in the Co-op and plans put in place to hang one on the GPO. A sympathetic Glaswegian sailor aided them and promised them he would ensure that it would stay in place for hours. Pots of glue and flour paste were made up for postering, but the facsimiles did not arrive as arranged, and Molony later dramatised the scene as she confronted Walker,

> I was raging and frothing at the mouth. I said: 'What about the posters?' He said: 'What posters?' I said: 'The posters – you said you would send them yesterday'. He said: 'What posters?' I said: 'The posters that I ordered'. He said: 'You called that off'. I said: 'What do you mean – called that off?' He said: 'Miss Plunkett came in, and said they were called off'.'Surely that is not true', I gasped, 'and if you don't want to print them, Can't you say so?' He said: 'I was told not to print them. Will I go on with them?' I said: 'Go on with them'. I held it over him. I put him on his metal.

Fiona Plunkett told her that Cumann na mBan were 'under orders' to call off any demonstration or flag flying. Molony was furious with whoever had issued the order. As much of the leadership was still in prison at the time, Molony ascribed it to IRB influence on the Army and Cumann na mBan. In the event, once the Proclamation was printed a group of 'Cumann na mBan, the Plunkett girls and boys, well known extremists' came together and posted it all over the city. In fact she recalled that their flour and glue mix was so effective that 'one poster on Grafton Street stayed up for six or eight months'.

The *Irish Times* reported that Easter Sunday in Dublin was quiet but that at 9am on Monday morning a crowd began to gather at the GPO and 'There was great excitement and much speculation ... when it was discovered that the tricolour or Sinn Féin flag as it was known had been hoisted surreptitiously'.[10] In fact the authorities were unable to get it down until 6pm when they cordoned off the large enthusiastic crowds and sawed off the flagstaff. Meanwhile, Molony and Madeleine ffrench-Mullen had also made their way to the College of Surgeons with a second flag wrapped under ffrench-Mullen's coat. They managed to persuade a next door neighbour to hang it out. Although it only stayed out for an hour, Molony, alert to the symbolism and the fact that the position was not as strategically important as the GPO or Liberty Hall, concluded that that was enough.

Molony was also determined to mark the execution of James Connolly, in as visible a manner as possible, from the rebuilt Liberty Hall. She made a huge banner that proclaimed, 'James Connolly Murdered May 12th, 1916', which was rapidly taken down by police. Molony, 'full of indignation at being circumvented in a quarter of an hour', remade the banner with a roll of calico from the Co-op shop.[11] Rosie Hackett recalled that 'Miss Molony called us together Jinny Shanahan, Brigid Davis and myself ... Getting up on the roof, she put it [the banner] high up, across the top parapet'.[12] The four women then barricaded the windows and managed to shoot nearly a ton of coal in front of an access door. They watched from the roof of

Liberty Hall as crowds gathered and the police questioned ITGWU representatives. Most of them were against the demonstration and Molony was scathing, both of their politics and of their caution: 'We knew we had unsympathetic members in the back, and enemies in the front'.[13]

Thinking that there was a detachment of Irish Citizen Army men on the roof, a large force of police was mobilised with military reinforcements from Dun Laoghaire, and Liberty Hall was cordoned off. Liam Clarke [National Aid organiser and de facto commander of the Volunteers] was on the steps of Liberty Hall when he spotted Shanahan up on the roof. Molony recounted the exchange and what happened next,

> He said: 'What are you up to? They are going to open fire'...
> He was trying to tell them that there were only four girls. He
> said: 'Will you, for God's sake, come down. They don't believe
> me that there are only four of you there'. We could not get the
> coal away. We said: 'We can't.' The scroll remained on Liberty
> Hall for several hours. It attracted great attention and crowds
> gathered – the same as happened in O'Connell Street when the
> flag was flown ... it was the four girls inside Liberty Hall, and
> four girls who were on the wrong side of the door, who were
> responsible for all this. It was not until about six or seven
> o'clock in the evening that they broke down the door of this
> room in Liberty Hall. The police had to shovel the coal
> themselves. We sat like perfect ladies, waiting for them.

Their object had been achieved and the image of Liberty Hall with 'James Connolly Murdered' in huge letters across the front of the building appeared widely along with accounts of the incident. None of the women were arrested – as Rosie Hackett later put it,

> Of course, if it took four hundred policemen to take four
> women, what would the newspapers say? We enjoyed it at the
> time, all the trouble they were put to. They just took the script
> away and we never heard any more. It was Miss Molony's
> doings.[14]

Liberty Hall, 1917 commemoration, crowds gather to see banner as
Helena Molony, Rosie Hackett and others are barricaded on the roof
courtesy National Library of Ireland

Molony (who estimated the force at a more modest 200) concluded her own account with, 'That celebration established the 1916 commemoration'.[15] Although they were not arrested, their actions did have an unintended consequence, and the food kitchen in Liberty Hall was shut down temporarily. Molony wrote to Mrs Cunningham, who ran it for the Relief Fund, and to the authorities, to express her regret at what had happened (but not at her actions) and to stress that she alone and not the organisers of the food kitchen, was responsible.

Following on from the demonstration, Molony was kept under close surveillance and described as, 'A dangerous woman who is evidently once again in the thick of the disaffected and whose doings and correspondence should be daily watched'.[16] Molony's sister-in-law was very involved with National Aid fundraising in the US and this contact with her brother and sister-in-law was also of interest to the authorities over the next two years.[17] Two weeks later an intelligence report was submitted and along with details of the events of the anniversary and attendance at the Sinn Féin conference, it was recorded that, 'She attends almost daily at the office of the Irish Women Workers' Union in connection with her business as secretary'. It was further noted that she assisted in directing operations at the communal kitchen in Liberty Hall along with ffrench-Mullen, Perolz and Bennett. In the last week of April she was also performing at the Irish Theatre on Hardwicke Street.[18]

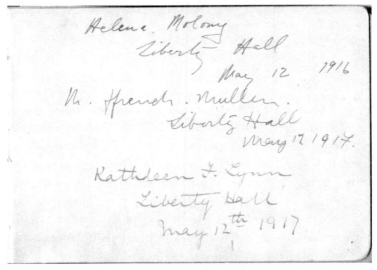

1917 commemoration autograph book, signatures of Helena Molony, Kathleen Lynn and Madeline ffrench Mullen
courtesy Kilmainham Gaol Museum

THE WOMEN KEPT THE SPIRIT ALIVE ... THE FLAG FLYING[19]

The 1917 commemoration that Molony had initiated and followed through with was a significant one and she later saw it as such. It also typified the methods of her public involvement and that of many other women in the nationalist movement. Their emphasis was very much on the raising of public consciousness through publicity and propaganda, regardless of the dangers involved. In May, Molony and Hanna Sheehy Skeffington were arrested after addressing a public meeting. Although charged, they were,

> only detained for 8 or 9 hours … [and she surmised] released through orders from above because they were contemplating the general release of prisoners and of course making some capital out of it.[20]

Molony returned to Aylesbury in June to accompany Markievicz back to Dublin as part of that general release. She sent a postcard of Aylesbury Prison to Nell Ryan saying 'Here I am again – on the right side this time!'[21] The jeers that had greeted some of the insurgents immediately after the Rising had been replaced by acclaim and Lynn recorded that Markievicz's homecoming attracted greater crowds than royalty.[22] This turnaround was largely a result of the executions and the subsequent propaganda campaign carried out by the women of the movement. Cathal Brugha later paid them tribute for this and keeping the flag flying was also a literal description in Molony's case. She recalled that,

> The opinion of the country rapidly changed and instead of sneering at Liberty Hall and all it stood for the people came to regard it with the Co-op and its activities with affection and respect.[23]

Before her death, Molony spoke with humour and frustration about being asked about the role women played during this period,

> I feel they might as well ask me what did the tall fair-haired men do in the wars and what did small dark men do? My answer in both cases is the same: they did what came to their hands to do – day to day, and whatever they were capable of by aptitude or training.[24]

It reflected her belief that gender, as a category of

difference, was absurd in the face of a common enemy, whether that was Britain or the capitalist system. She was well aware that, in reality, the situation was not so straight forward and spent much of her life defending the right of women to participate fully and be represented equally in the nationalist movement, the workforce and civic society. While many of the women of Cumann na mBan and other nationalists had been radicalised by the events and aftermath of the 1916 Rising, getting their male colleagues in the movement to accept them as equals would continue to prove more difficult.

This was in evidence when a newly reconstituted Sinn Féin party was established in May 1917, to provide an umbrella organisation for nationalists. Molony and Marie Perolz had attended the Mansion House Conference on 19 April as representatives of the IWWU. Only one woman, Countess Plunkett, was included on the new executive. In response, Molony and Jennie Wyse Power, Hanna Sheehy Skeffington and others (representing Inghinidhe na hÉireann, Cumann na mBan, the IWFL as well as other women's organisations), formed a coordinating body of all women delegates to future nationalist conferences. In July, when the Sinn Féin executive was expanded to include returned prisoners and still no further women were included, they protested. They lobbied the Sinn Féin executive and Molony, Áine Ceannt, Grace Plunkett and Jennie Wyse Power were co-opted on but only as members of Sinn Féin.

The tussle between Arthur Griffith and Count Plunkett for control of this new Sinn Féin intensified in advance of a convention called for 25 October. It was an indication of Molony's standing at the time, that the newly-elected Clare MP, Éamon de Valera, turned to her and Kathleen Lynn 'as certain representatives of Liberty Hall', for support in his bid to become President of the new Sinn Féin. She gives a wonderful account of a pre-Presidential de Valera, who called to 9 Belgrave Road one evening just before the Convention,

> He said that he himself was not anxious for it – he was very modest and retiring – but that that was the decision of the boys – that he would be the compromise. That was put forward as a solution. He asked would he be acceptable to our lot. We said he would be, so long as he shared our opinions. It was agreed our lot would support his candidature at the meeting. While Count Plunkett was Joe's father, and very good, de Valera was the better leader.[25]

Molony and her colleagues were also developing policy and discussed a resolution specifying that, 'in all speeches and leaflets etc ... men *and women* should be mentioned'.[26] On the eve of the October Convention they took the name Cumann na dTeachtaire. They also decided to bring forward a resolution, which would explicitly formalise the political equality of men and women, based on the 1916 Proclamation. At the Convention which took place in the Mansion House, de Valera was elected leader and the Cumann na dTeachtaire resolution was passed. It was agreed 'that the equality of men and women in this organisation be emphasised in all speeches and leaflets'.[27] Molony along with Jacob and ffrench-Mullen were now anxious that the Convention 'declare for a Republic' and concerned about Griffith's 'non-republicanism, autocratic spirit and the extreme trouble they had in forcing 6 women on to the executive'.[28] Ten years previously *Bean na hÉireann* had been established because of just such disagreements with Griffith. Molony was concerned enough to persuade Jacob to specifically bring up the question of the franchise. Jacob recorded in her diary that 'Griffith answered plainly that whatever the franchise was, it would include them, which is the straightest statement he has ever made on the point'.[29] Although, Molony did not stand for re-election, Lynn and Markievicz were among the four women elected to the new 24 person Sinn Féin executive.

That winter Molony recalled there was a very real 'fear of a second famine' and that the food kitchen in Liberty Hall was more necessary than ever.[30] Throughout 1918 she appeared on public platforms and canvassed all over the country as opposition to the introduction of conscription escalated and support for the newly-reconstituted Sinn Féin party gathered momentum. In May, she cycled to Cavan with Maeve Cavanagh, Robert Brennan and others from the ICA to campaign for the Sinn Féin candidate. Cavanagh recalled that when they reached Virginia they were met with 'great hospitality and kindness, and the people generally were very enthusiastic'.[31] Addressing public meetings became considerably riskier and Annie O'Brien recalled a Sunday morning meeting at Foster Place. She had attended, with others from Cumann na mBan, to protest against the continued detention of Maud Gonne MacBride, Constance Markievicz and Kathleen Clarke in English prisons,

> The speakers were all women and they spoke from a jaunting car. The speakers I remember were Mrs. Sheehy-Skeffington and Helena Molony, who continued to speak in spite of interference by the police. Finally the police dispersed the meeting with their batons.[32]

Even though Molony had not yet returned to the Abbey stage, it was clear that neither her skill as an orator nor other aspects of her theatrical training were going to waste in her work as a publicist for the cause of Ireland. Kathleen Lynn, as a member of the standing committee of Sinn Féin, was on the run between May and November of 1918. To allow her to move more freely about the city and make occasional visits to her patients in their own homes she explained how,

> Miss Molony got a beautiful rig-out for me. I was supposed to be a war widow, the military badge of my husband's regiment

on my coat. I had my hair powdered and dressed up v beautifully in a way that I ordinarily never wore it.[33]

Ironically, Molony herself had been fooled the previous year when she went to meet Maud Gonne MacBride off the mailboat on her return to Ireland. Gonne MacBride, in an elaborate disguise provided for her in London by Eva Gore-Booth and Esther Roper, walked straight past Molony and some waiting intelligence officers.[34]

In December 1918 the first post-war election was held and it was also the first in which the franchise was extended to women (albeit partially, to women over the age of 30). Molony canvassed extensively around St Patrick's Ward in Dublin for her friend Constance Markievicz, who became the first woman to be elected to a Westminster parliament. She never took her seat in London as Sinn Féin's sweeping victory enabled them to abstain en masse and the First Dáil was established. On the day of its first sitting in January 1919, the first shots were fired in the War of Independence which would continue until June 1921.

THOSE TERRIBLE YEARS[35]

Molony recalled how 'every day was full of incidents in the Tan War. I cannot remember a single day when I was not doing something, going down to election meetings, publicity'.[36] It was a busy and fractured time. In between her publicity work, her organising work with the IWWU, as well as sporadic appearances on the Abbey stage, she was 'working for the Republic'. She provided a safe house and first aid for republicans on the run; undertook occasional intelligence work and moved small quantities of arms; spoke and organised with the Women's Prisoners' Defence League; assisted Markievicz in the Ministry of Labour; was a District Justice for the Sinn Féin courts; was involved in organising the Belfast Boycott and canvassed extensively for Sinn Féin in elections.

Molony lived at 9 Belgrave Road and rented a room beside Grace Plunkett's studio on Westmoreland Street for 5/- a week as a base in the city centre. Both her home and her office were raided constantly, in fact she said 'it would be easier to say the times they were not raided'.[37] The Co-op on Eden Quay became a crucial hub once more, its proximity to the Liffey made it useful for intelligence gathering and dissemination, as arms and ammunition arrived off boats from Glasgow and Liverpool. Details of what had come in, and when, were passed through the women of the Co-op. 'It was a well-known channel',[38] Molony said. Meanwhile the food kitchen in Liberty Hall had other uses, as recalled by Rosie Hackett,

> When Miss Molony succeeded in getting the soup kitchen going again, it was a great cover-up, and we were able to carry on our activities, where a lot of other places were not. I remember when [Dan] Breen and those people were on the run, they would come to the place … They were able to sit in this place and meet people they wanted to see, very important men and it was not found out.[39]

Local elections in 1920 must have kept her busy, especially as her good friends and housemates, Kathleen Lynn and Madeleine ffrench-Mullen, both ran for and were elected to Rathmines Urban District Council. Further elections followed in 1921 under the Government of Ireland Act. Sinn Féin called for the election to the proposed six county parliament to be fought as an anti-partition plebiscite. Molony and Lynn went to Derry to campaign at the end of May amidst serious sectarian violence. Lynn described the city as an 'armed camp' in her diary.[40] On her return to Dublin, Molony worked closely with Lily O'Brennan of Cumann na mBan to organise the Belfast Boycott, undertaken in protest at sectarian attacks on Northern Catholics. Also at O'Brennan's request, Molony became a

District Justice for the Republican Courts in Rathmines for much of the period. The court only sat once a month in the Town Hall and dealt with minor cases but, as she pointed out the significant thing was that people acknowledged their jurisdiction.

A large part of her propaganda and publicity work was carried out through the WPDL. It was founded by Maud Gonne MacBride and Charlotte Despard to provide much needed support for prisoners, their families and to promote the republican cause. Molony was one of its original and most prominent members. She later recounted how,

> I was ... addressing public meetings. There were public meetings held on behalf of the prisoners. Women, in that case, played a good part, we were busy mostly organising the Prisoners Defence League ... there were a lot of spasmodic meetings held all along, just to keep the flag flying. On any pretence we would hold a meeting – probably because it was forbidden. We would draw attention to the perfidy of the British. I was usually asked to participate in the meetings because I happened to have the misfortune to be able to speak.[41]

However, she also recalled the risks involved and how on one occasion she 'was presiding at a meeting in O'Connell St ... (under Army orders) when a woman was shot dead, and a boy standing beside me shot through the head and 6 others wounded'.[42]

When Molony was asked by Lily O'Brennan to join Cumann na mBan in order to help her organise the Belfast Boycott she refused as she was 'attached to the Citizen Army'. She was made an honorary member of the Ranelagh branch to overcome this but it was clear her allegiance was to the ICA. Molony was described as 'one of a special group of women who were always available for "special service" for the Citizen Army between 1916 and 1923'.[43] However, the ICA was torn by splits and never achieved the cohesion or prominence that it had during the Rising. Many of its members, Molony included, carried on their activity with the IRA.

In the post-Rising reorganisation of the ICA women were admitted on equal terms constitutionally but initially this was far from a reality. Minutes revealed that throughout 1918 and 1919 tensions concerning use of a 'card room' in Liberty Hall dominated the organisation. Women members, excluded from its use, were being reprimanded for rowdy and disorderly conduct and 'giving impertinence to the officers'.[44] One can only imagine what Molony made of this. In late 1920, Padraic O'Broin reorganised part of the ICA into a South County Unit, and in 1936 he testified that,

> my duties brought me in close contact with these ladies [Molony, Lynn and ffrench-Mullen] – owing to the necessity of having need of their services at all times of day or night during the Black and Tan and Civil wars. This lady's house was constantly a meeting place for Army work, Arms dump, Wounded men, and those then on the Run. [sic] She was on the South Co. Dublin list for 'Special' services.[45]

Her full membership of the ICA after 1918 would later be challenged by James Hanratty, a member of the Army Council but not a member of the South County ICA.[46] Hanratty was also part of the reformed ICA committee involved in the petty disputes that occurred in 1918 and 1919. Given all this and the fact that Molony herself went on to be a referee for the head of the Women's Section of the South County ICA, O'Broin's testimony is probably more accurate than Hanratty's.

In her pension application Molony also recorded that she was in active cooperation with republican forces. She carried out occasional duties for the IRA which included the delivery of ammunition. She went to County Longford, ostensibly to 'hold a meeting of protest against the torture of prisoners of war' but also to deliver a parcel of ammunition to the IRA commanding officer of the Granard area. Molony now had rooms at 4 Leeson Street where aside from her own gun she 'constantly had [up to five or six arms] ... either to pass them on or keep ... in safety'.[47] On one such occasion her rooms were raided and a small arsenal found. As she was out at the time, her elderly landlord, who had no connection with the movement, was arrested. She recalled being very upset by this and wrote to plead for his release and took full responsibility for the cache.[48]

On 4 February 1919, Molony returned to the Abbey stage and appeared as the Singing Woman in Yeats' *On Baile's Strand*. It was her first appearance in three years and she followed it up in March with a performance as Anne Forde in *The Rebellion in Ballycullen* by Brinsley MacNamara. On 17 March, in a production of *Cathleen Ní Houlihan*, she played the mother to Augusta Gregory's Cathleen. Máire Nic Shiubhlaigh (who was meant to have played the part), later recalled the production and Gregory's rare stage appearance with glee, and compared her to Queen Victoria.[49]

Molony acted in five further productions that year. It appeared that she was still on contract and paid even when she was not working. 'Some weeks I was on, and some weeks I would not be on. However, as I had a contract with the Abbey, I was paid all the time'.[50] However, in 1920 she only appeared in three productions and four the following year, which does seem very few given this fact.

In 1920 the critic Lawrence, in *The Stage* noted that Molony was an 'artist [with] a curiously individual style and capacity for self-obliteration'.[51] It was an insightful and revealing comment which spoke to her work as an actor, to the myriad roles she took on in her political and trade union work, but also perhaps to a streak of self-destructiveness, one that would become more evident over the coming years. Another insight into the woman behind the agitator and orator came from the late Francis Stuart. It was during this period that he first met Molony, who played an important role in the developing relationship between Stuart and Iseult Gonne. Molony appears in *Blacklist Section H* (Stuart's semi-fictional autobiography) as a 'friend of the Gonne's, a small plain woman with an old fashioned turn of phrase … and a sensible manner'.[52] She defused the tension that the couple's disappearance to London had caused. When marriage was agreed upon, it required Stuart's conversion to Catholicism and Molony reassured the nervous Stuart 'in a few whispered words … by seeming to treat the ceremony as a piece of church bureaucracy not worth making an issue of by refusing to submit to'.[53] The small wedding party then adjourned to Molony's rooms on Leeson Street for tea and cakes. Stuart recalled Molony with a deep affection. He was struck by an 'ageless' quality about her and her emotional generosity. He was also impressed by her ability to hold her own with Gonne MacBride whose forceful personality often swamped those around her. Molony was Iseult's closest friend whom Iseult affectionately called 'Chick'. She also apparently shared Molony's predilection for alcohol; the two women would raid Gonne MacBride's drink cabinet. For Stuart, the abiding impression he got from her involvement in public life was that she was 'a practical not a theoretical politician'.[54]

WOMEN WERE SUBMERGED AND INARTICULATE[55]

The range of Molony's activities were having an effect on her duties as General Secretary of the IWWU. Her apprenticeship as a trade unionist had been served with James Connolly and over that first year her role as a nationalist revolutionary and trade unionist merged into one while she was at the centre of Irish Citizen Army preparations for the 1916 Rising. The union was now establishing itself as an institution and full time administration was required if it was to avoid the kind of upheaval which had characterised its first seven years of existence. Ultimately, Molony was not an administrator – she viewed the amelioration of horrendous working conditions as a necessity but one which must be connected to wider changes. Her desire for this more fundamental change in Ireland, political and social, was too pressing to allow for her exclusive concentration on the day to day running of a trade union at such a crucial time. Louie Bennett and Helen Chenevix (who had also come to the IWWU via suffrage societies) stepped into this role and by March 1918 were established as Honorary Secretaries of the union. Neither was as involved in the nationalist movement so 'by default, established the priorities for the organisation of women workers', adopting a more conciliatory tone.[56]

Louie Bennett was also determined to establish the young union in premises separate from Liberty Hall, at 21 Denmark House, while a substantial part of Molony's activity was still centred on the Connolly Co-op and at Liberty Hall. With the exception of a short period in 1920, Molony did not resume her position as General Secretary of the IWWU and Bennett remained there until 1955. There is no evidence to suggest that she resented her demotion. Molony was not personally ambitious and being relieved of overall responsibility for the union gave her time and scope to follow her other activities and also concentrate on those to whom she had always been drawn – the most vulnerable sections of women workers, and hence the most difficult to organise.

Over the next twenty years she remained a vocal voice of dissent within the union, ensuring that the union remained vibrant. So by 1918 Molony had 'retreated' to the position of official with responsibility for organising domestic workers.[57] It was a notoriously difficult task and one which she would return to several times in her long trade union career. To attract potential members she rented the Sinn Féin Hall every Sunday and invited prominent speakers such as Hanna Sheehy Skeffington. In a letter headed 21 Denmark House, March 1919, she invited Sheehy Skeffington to,

> come and say a few words on the value of trade unionism and organisation generally on next Sunday 6th? If not perhaps you could manage on the following Sun the 13th. I would not want you to stay more than half an hour so that you might be able to fit it in with other engagements. Drop me a note at No 9.[58]

Helena Molony to Hanna Sheehy Skeffington
re organisation of domestic servants, 1919
courtesy Sheehy Skeffington Estate and National Library of Ireland

The letter gives a good idea of just how busy these women were, how connected the various causes they worked for were, but also how physically close together many of them lived. Belgrave Road was known as Rebel Row; Hanna

Sheehy Skeffington lived at No 7 (and rented from the Plunketts), two doors down from Lynn and Molony while Robert Brennan was also living a few doors away.

The job of organising domestic servants also involved extensive door to door recruitment. Molony and Theresa Behan (an official of the Laundresses Section of the union) spent long days in the wealthy Southside suburbs. The proximity to the sea was a great relief to the two foot-weary women who often paddled when finished for the day.[59] Molony loved the sea throughout her life and later told a journalist that,

> whenever she was feeling low she found nothing would do her more good than a trip on the mail boat. 'I'd get a five-shilling ticket in the morning. I'd have my lunch at Holyhead and I'd be home again by evening feeling marvellous!'[60]

According to the same interview, she also played a central role in setting up the Irish Nurses Union, which became a branch of the IWWU in 1919.[61] Molony was evidently very popular within the union. A friend recalled that she was a 'wonderful negotiator – she would ... keep everyone moving – keep everyone's feet on the ground ... they weren't allowed to go off into flights of fancy'.[62] In April 1920, the executive minutes recorded that complaints were aired about officials with 'soft jobs and big wages', although, as Mary Jones has pointed out, the big wages were non-existent and this was a perception. However, it was clearly not a perception held about Molony as, at the same meeting, she was unanimously accorded a pay rise which brought her wages up to parity with Bennett, the General Secretary.[63] She was now effective deputy of the union.

It was as an IWWU representative that Molony came to prominence in another forum, the Irish Labour Party and Trades Union Congress (ILPTUC, later ITUC). Her association with Congress continued until 1941 and she was elected President in 1936. Annual reports show that

Molony was one of the most prolific speakers over the period that she attended Congress. Her frustration with her colleagues' inaction during the period of the War of Independence was palpable. Her impatience was particularly evident at her third Congress in 1921, which occurred at a time when independent rank and file action was at its height. The upsurge in agrarian and industrial radicalism during the War of Independence was an embarrassment to the cautious leadership under Tom Johnson, despite the professed socialist aims of the Congress. Molony accused them of making 'mere pious expression of opinion'.[64]

Molony and the other IWWU representatives were the only ones to put forward motions calling for practical steps to be taken to support such ventures as seizures by workers of the Knocklong Dairies and the Arigna mines and their (short-lived) attempts to establish soviets. She declared that 'she believed in practice and if any of these things were put into operation it would do more good than half a dozen Congresses'.[65] Defending the Women's Labour Council against opposition, on charges of segregation, she countered that,

> it was not the idea to segregate. Labour had granted equality but how did it work out? Women were submerged and inarticulate and their desire was to lead them to express themselves. Women were not the equal of men and if there was to be fraternity they must be equal.[66]

Just as she insisted on the need for equal political representation of women in Sinn Féin, so Molony would continue to work for the equal representation of women in the trade union movement and wider civil society. Throughout her career she defended the need for a separate women's union, until such time as full equality was established.

For Molony, an even more immediate and divisive issue was the attitude being taken by other labour leaders to the Anglo-Irish Treaty and subsequent Civil War. The years between 1921 and 1923 were among the most contentious and bitter for her in the labour movement. Even though these debates continued well into the 1920s, it was a measure of her ability to work with others that Cathal O'Shannon of the ITGWU, who vigorously opposed her, recalled that 'she bore no ill will to us in all our differences, nor did we to her'.[67] Molony had been elected to the ILPTUC National Executive in 1921 and was part of the decision-making process over the next, crucial year. For the executive the main question in the opening weeks of 1922 was whether or not they would contest the June general elections. Labour stood aside in 1918, at the request of Sinn Féin, but the general feeling was that this was not to be repeated. The executive's recommendations would be crucial in determining which way delegates would vote on the issue at the Special Congress of all unions to be held in the Abbey Theatre in February. Feeling that neither of the parties represented Labour's aspirations, a majority recommended participation. Molony was the only executive member to oppose this and at the Special Congress she argued passionately that Labour should stand aside once more, as the election could only be fought on the issue of the Treaty. She tabled a motion to that effect but, despite the cheers of 'Hear, hear' which followed her assertion that 'the first claim on all of them was the country to which they belonged'; her motion was defeated by 115 votes to 82.[68]

It was one of the forums where her anti-Treaty position was outlined and similar bitter debates happened all over the country. Propaganda and publicity were crucial to both sides and again Molony played a significant part. In

January 1922, an appeal to Irish women was published in the *Irish Independent* signed by Molony, Lynn and others. It was a good indication of how a significant majority of female republican activists felt about the Treaty. In their appeal they called on Irish women who, as

> guardians of the race spirit, should be mindful of their sacred trust and remember that freedom is the birth right of every nation ... they should hesitate before they abandon that right for any mere concessions short of complete independence ... [and] maintain an unbroken front towards the common enemy.[69]

ABBEY THEATRE
— DUBLIN. —

Proprietors	THE NATIONAL THEATRE SOCIETY, Ltd
Directors	W. B. YEATS, LADY GREGORY
Manager	LENNOX ROBINSON

Tuesday, 31st January, 1922, and following Nights at 8.15 p.m. Matinee Saturday at 2.30.

FIRST PRODUCTION OF

THE ROUND TABLE

A Comic Tragedy in Three Acts by LENNOX ROBINSON

MRS. DRENNAN		Helena Moloney
DE COURCY DRENNAN		Barry Fitzgerald
DAISY DRENNAN	her children	Eileen Crowe
BEE DRENNAN		Eileen O'Kelly
JONTY DRENNAN		J. Hugh Nagle

Cast list for Abbey Theatre production of *The Round Table*, 1922
courtesy Abbey Theatre Archive

Molony's theatrical, trade union and republican activities tipped off each other once more. Just a week before the controversial Special Congress in the Abbey, she appeared onstage as Mrs Drennan in *The Round Table* by Lennox

Robinson. Throughout 1922, Molony performed in the Abbey on a much more regular basis and was cast in 15 productions that year. In April she was again playing the role of Mrs Drennan and planning a trip to Brussels and Germany with Lynn and Madeleine ffrench-Mullen, when anti-Treaty republicans entered the Four Courts. Over the next month the three women tried to decide whether or not to take the trip after all.

> There was a great deal of uncertainty and a great deal of talk about peace and truces. We finally decided we would go away and we would be away for three weeks.[70]

It was the first break Molony had taken since 1915 but a week in, Lynn and ffrench-Mullen assessed the worsening situation at home and decided to return. Molony's financial situation was always more precarious than that of her friends, so she remained in Brussels. She was there as Free State forces began to bombard the Four Courts at the outbreak of the Civil War in June 1922. It is the only absence from duty which she recorded over the period and as she explained later,

> I was a bit tighter with money and thought I would remain until the next week. I did not see the force of spending £2 or £3 on a ticket and I decided to remain. I stayed away until the end of the week; of course it had well taken place.[71]

Molony spent what limited funds she had left on two revolvers, returned to Dublin and 'reported for duty on July 4th' on the anti-Treaty side. She gave one of the guns to Francis Stuart but it was seized soon after when he was arrested. She later recalled her annoyance. 'As I bought this with my money I felt very sorry about it going so easily'.[72] Thomas Behan, new Commanding Officer of the South County Dublin ICA testified,

> I have known Miss Helena Molony to be a member of the I.C.A South Co Dublin. During my time with that unit from 1922 onwards, she was one of the most trusted women, [she

was] capable and rendered valuable and esteemed services to the Republican forces.[73]

A. Prisoners, First Aid and the care of prisoners. With Madame Gonne McBride, Mrs. Despard, and Mrs. Skeffington, I was at the very first meeting of the Prisoners Defence, a very serious situation with regard to prisoners, more particularly to prisoners dependants. That has gone on of course ever since.

Q. You gave a revolver to Frank Stewart and you think you gave one to Sean McBridge?
A. Certainly one to Frank Steward there is no question about that. He was arrested quite soon afterwards with it on him. As I bought this with my money I felt very sorry about it going so easily.

8th Period:

Q. You attended to wounded man and prisoners procuring and concealing arms. That was at the start of the fighting in the Civil War?
A. Yes.

Q. Were you in any outpost?
A. No. I was away, Dr. Lynn, Mrs. French Mullen and I were away at the week of the Four Courts. We were in Brussels, we were on our way to Germany. They came back I did not come back at the period There was a great deal of uncertainty and a great deal of talk about peace and truces. We finally decided we would go away, and we would be away for three weeks and nothing happened. They got a copy of "The Sketch" one day and they decided to come back. I was a bit tighter with money and I thought I would remain until the next week, I did not see the force of spending £2 or £3 on a ticket and I decided to remain. I stayed away until the end of the week, of course, it had well taken place, I think it was Wednesday, was the day of the opening. I did not return until Monday night.

Q. That was the 4th July?
A. Yes. Then I immediately reported for duty and resumed my work such as it was.

9th Period:

Q. You helped and harboured Republican soldiers, procuring and concealing arms. Assisting Publicity, Dept. of Republic etc. etc.?
A. Yes.

Q. Give us an idea of how much activity you had from the 4th July onwards up to the end of March 1923?
A. General activity and co-operation with the Army as before caring dumps, caring individual arms, providing First Aid Equipment, publicity very largely. My rooms were hqrs., naturally I had a good deal of work in connection with this.

Helena Molony giving evidence in 1936 about her activities
during the War of Independence and Civil War
courtesy Military Archives, Ireland

She later recorded that her work at that time involved 'helping and harbouring Republican soldiers, procuring and concealing arms, assisting Publicity Department of Republic'.[74] Her rooms in Westmoreland Street became the publicity headquarters for the anti-Treaty movement and much of her property there was destroyed in raids. She subsequently exchanged these rooms for ones that Cumann na mBan used on Bachelors Walk. These were also raided regularly, with 'a good many things taken out of it, not of much value'.[75] The majority of female republican activists, and Cumann na mBan as an organisation, were on the anti-Treaty side and a large number of women (over 400) were imprisoned during the Civil War. This was significantly more than in the War of Independence and was recognition by their former colleagues, now opponents, of their value in the war. Many went on hunger strike and though Molony herself was not arrested, she agitated for their release and spoke regularly at Women's Prisoners' Defence League meetings. In Molony's own later accounts very little detail was provided about her activities during the Civil War.[76]

All of this publicity and military work was carried out alongside her trade union work and performances on the Abbey stage. In August, as the Civil War continued, Molony appeared in five Abbey productions, largely in supporting roles. They included an appearance as Bridget Gillane in a revival of *Cathleen Ní Houlihan*, and as Hannah the servant in Lennox Robinson's *The White Headed Boy*. Molony was then cast as the lead in a new play by Robinson, *Crabbed Youth and Old Age*, which premiered in November 1922. The character was a 'delightfully loquacious and brilliant woman – who keeps attracting the suitors of her dull daughters'.[77] The *Evening Herald* described her performance as 'deliciously humorous'. It was seen as her finest role and later performances were compared to hers. Just as in 1913, as her profile rose, her acting career took second place to her political and trade union activities. Her career slowly began to wind down from 1923, apparently under pressure from the IWWU. Although she would continue to act on the Abbey stage until 1927, her appearances were sporadic.

Meanwhile, anti-Treaty forces were in retreat and when a ceasefire was agreed that summer, an election date was set for August 1923. Molony went down to Mayo where she was publicity director for Patrick Ruttledge, now Vice-President of Sinn Féin. He won his seat by a significant margin while in Dublin, Kathleen Lynn was also returned as an anti-Treaty Sinn Féin candidate. Anti-Treaty Sinn Féin failed to gain a majority in the election, and refused to take their seats in the new Free State Parliament.

It was the end of 'the terrible years' but they had left their mark on many of the men and women who lived and worked through them.[78] Before 1918 all the different strands of Molony's activity coalesced, but by 1923 her life had changed significantly. Events had forced her to choose between political loyalty for the labour and republican movements, and between her career as an Abbey actor and her work in the IWWU, a choice that would become final in the following years. In 1917, Molony spoke and agitated publically, often at great risk, to declare that the Republic proclaimed in the Rising still lived. In 1923 she was engaged in many of the same activities. This time however she, along with most of the women of the republican movement, was in the position of dissident against an Irish administration. The fact that so many active women had been on the anti-Treaty side in the Civil War would be entwined with attitudes and legislation in the reactionary and conservative post-revolutionary State. Molony was one of the small number of women in public life who through their actions and their very presence would challenge this conservatism. The support and framework provided by James Connolly, and the declaration of equality in the Proclamation, provided powerful legitimising forces for Molony and other women throughout the Free State years.

SOURCES
1   Helena Molony: BMH WS 391.
2   Interview with Máire Comerford, Sound Archive, Fawcett Library, London.
3   Military Service Pension Collection File 11739, Helena Molony, 1935–1967; hereafter Helena Molony, MSPC 11739.
4   Helena Molony: BMH WS 391.
5   *Saturday Evening Post*, 3 February 1917.
6   14 April 1917, CO 904/201/305, National Archives UK, reproduced in McGarry, *Abbey Rebels*, p. 249.
7   Helena Molony: BMH WS 391.
8   *Ibid.*
9   Helena Molony: BMH WS 391. Her version, as retold by Joseph Bouch (NLI), in 1936 has been contested by print historians on the basis that the extant 1917 Proclamation is a form of photographic reproduction (see http:typefoundry.blogspot.ie/2010/01). However it is possible that Walker either did not use the type as collected (and did not inform Molony) or there is another version which may not have survived. My thanks to Theresa Breathnach for access to her unpublished paper 'Matthew Walker, the Gaelic Press and the 1916 Rising'.
10   *The Irish Times*, Tuesday 10 April 1917.
11   Helena Molony: BMH WS 391.
12   Rosie Hackett: BMH WS 546.
13   Helena Molony: BMH WS 391.
14   Rosie Hackett: BMH WS 546.
15   Helena Molony: BMH WS 391.
16   McGarry, *Abbey Rebels*, p. 252.
17   Frank Robbins, Bureau of Military History Witness Statement 585.
18   30 April 1917, DMP Report, reproduced in McGarry, *Abbey Rebels*, p. 251.
19   Cathal Brugha, quoted in Regan, 'Helena Molony', p. 154.
20   Helena Molony: BMH WS 391.
21   Undated postcard of Aylesbury prison from Helena Molony to Nell Ryan, MS 48447/2, NLI.

22   Kathleen Lynn diary, 21 June 1917, quoted in Pašeta, *Irish Nationalist Women*.

23   Molony, 'Years of Tension'.

24   Interview with Helena Molony, 'Women of the Rising', 1963, RTÉ Sound Archives.

25   Helena Molony: BMH WS 391.

26   Pašeta, *Irish Nationalist Women*, p. 227.

27   *Ibid*, p. 229.

28   *Ibid*.

29   RJD, quoted in Pašeta, *Irish Nationalist Women*, p. 229.

30   Helena Molony, MSPC 11739.

31   Maeve Cavanagh MacDowell: BMH WS 258.

32   Annie O'Brien, Bureau of Military History Witness Statement 805.

33   Kathleen Lynn: BMH WS 357.

34   Maud Gonne MacBride, Bureau of Military History Witness Statement 317.

35   Helena Molony, MSPC 11739.

36   *Ibid*.

37   *Ibid*.

38   *Ibid*.

39   Rosie Hackett: BMH WS 546.

40   Kathleen Lynn diary, 21–23 May 1921, quoted in Mulholland, *Kathleen Lynn*, p. 72.

41   Helena Molony: BMH WS 391.

42   Helena Molony, MSPC 11739.

43   *Ibid*.

44   Matthews, *The Irish Citizen Army*, p. 166.

45   Helena Molony, MSPC 11739.

46   Helena Molony, MSPC 11739: Hanratty Evidence.

47   Helena Molony, MSPC 11739.

48   Helena Molony: BMH WS 391.

49   McGarry, *Abbey Rebels*, p. 196.

50   Helena Molony: BMH WS 391.

51   *The Stage*, 21 November 1920.

52   Francis Stuart, *Black List Section H* (Dublin, Lilliput Press, 1995), p. 16.

53   *Ibid*, pp 29–30.

54   Francis Stuart, interview with author, 1991.

55   ILPTUC Report of the 27th Annual General Meeting, 1921.

56   Mary Jones, *These Obstreperous Lassies: A History of the Irish Women Workers' Union* (Dublin, Gill and Macmillan, 1988), p. 26.

57   *Ibid*, p. 29.

58   Helena Molony, letter to Hanna Sheehy-Skeffington, Sheehy-Skeffington Papers, MS 33605 NLI.

59   Jenny Murray (daughter of Theresa Behan), interview with author, 1995.

60   *The Irish Times*, January 1965, Candida column.

61   *Ibid*.

62   Louie Coghlan O'Brien interview with author, 1991.

63   Jones, *Obstreperous Lassies*, p. 48.

64   ILPTUC Report of the 27th Annual General Meeting, 1921.

65   *Ibid*, p. 132.

66   *Ibid*.

67   Cathal O'Shannon, 'Recorded Voice of Helena Molony' *Evening Press*, 3 February 1967.

68   ILPTUC Report of the 28th Annual General Meeting and of the Special Congress on Election Policy, 1922, p. 69.

69   *Irish Independent*, 7 January 1922.

70   Helena Molony, MSPC 11739.

71   Helena Molony, MSPC 11739.

72   *Ibid*.

73   Helena Molony, MSPC 11739.

74   Helena Molony, MSPC 11739.

75   *Ibid*.

76   The Bureau of Military History only sought testimony up to 1921 but many interviewees gave more detail about the post-Treaty period.

77   *The Evening Herald*, 15 November 1922.

78   Helena Molony: BMH WS 391.

Helena Molony, 1930s
private collection

TRADE UNIONIST
1923–1941

> Our next move forward must be accompanied by clear
> knowledge and determination to deal with poverty,
> unemployment and industrial servitude.[1]

From the end of the Civil War until her retirement from
public life in 1941, Helena Molony's primary work was as
a trade unionist. She was a long time official with the Irish
Women Workers' Union and prominent in the Dublin
Trade Union and Labour Council and the Irish Trade
Union Congress. She still appeared on the Abbey stage
(albeit sporadically) and continued to agitate against
whichever administration was in power. However when it
came to a decision (often made under pressure) over
which to prioritise, she consistently chose her trade union
work. Her acting career finally ended in 1927.

In the 1930s, Molony was instrumental in trying to move
the republican movement to the left and was widely
known as a 'revolutionary'.[2] She was in regular
disagreement with the majority of trade unionists (both in
the IWWU and the wider movement) on republican and

socialist grounds. She was also a vocal opponent of her male colleagues who supported the extensive restrictions being placed on women in public and working life, through legislation and expectation.

It was a mark of her authority and standing as a trade unionist that, despite all of this, she was a leading executive member of the Dublin Trades Union and Labour Council and the Irish Trades Union Congress throughout the 1930s. She was elected President of the ITUC in 1936, only the second woman to have achieved this position (Louie Bennett being the first). Although less dramatic and not as well documented, it could be argued that her defence of the rights of working women in these conservative years was as significant as her role in the independence movement's early years.

EQUALITY OF OPPORTUNITY FOR ALL MEN AND WOMEN[3]

Helena Molony still lived at 9 Belgrave Road when the Civil War ended and was a familiar figure in Rathmines. She caught the Number 25 tram to the city centre every morning as she went into the IWWU headquarters and again, at weekends, as she went to address meetings of the Women's Prisoners' Defence League on O'Connell Street.[4] By 1923 Louie Bennett was fully established as General Secretary of the IWWU and her close friend Helen Chenevix assumed the duties, if not the salary, of her assistant. Although Molony's position was that of a salaried official, she remained one of the three effective leaders of the union until her retirement in 1941. As Cullen Owens, social historian and biographer of Louie Bennett points out,

> Together Bennett, Chenevix and Molony would form a formidable triumvirate on behalf of women workers. Gains achieved by the IWWU over the coming decades in many ways were disproportionate to its membership and were to a

large extent the result of the commitment of these women to the rights of women workers and women generally.[5]

Cumann ban Oibre éineann

(IRISH WOMEN WORKERS' UNION.)

Irishwomen, take your place in the ranks of Labour by joining the Irish Women Workers' Union.

This Union is run by women, for women, and puts the interests of women workers in the forefront of its programme.

In addition to Strike, Lock-out, and Victimisation Benefits, we pay :—

Sickness Benefit ... ... **6/- to 10/- per week**
(apart from National Health Insurance)

Hospital Benefit ... ... **6d. per annum**
which entitles Members to free treatment, intern or extern, at ten Dublin Hospitals.

Marriage Benefit **£5**

Mortality Benefit **£5**

We have a **Benevolent and Loan Fund** which all may join, an **Unemployed Fund** which all our Unemployed Members share at Christmas, a **Library** and **Social Club** open to all our Members and friends.

OFFICES :

7 & 8 EDEN QUAY, DUBLIN

IWWU advertisement, reproduced from the *Dublin Labour Year Book*

IWWU records reveal just how small the union was and it went from 5,300 members in 1918 to 2,553 in 1929. While all trade unions experienced a drop in membership in the 1920s (and often, an even more dramatic percentage drop than the IWWU) new female entrants were more likely to join a mixed general or clerical union than the IWWU. Despite this, the majority of female delegates to Annual Congress conventions and those elected to its national executive were from the IWWU. Social historian Mary Daly concludes that the IWWU were 'the sole voice within the trade union movement which spoke for women's interests'.[6]

There were occasional tensions and differences of opinion between Bennett and Molony during the 1920s, however they were confined to organisational matters and did not spill over into the public arena until the 1930s. In fact, Molony's close friend Máire Comerford recalled that the two women were on good terms but that there may have been rivalry in union elections. Because of the nature of the work it is often difficult to gauge a trade unionist's efficacy and contribution and it is hard to identify Molony's exact position or role prior to 1929, due to scant records. What does emerge clearly from the IWWU executive minutes was the contribution Molony made vocalising problems and pushing for solutions. She showed a consistent commitment to the most vulnerable sections of women workers; home workers, those affected by increasing mechanisation and the rising numbers of unemployed members. Her negotiation skills were renowned as she solved seemingly intractable disputes rapidly.

In 1924, Molony took up the issue of bag-makers and the increased use of home workers in the trade. Employing women to work from home had long been common practice in the areas of clothing and textiles. It involved poorly-paid piece work and, as with the case of the domestic workers, was a virtually impossible sector to organise. Molony led a delegation to Dublin Corporation to register the 'Dublin Workers Grievance'. In her submission she emphasised the dangers to the public of the 'unhygienic practice of bag-making in private homes'.[7]

Throughout the 1920s the introduction of increased mechanisation was affecting the women Molony and the IWWU represented. This regularly resulted in wage reductions and layoffs. It was a particular problem faced by those working in the printing and laundry industries, who made up nearly 4/5 of the union's membership at that stage. In July 1924 Molony reported that machinery in the printing trade was displacing workers and that a wage reduction was being imposed by employers. As the union had reluctantly agreed to a reduction the previous year, they were not prepared to accept this. An increase was sought and strike notice served. At the 1926 IWWU Annual Convention Molony reported on how a similar problem was faced by laundry workers. She told the Convention that a 'grave crisis' was imminent because of the introduction of pressing machines. Male juvenile workers were operating the machines at the same time as women with years of experience were being laid off. Molony accused employers of 'dehumanising human life', as in areas where women had previously exercised skill they were now just 'machine attendants'.[8]

Molony also highlighted the issue of the 'Magdalen' laundries, established by charitable and penal institutions, which used inmates as unpaid labour. Molony, in common with her contemporaries, did not investigate or address the status and conditions of the 'penitents' in those institutions. Her concern was for the women workers she represented in the laundry trade. Even the government was contracting work out to the 'Magdalen' laundries and Molony was scathing that 'In the sacred name of charity, wage earning women were being deprived of their employment'.[9]

As emigration and unemployment numbers rose in the early years of the Free State, Molony and the IWWU were among those who put pressure on the government to respond to the crisis. In November 1925 Molony and another IWWU member, Mary O'Connor, organised a poster parade outside the Dáil at the opening of the new session which attracted 'great interest'.[10] The IWWU were deeply critical of their trade union colleagues who had not involved themselves in a significant campaign. That same year they resigned from the Dublin Workers Council because of their failure to 'carry out any strong agitation on behalf of the unemployed'.[11]

Molony's career in the Abbey was now coming to an end and she retired completely from acting at the age of 44. Between the end of the Civil War and April 1927 she appeared in only eight productions. In more than half of these she took on roles that she had played previously, in fact this included three appearances as Mrs Swan in *Crabbed Youth and Old Age*. However her range and adaptability as an actor meant that she was still much in demand. In 1926 Seán O'Casey wrote to the Abbey about the casting of Mrs Gogan in his new play *The Plough and the Stars*. He wrote that he 'would of course like Helena Molony but I suppose this is out of the question'.[12] As the Abbey regularly fielded and refused O'Casey's casting suggestions, the fact that Molony did not play the part may have had as much to do with this, as her availability. (Or indeed any political objections she may have had about the play given the later protests).

In 1926 and 1927 she took on two new roles; Madame Pons in *Doctor Knock* by Jules Romains and Mrs Whitefield in George Bernard Shaw's *Man and Superman*. However, it was not possible, even for Molony, to combine an acting career and one as a full time official of the IWWU. It would seem that her final decision to leave the theatre came under pressure from Bennett, and Molony elected to stay with the union.[13]

Her final role was one that she had played twice before and, not for the first time, the theme on stage would chime with her public activism. On 28 April 1927 after playing Hanna Cooney in *The Land for the People* by Brinsley MacNamara, Helena Molony changed out of her costume and retired as an actor. She had appeared in over 100 productions since joining the Abbey in 1912, toured nationally and internationally and achieved a substantial level of acclaim at two separate points in her acting career. The claims made in her obituaries that, had she remained a full-time actor, she would have become 'one of the greats' rang true.[14] It is impossible to know what leaving the stage cost her but, in 1934, she sounded a note of regret when she described theatre as the 'one and only sphere in which woman has succeeded in holding her own'.[15] It was an interesting comment from a woman active in the spheres of theatre, trade unionism and nationalist politics. It provided an insight into her own experience but also spoke to the fact that there were no lead roles envisaged for women in the public life of the Free State. Letters and articles written after her retirement showed that she retained an active interest in the world of the arts and a fondness for the Abbey. She had enjoyed the atmosphere, the gossip and the intrigue. Although the end of her acting career left her without a creative outlet, this facet of her personality surfaced occasionally on public platforms and in the imaginative approach which she brought to solving problems.

In 1929 Molony was appointed as Organising Secretary for the IWWU and she held this post until just before her retirement. At successive Annual Conventions throughout the 1920s she had argued that the union needed to take a more active approach to the organisation of women workers. In June 1929 a Special Convention was held to elect a vice-president and president for the union and to hear her plans for reorganisation. Molony proposed targeting particular industries to recruit all of the workers in them; shirt-making and textiles were to be prioritised. She also highlighted a problem affecting the printing trade, the fact that non-union shops outside Dublin were undermining advances which had been made by organised labour inside the capital. Consequently a particularly strenuous effort was to be made to organise these and over the next few years she travelled to different towns recruiting for the IWWU. Apart from the usual factory gate recruitment, methods were to include public meetings, the use of cinemas for propaganda and a weekly manuscript journal.[16] In fact, an IWWU monthly paper, *An Bhean Oibre*, had ceased production the previous year and there is no evidence that a replacement along the lines proposed by Molony (or indeed cinema advertising) resulted.

Equality of opportunity for all men and women was the first principle of the IWWU and formed 'the basis of its general policy'.[17] To this end they were involved in housing initiatives, adult education and also had an active social and civic committee. Molony apparently directed performances of the union's 'Dramatic and Concert Troupe'. Molony was also an Urban District Councillor on the Rathmines and Rathgar Council and was involved in trying to set up affordable housing schemes there. She was assistant librarian for the IWWU but complained that members were only borrowing fiction material; she suggested public lectures and readings be held and inaugurated a study circle and summer school. However, this was not to be seen as a replacement for a more comprehensive approach. In 1929 when the question of adult education arose at the annual delegate conference of the Irish Labour Party and Trade Union Congress

(ILPTUC) members deplored the lack of a nationwide system and Molony agreed saying 'individual local activities are not satisfactory, the position in Dublin is disgraceful'.[18] Thus while she initiated schemes at a local level she remained aware of the need for more radical and far-reaching action.

Molony and the IWWU were very involved in the attempts to reunite the Dublin Workers Council and the Dublin Trades Council. These splits were ideological as well as personality based and involved the ITGWU and the Workers Union of Ireland. The WUI had been established in 1924 by Jim Larkin after his return to Ireland and his failure to regain control of the ITGWU. Molony was a member of a unity committee drawn from non-aligned unions which successfully achieved this in 1928. She was elected to the executive of the new Dublin Trade Union and Labour Council (hereafter Trades Council) in 1929 and remained a leading member until 1939.

Dublin Trades Union and Labour Council Executive Committee, 1930–31. Helena Molony centre row with dog
Reproduced from the *Dublin Labour Year Book*

Detail reproduced from the *Dublin Labour Year Book*

The other major development in the Irish labour movement of the time was the amicable separation of its industrial and political sides into two separate organisations, the Labour Party and the Irish Trades Union Congress (ITUC). It marked the effective end of James Connolly's syndicalist vision. When Molony refused, in May 1930, to appear on a Trades Council platform with the Chairman of this new parliamentary Labour Party, the anti-Treaty and syndicalist crosscurrents in her thought were evident. Her view that the unity just achieved by the Trades Council could not come at any cost and should not be seen as repudiation of Connolly's thought was forcefully stated,

> After many years of disunity, the Dublin Labour Movement is able to present a united front. In order to achieve this unity the Workers Republicans, whom I represent, tacitly agreed to avoid contentious politics, and to work loyally with all other workers' parties towards industrial solidarity and militant Trades Unionism, and so to stem the wave of disorganisation which was sweeping over the Labour Movement. If some people foolishly imagine that this quiescence is a sign of repentance or change of outlook, they are likely to get a rude awakening in the near future, and if the Dublin Trade Union and Labour Council accept the position of being a background and a platform for Labour Imperialism, they will have the credit of again disrupting the Dublin Labour movement on the Industrial field – the real venue of the workers' struggle.[19]

She signed off as a self-styled member of the remnants of Connolly's followers.

WE CAN NO LONGER LOOK OUT ON THE WORLD EVEN AS WE COULD IN 1915

In fact Molony had been in political transition. Before 1918 her trade union and radical nationalist activities merged as one. Over the next decade they increasingly diverged. In the 1920s she was at the centre of bitter debates at ILPTUC congresses over the political participation of labour in the new Free State. Meanwhile, in parallel with her job as a union official she opposed the government at Women's Prisoners' Defence League meetings. Most Sundays throughout the 1920s and 1930s Molony was to be found speaking at their meetings on O'Connell Street or Cathal Brugha Street after 11 o'clock mass. The women usually addressed crowds of between two and four hundred from the back of a horse-drawn platform. Intelligence records reveal that the authorities kept a close eye on the meetings but, apart from 1931, gauged that they were more of a nuisance than a serious threat.[20] Molony used this platform to lambast the new Free State administration (and later the Fianna Fáil government) and kept her audiences informed on a range of national and international issues.

Along with other anti-Treaty republicans her political views and involvement developed in the early years of the state. She was beginning to examine other ways of furthering the ideal of a workers' republic within republican structures, as well as through labour ones. Molony was one of the major figures who attempted to bring the anti-Treaty movement leftwards. The year after many of her old friends and colleagues, including Markievicz, established Fianna Fáil, Molony published an article in *Irish Freedom*, the Sinn Féin paper. It showed just how she had reassessed and regrouped. In an article titled 'Unemployment – a solution' she addressed republicans saying that,

> The new menace to us small nations is not big armies or big navies but Big Business – except it is controlled in the interest of the nation. We can no longer look out on the world as we could even in 1915. We who have been through a welter of military war have (necessarily) lost sight of certain economic developments.[21]

It was an interesting admission and one that signalled a crucial development in her thinking; neither the current composition of the IRA and Sinn Féin, or the new Fianna Fáil party, would yield the vision for Ireland she believed in. This shift of emphasis was to be crucial for the direction her work would take throughout the 1930s. Molony never actually identified herself as a communist but it was often levelled against her as a charge by opponents, especially in the IWWU.

In 1921 she had advocated support for the Russian Revolution and urged that more education should be undertaken on this. On the 12th anniversary of the revolution she got the opportunity to see Russia first hand when she visited as part of a Trades Council delegation. In November 1929 she and nine colleagues sailed from London to Leningrad. For the next six weeks they travelled as guests of the Soviet trade union movement, along with French and British delegates to Moscow, Rostov and Kharkov. When Molony returned from Russia she became increasingly prominent in left wing groups and was a central target of the 'Red Scare' that swept Ireland in the early 1930s.

Miss Molony, That Shrewdest of Socialist Propagandists[22]

The Trades Council delegation sailed back to Ireland at the beginning of a new decade, as the worldwide depression was taking a tighter hold of the country. Molony, Robert Tynan and P.T. Daly, the three executive members on the delegation, produced a report which was enthusiastic about the Soviet state but not uncritical. They concluded that,

> Russia is not a paradise and we do not want to create the impression it is. The delegation submits to the Irish Labour movement that it should support the Russian workers in their struggle for human progress which is essentially the same in all lands.[23]

Molony's approach to the issue of equality was clearly reflected in the section on the role of women,

> Women are taking their full part in all this work and occupy many responsible positions. Russians do not consider whether it is a man or a woman, they are only concerned with getting the best person for the job.[24]

Soon after her return, Molony was involved in establishing the organisation the Friends of Soviet Russia and lectured extensively on the Soviet Union.

This new direction that her involvement was taking quickly brought her into serious conflict with many of her trade union colleagues. The trade union movement was beginning to reflect a wider hysteria surrounding radical organisations that was current in the Free State. The Russian Delegation's report proved controversial in the Trades Council. It then ignited a row in the IWWU which quickly centred on Molony's 'public connection with Communists'.[25] Molony proposed that the IWWU take 100 copies of the report on a sale or return basis. The majority of the executive refused and Molony, furious,

> wished it to be recorded that she thought it disgraceful that the IWWU should refuse to take cognisance of the report of their own fellow workers in preference to the reports of the capitalist press.[26]

By May 1930 the Trades Council was refusing to send delegates to a conference organised by the Friends of Soviet Russia. That same month the dispute over the report flared up again at the IWWU Annual Convention when Bennett tabled a motion which regretted that 'certain principles of religion and liberty are not upheld by Soviet Russia', while Helen Chenevix declared 'communist affiliations are undesirable'. The debate rapidly became an attack on Molony and the motion was carried by 40 voters to 15.[27]

Advertisement for the controversial Report of the Russian
Delegation. Reproduced from the *Dublin Labour Year Book*

The relationship between Bennett and Molony was increasingly a fraught and complicated one, but this episode seemed to bring matters to a head. Bennett had also suggested that the executive take over the role of organisation, a post held by Molony. Molony successfully resisted this move but the tensions continued. Two weeks after the Annual Convention, Bennett dropped a bombshell at an executive meeting and said she intended to resign citing 'health reasons and ... friction with staff'.[28] Jones, historian of the IWWU, frames this episode in the context of Bennett's move to re-establish authority within the union. She argues that Bennett used the threat of resignation to this end on more than one occasion. Cullen Owens, Bennett's biographer, has shown that while this was partly true, Bennett's genuine health problems and a mounting workload in the union and other areas were also factors.[29] It was Molony who persuaded Bennett to stay on for another six months and a series of meetings between Bennett and the IWWU staff, including Molony, was held. When the matter arose again in September Molony said that 'she [Bennett] and they [members of staff] had agreed to let bygones be bygones'.[30] Bennett agreed to stay on as General Secretary and requested that she be allowed take short breaks on unpaid leave.[31] However, Molony's non-union activities would soon come up again and her lack of authority within the union and her status as a member of staff would be publicly and firmly stated by Bennett.

In April 1930 the government carried out their first detailed examination of revolutionary organisations. The resulting internal memorandum stressed the links between the Irish groups and international communism but acknowledged the small numbers of people actually involved and the considerable overlap of those individuals. Molony was named as a committee member of the Friends of Soviet Russia, the Women's Prisoners' Defence League and as 'an active sympathiser with the irregular organisation'.[32] It was also noted that she spoke at meetings organised by the League Against Imperialism.

The visit of the Trades Council delegation to Russia was the subject of a lengthy intelligence report and Molony was described as 'that shrewdest of socialist propagandists'.[33] Comintern records reveal that Molony also wrote to Moscow about the communist paper *The Workers' Voice*, edited by Scottish nationalist Tom Bell, which she felt 'left much to be desired'. Clerical hostility was best addressed by the Friends of Soviet Russia who, she explained, were led by 'people familiar and sympathetic with the National and religious psychology'.[34] From the ten Trades Council delegates Molony and Kathleen Price were singled out as 'noteworthy' because of their association with the IRA.[35] From this point on surveillance increased dramatically. A seeming alliance between the IRA and the left caused the government most concern, and Molony was to the fore in trying to achieve this. The culmination of this process was the founding of Saor Éire in September 1931 when 150 delegates met in Dublin. Molony was elected to the executive, along with George Gilmore, Frank Ryan, Seán MacBride, Sheila Humphries and its leading personality Peadar O'Donnell. Saor Éire aimed to create 'an independent revolutionary leadership for the working class and working farmers' with the ultimate aim of achieving 'the overthrow in Ireland of British Imperialism and its ally Irish Capitalism'.[36]

Within the IWWU Bennett immediately objected to Molony's involvement in Saor Éire. Molony was then put in the position of having to 'ask for the confidence of the executive in view of her Labour record'.[37] At a special meeting of the executive Bennett suggested that Molony would either have to resign as the IWWU representative on the Trades Council, or as an executive member of Saor Éire. Molony resigned her position as an executive member of Saor Éire, but declared that she intended remaining a member. It was significant that, again, when forced to choose between her trade union work and non-union involvement, she chose the union.

The strength of these radical groups was being greatly exaggerated, both by those involved and the government, since it was largely a leadership without a movement. A combined church-state offensive was launched and Saor Éire disintegrated under the pressure. An amendment known as Article 2A was introduced into the constitution on 23 October 1931 and twelve different groups were banned. Many of their members were arrested or driven underground. As surveillance had accurately recorded, Molony was a member of at least three of these, namely the Friends of Soviet Russia, Saor Éire and the Women's Prisoners' Defence League. The latter was the only group to openly defy the Act. The Sunday following its promulgation, crowds assembled on O'Connell Street in anticipation and a lorry drew up bearing the banner, 'The People's Rights Association', thus leaving the police unable to act. In case there was any doubt that this was, in fact, the WPDL, Molony opened the proceedings by declaring that 'a rose by any other name would smell as sweet'.[38]

The Minister for Justice, James FitzGerald-Kenney, declared that 'we are going to put people like these in prison, and if they persist and if it is necessary we are going to execute them'.[39] He did not get a chance since, in March 1932, Fianna Fáil entered government with an overall majority; Article 2A was suspended and political prisoners released. Immediately Molony, Charlotte Despard and Hanna Sheehy Skeffington, along with Robert Stewart, Peadar O'Donnell and Sean Murray set about reviving the Revolutionary Worker's Groups which led to the founding of the Workers' College in Eccles Street.

Molony moved from 9 Belgrave Road in the mid 1920s into Frankfort House, Rathmines. It was a lodging house run by the Coghlan family who had republican sympathies and where her old friends Constance Markievicz and Sidney Gifford Czira (with her young son Finian) also lived. Molony made a lasting impression on Louie Coghlan, the young daughter of the house, who recalled that,

> she was wonderful – very soft spoken … I think she was very disappointed about all the other women [who] got great publicity … [she] gave the impression of being a sad woman – not being fulfilled in the way that she wanted to be.[40]

It was to Coghlan that Molony confided about her earlier 'understanding' with Bulmer Hobson and how he had 'broken her heart'. She also told her that this was the reason she drank. Constance Markievicz's death in 1927 affected Molony deeply and she apparently disappeared on periodic drinking binges around this time. These may account for some of her frequent absences from IWWU and Trades Council meetings, always noted as being due to ill health. However at this stage, her skills overrode her erratic habits. Coghlan got the impression that within the IWWU she was 'so important for negotiations, she couldn't be done without … [she was] too important to sack'.[41]

MISS MOLONY AND THE POPE[42]

In the summer of 1932 Molony was again involved in a major public controversy. 'Miss Molony and the Pope' correspondence filled the *Irish Independent's* letters page for over a week. On 18 July 1932 she addressed a WPDL meeting (they had reverted to their original name after the suspension of Article 2A). She referred to de Valera's recent negotiations in London, the unsuccessful attempts to resolve the Anglo-Irish Trade War and to the 'hair brained and irresponsible scheme' of an English MP who had called for the Pope to intervene and arbitrate. Molony continued 'that if Ireland learned anything from her unhappy history, she had no reason to look with confidence for Papal intervention in Irish secular or political affairs'. Her remarks were reported in the Monday edition of the *Irish Independent* under the headline 'Strange Outburst: Attack on the Pope'.[43] The article brought the full fury of post-Eucharistic Congress Ireland down on Molony, despite the fact that she criticised the reporter for misrepresenting her remarks in a letter published the following day.

'The Catholics of Ireland are not going to submit tamely to these insults', wrote Louis A. Tierny, who suggested that 'all meetings addressed by communists, either male or female, should be attended and hymns such as "Faith of our Fathers", etc., sung'. He at least was prepared to sign his own name. 'A True Republican' wondered was it an Orange meeting she was addressing; 'I, for one, did as much as Miss Molony for Ireland and would do so again, but God first and Ireland after'. 'Papal Colours' said that the attack was 'tainted with communism' and called for a mobilisation of Catholic Action to get 'rid of many of the diseases from which the country is now suffering', while 'Disgusted' expressed horror and indignation that this had taken place so soon after the Eucharistic Congress, and called for the formation of a Catholic Defence. The IWWU was publicly drawn into the debate when 'Catholic Editor' said that Molony would do well to bear in mind that,

> Catholic Ireland will have no patience with those who make open attacks on our Catholic faith in the streets of Dublin. Miss Molony is President or Secretary of the Irish Women Workers' Union. What do its members think?

IWWU General Secretary Louie Bennett and President Sarah Kennedy moved rapidly to respond and wrote,

We beg to say that she [Helena Molony] is on the staff of the Union but is not an officer. The Executive have no responsibility for the personal or political views of the staff.

A letter was also published from Molony which clarified that she was neither President nor Secretary of the IWWU. It was significant that her public profile was such that it was widely assumed that she was still in a leadership position within the union.

On 23 July Molony wrote to the paper again, hoping to end the 'unpleasant correspondence arising from a statement alleged to have been made by me'. She pointed out that the majority of the listeners were Catholic and would hardly have stood for such an 'attack'. She concluded that she wanted to,

> completely disassociate from myself in this matter all persons with whom I work in politics or the trade union movement. I am well aware that my political views are not shared by many of the latter and that many are in strong disagreement with me. But in these matters I claim the right to hold my own views much as I regret at times opposing the opinion of people I respect.[44]

The necessity of separating her radicalism and trade unionism was in part due to the overwhelming need for unity at a time of relative weakness. The personal strain involved in maintaining such a separation was apparent at the Irish Trade Union Congress in 1933. Molony proposed a vote of thanks to a visiting Scottish delegate who had proudly declared himself a communist and a trade unionist, saying that,

> They stepped sometimes on very dangerous ground in Ireland because of the various political camps and hesitated to nail their flags to the mast. Mr. Stevenson's address encouraged them to do so without being afraid of being dubbed with this or that 'ism'. They could all engage in a common struggle against that common enemy, the capitalist class.[45]

Although Molony spoke regularly on anti-fascist platforms and opposed the Blueshirts vigorously at WPDL meetings, she was not prominent in the next major left republican organisation, the Republican Congress. However, she was, as the late Nora Harkin recalled, a regular attender at Republican Congress and Spanish Civil War meetings.[46]

Within the IWWU the ideological and personal tensions between Bennett and Molony now spilled over into organisational matters. For a time these centred on the Unemployment Committee which Molony chaired. In 1931 she had established a Grand National sweepstake to raise money for a fund to help their unemployed members. Helen Chenevix questioned its legality and resigned in protest. The sweepstake earned over £1,000 for the fund but in 1933 tickets for the draw (20,000 of which had been printed) were not distributed. Molony questioned the executive's interference and the minutes delicately record that 'there was considerable heat during the discussion and finally Miss Bennett and Miss Chenevix withdrew'.[47] After further discussion the executive of the union 'expressed its confidence in the Unemployed Fund Committee and instructs them to use their discretion in the prize draw'.[48] It was significant that when ideological tensions were not concerned it was Molony rather than Bennett who had the support of the executive. Molony was also rapidly becoming as influential as Bennett in the wider trade union movement.

LEADING TRADE UNIONIST

Helena Molony rose to her greatest prominence within the trade union movement during the 1930s. Given her regular disagreements with colleagues over republicanism, socialism and the rights of women workers, it was a recognition of her effectiveness and talent as a trade unionist, as well as an indication of her ability to work with those whom she differed sharply with. It was also a reflection of her personal popularity among her colleagues. The late John de Courcy Ireland recalled that Molony's standing in 1930s Dublin was very much that of a revolutionary. Her name always cropped up as 'someone who would do something'. He also recalled how impressive it was that she could disagree sharply on political grounds with trade union colleagues but did not engage in any personal attacks.[49]

Molony was an executive member of the Trades Council until 1939. The organisation performed many of the functions of the present day Irish Congress of Trades Unions and was recognised as the primary arbitration forum for inter-union disputes as well as union-employer disputes. Its brief was far-reaching and Molony was on Trades Council delegations which met with national and local government officials on a wide range of matters from housing to protected industries. In 1930 Molony was instrumental in initiating and organising the 'Back to the Unions' campaign and also the inauguration of a 'Connolly Day' in 1929. The first Connolly Commemoration was highly successful according to Trades Council reports. On 24 May a vote of thanks to her for 'great attention to every portion of work' was proposed by one of those who had been pessimistic about the idea. Moreover, he was glad the 'optimists like Miss Molony ... and her colleagues had been proved to be right'.[50] The commemoration continued throughout the 1930s.

Molony was also the Trades Council delegate to many outside bodies, including the Irish Trade Union Congress (ITUC), another forum in which she rose to prominence. In 1933 Molony was elected to its National Executive. A month later she was appointed to the Permanent Joint Committee of the Labour Party and the Irish Trade Union Congress, which had been established to examine matters of joint political and industrial importance. The collapse of Saor Éire and changing political landscape may have persuaded her to work more closely with the Labour Party. For her first term on the executive, the Joint Committee concentrated on examining legislation going through the Dáil, such as the Workman's Compensation Bill and the proposed Shops Legislation. They produced proposals for extensive amendments and met regularly with the Minister for Industry and Commerce, Seán Lemass and his officials to discuss these. Molony was also on the subcommittee that made an extensive examination of the banking, currency and credit system of the Free State and advocated nationalisation. Molony was elected the ITUC Vice-President in 1935 and President in 1936. She was only the second woman to be elected President; the first was Louie Bennett in 1932. As President, Molony represented Ireland at the International Labour Conference in Geneva.

Helena Molony (centre), ITUC delegate to the International Labour Organisation, Geneva
courtesy Imogen Stuart

Molony was allocated a council house in 1933 in Kimmage, where she lived until 1940. If Belgrave Road, Rathmines had been known as Rebel Row, then Larkfield Grove in Kimmage might well have been called Rebel Terrace. Jane Shanahan lived in Number 71, Maeve Cavanagh (now MacDowell) in Number 53 and two doors down, in Number 51 was Molony. She regularly visited the Gonne MacBrides and Stuarts and went on holidays with her old friend Sidney Gifford Czira and her son Finian. He recalled that Molony was convivial company, a good mimic and a 'wise cracker'.[51] She continued to be an unorthodox figure; a 1930 photograph of the Trades Council executive shows her with a small dog on her lap and cropped hair, unusual for the time. However, Molony was not above taking editors on for using unflattering photographs of her. On one occasion she even went in to the offices of *An Phoblacht*, then edited by Frank Ryan. A young activist recalled that she took Ryan,

> to task for a photo he used of her in several of our issues – it was an old fashioned photo taken years ago – Helena wearing an awful hat. Frank explained that he had "the block". She asked him to burn it for God's sake and she'd get him a new one.

He also recalled that 'She appeared to me as an old woman (I was in my twenties) but full of life. Small and inclined to be stout if I remember right'.[52]

THE SORRY TRAVESTY OF EMANCIPATION

In the mid-1930s Molony was at the centre of public debates about the rights of women to equality whether as citizens, workers or soldiers. Legislation and attitudes had increasingly restricted women's role in Irish society since the establishment of the Free State, despite the extension of the franchise to women. In 1930 in an article entitled 'James Connolly and Women', Molony reflected on,

> the sorry travesty of emancipation ... Women, since [Connolly's] day have got that once-coveted right to vote, but they still have their inferior status, their lower pay for equal work, their exclusion from juries and certain branches of the civil service, their slum dwellings, and crowded and unsanitary schools for their children, as well as the lowered standard of life for workers which in their capacity as homemaker, hits the woman full force.[53]

She also wrote that the women's movement,

> now unhappily long spent, which aroused such a deep feeling of social consciousness and revolt among women of a more favoured class, passed over the heads of Irish working women and left her untouched.[54]

Female trade unionists, including Molony, found themselves in a difficult, defensive, often contradictory position when defending the right of women to work in industry. In reality that right usually entailed badly paid and unskilled labour. Increasingly a part of their argument was that women would be better off if it *was* economically viable for them to concentrate on their duties in the home. As Mary Daly puts it, 'Bennett and other trade unionists of the 1930s tended to defend women's work, not as a right, but as a necessary evil'.[55] Less than 6% of all women employed were married and a marriage ban had already been introduced into the civil service and teaching profession (with the aquiescence of the INTO). For female trade unionists this did not however entail women's exclusion from civil and political society since, even in her role as homemaker and primary carer of children, her contribution was vital. By 1934 even Molony seemed to be putting increased emphasis on the role of women in the home. She gave a talk on 'Technical Education in Women's Work' to the Irish Technical Education Association. In it she pointed out that 'Educating for Industry', in the sense demanded by industrialists, left women in a vulnerable position as 'so much raw material in the manufacturing process'. With the exception of printing and stationary and laundry work, none of the skilled trades were open to women. She suggested that increased mechanisation would mean shorter and shorter working days and concluded that the,

> imperative need for women is to educate them for life and the proper use of leisure and cultural activities. Vocational instruction ... will equip her for her special and permanent vocation as homemaker ...[56]

She asserted that,

> While it is good that boys should be trained to lay bricks, carve wood and make machines, it is better that girls should play tennis, grow roses and read poetry with intelligence.[57]

It is hard to reconcile these statements with comments that she made the same year in a scathing letter to Seán Ó Faoláin. Ó Faoláin had interviewed Molony, among others, for his biography of Constance Markievicz. Molony was horrified at the resulting account. The misleading portrait of Markievicz and her motivations that had been created by Ó Faoláin was seemingly backed up by statements attributed to Molony. Molony was succinct: 'You would make it appear that love of publicity was the keynote of her character. That is the last thing that would be true of her'.[58] She called lines 'catty' and questioned Ó Faoláin's own judgement. She continued with a devastating critique of male prejudice,

> It is a curious thing that many men seem to be unable to believe that any woman can embrace an ideal – accept it intellectually, feel it as a profound emotion, and then calmly decide to make a vocation of working for its realisation. They give themselves endless pains to prove that every serious thing a woman does (outside nursing babies or washing pots) is the result of being in love with some man, or disappointed in love of some man, or limelight, or indulging their vanity.

Having made the wider point, she then addressed Ó Faoláin directly,

> You do not seem to have escaped from the limitations of your sex. Therefore you describe Madame as being 'caught up' by or rallying 'to the side of' Connolly, Larkin, or some man or other whereas the simple fact was that she was working, as a man might have worked, for the freedom of Ireland.[59]

She pointed out that herself and Markievicz had been involved in – and had written about – labour matters and women's labour in particular, years before there was publicity attached to these ideals and causes. It was a final indignity that Ó Faoláin got Molony's own name wrong in the book. She spelt it out in capitals and requested that he spell it properly. Molony had feared correctly; the assessment of Markievicz that Ó Faoláin published informed much of the later historiography. It coloured popular opinion of her as a vain, limelight-seeking woman.[60] The political, cultural and military work that Molony, Markievicz and other women had done prior to 1923 was being minimised, at the same time as women's role as citizens was being restricted.

CONDITIONS OF EMPLOYMENT BILL

In 1935 Molony was to the fore in opposing a move by the state to limit the rights of women to work. The Conditions of Employment Bill was published by Seán Lemass, Minister for Industry and Commerce, that year. He had refused to consult with the IWWU on the drafting of the Bill and their worst fears were realised in a proposed section. Section 12 would give the Minister the authority to bar women from industry in cases he saw fit. The union passed a resolution condemning it and launched a public campaign opposing it. It fell to Molony, the only woman and IWWU representative on the ITUC executive, to persuade her male colleagues to support this.

IWWU delegation to Minister Seán Lemass re Conditions of Employment Bill, May 1935. Helena Molony back row left and Louie Bennett front left

Male trade unionists and others tended to argue that a solution to the problems of mass unemployment and low wages would be to restrict the rights of women to take up paid employment. This had been faced by the IWWU since their foundation in 1911, but was increasingly being vocalised in the 1930s. Addressing a WPDL meeting that year, Molony pointed out 'that men may be foolish enough to think that they were gaining something but in her opinion the object was to cut down wages'.[61]

Molony and the IWWU were on the defensive on the issue. A majority of the ITUC executive were prepared to accept the assurances of the Minister that Section 12 of the Conditions of Employment Bill was being introduced to protect the health of women. In fact, the Bill itself had made no mention of this. Molony was determined to keep Section 12 on the agenda. She raised it again at a meeting of the Joint Committee of the Labour Party and ITUC in Leinster House. The meeting had been convened to determine how the Labour Party would vote on the Bill in the Dáil. Molony declared that Section 12 was a 'reflection on females and on anti-progressive and anti-social limitations of their rights as citizens to earn their living as such'.[62] William O'Brien spoke in support of Section 12 and said that women were pushing men into unemployment. No compromise was reached and at the next meeting, in the absence of Molony, it was generally agreed that some form of protection was necessary and that the 'incursion of women was a serious social problem'.[63]

In August, at the annual Irish Trade Union Congress delegate conference, a heated debate surrounded a resolution on equal pay and opportunity tabled by the IWWU. The previous year a similar resolution had been passed unanimously and without need for debate. This time however, William Norton, leader of the Labour Party, launched an attack on Molony saying that he detected her hand behind the,

> subtle ingenious resolution they were discussing. It asked Congress to accept certain principles which they could accept in the abstract – if passed, they would be told it implied Congress was committed to opposing Section 12, was that so?[64]

Molony replied 'Yes'. Norton continued saying that she had 'confused' the National Executive on the issue who had been 'swayed by the energetic campaign Miss Molony had waged'. When he asked her,

> Whether she claimed that it should be within the right of women to be carpenters and blacksmiths, and when she answered in the affirmative, there was a notable lack of enthusiasm by the male members of the National Executive.[65]

A vote was taken and the resolution was passed, but so too was support for Section 12, thus making it meaningless. Molony was elected Vice-President at that same conference by a narrow majority and dryly remarked on the chivalry of Irish trade unionists who would make women 'queens of their hearts and homes – but would give them no jobs'.[66]

The IWWU campaign did not stop there and, in September 1935, a delegation met with de Valera. They reported that though 'he listened attentively he could not see that men and women could be equal' and that he did not seem to know very much about the Conditions of Employment Bill.[67] The issue was brought to the League of Nations and the International Labour Organisation in Geneva who blacklisted the Free State. In the Senate, Jennie Wyse Power and Kathleen Clarke led an attack against the bill but Labour deputies swung the vote and it was passed. The public campaign included protests outside the Fianna Fáil Árd Fheis during which the police intervened. In November a mass meeting was held and speakers included Molony, Hanna Sheehy Skeffington and

Mary Hayden. Molony was reported as saying that 'the Trade Union Congress had fought with all its power against the Bill and against that clause affecting women'. The Labour Party had also made representations to get the clause deleted but although Mr Lemass received the deputation with politeness he treated the application with contempt.[68] It was hardly a reflection of the debates, but Molony and the IWWU could not afford, as Daly puts it, a dispute with the rest of the labour movement.

By this stage the IWWU had accepted defeat on the issue – they were clearly fighting against the tide. As Cullen Owens has pointed out, although the practical effects of the 1936 Act might have been negligible 'the psychological effects cannot be underestimated and were embellished by the constitution of 1937'.[69]

Outside of trade union structures Molony made another attempt to campaign for equality and rouse the consciousness of Irish women. In December 1935, directly as a result of the restriction of working women's rights, she, Maud Gonne MacBride, Sidney Gifford Czira, Brigid O'Mullane, Mrs Kirwin, L Kennedy and Mrs Gifford Donnelly established a new organisation, Mná na hÉireann (Women of Ireland) that took as its inspiration the methods and aims of the earlier Inghinidhe na hÉireann. Their constitution declared that they were founded to 'advance the national cause and to ensure that women will take their place in the political, social and economic life of the country'.[70] That would involve the equal rights and opportunities which successive governments had restricted since 1921. Their inaugural meeting attracted only 15 people, and while letters and small articles appeared in the national press the organisation never got off the ground; conditions were not right. The Inghinidhe, as a group of young women, had flourished against a backdrop of a politicised society ripe for change. Ireland in the 1930s was stagnant. The large amount of headed paper printed for Mná na hÉireann lay around Gonne MacBride's house and was used as scrap paper. The daughters of Ireland had become the women of Ireland and it was clear that they were also being written out of their own history. For Molony, Ó Faoláin's biography of Markievicz was just one example of this. Another was the Military Service Pension process that followed. It was as crucial for Molony to establish recognition of women's work in war time as it was to defend their right to work in peace time. In fact, the two were closely linked given the erosion of women's citizenship rights since the establishment of the Free State. Their restoration was, for Molony and others, legitimised by the 1916 Proclamation and women's participation in the national struggle. Consequently there was a terrible symmetry to the debates around the Conditions of Employment Bill and her Military Service Pensions correspondence.

THE STATUS OF WOMEN SOLDIERS OF THE REPUBLICAN FORCES[71]

In 1934, under a Fianna Fáil administration, the Military Service Pensions Act was extended to include members of the IRA, the Irish Citizen Army, Cumann na mBan as well as several other organisations. That December Molony was on the executive committee of the 'Old Irish Citizens Army Comrades Association 1916–23', formed to advise members applying for the pension. They met twice a week to interview and dispense advice and other members included James O'Neill (ICA Commandant in the post Rising reorganisation), Nora Connolly O'Brien (ICA Council 1934) and James Hanratty (ICA Council 1922). Cumann na mBan had only been belatedly included in the provisions of the Act and its members were only eligible to apply for the bottom two ranks. Despite the fact that women in the ICA had held commissions, the surviving members, including Molony, had made a definite decision not to claim their ranks for pension purposes, although whether this was pre-empting a refusal was not clear.[72] Margaret Skinnider had previously encountered difficulty with the Pension Board who changed their definitions to deny her a claim.

In June 1935 Helena Molony made her initial application to the Minister for Defence for a Service Certificate, the first step towards the granting of a Military Pension. The tortuous two and a half year process that followed was as revealing of the attitude of the Department towards women, and its own bureaucratic procedures, as it was of Molony's personal life and state of mind. With the exception of Easter week 1916, she filled out the form (which divided the period 1916–23 into different periods) with the general statements; 'Obeyed all orders of superior officers; procured and collected arms and ammunition; in active cooperation with Republican forces; intelligence and publicity work; First Aid work'.[73] She recorded her dates of service with the ICA as 'continuous' with the exception of two absences from duty; her time in prison after the Rising and a week in Brussels at the outbreak of the Civil War. She provided the names of referees but did not provide written references as requested and this, combined with the lack of detail about specific events and engagement, caused problems for her. This was ironic given that Molony had not only advised other members on their applications; she herself went on to provide substantial written references for other ICA women.

Her initial call to interview was for 27 June 1936 but she was unable to attend 'due to illness' and instead made her sworn statement before the Advisory Committee on 3 July.[74] She had not kept a record of her original application and the resulting interview makes for often painful reading. 'Like a lot of men and women my brain has become very woolly it is so long ago' she explains early on.[75] She did go on to provide many specific details although the dates are often vague. More than anything the questioners wanted evidence of her work as a combatant, her involvement with arms and or arrest: 'We will have to concern ourselves purely with military work' they told her. She responded 'I was always in active cooperation. In the Citizen Army men and women were regarded on equal terms. It was unique'. This seemed to amaze one questioner who asked 'Some of them were actually under arms in 1916?'[76] She gave details about her involvement with arms, raids on her home, as well as her extensive publicity, propaganda and military intelligence work. At one point she said 'It was difficult to disentangle what was military and what was civil'.[77] The Committee members gave her short shrift saying 'We are expected to disentangle them?'[78]

Helena Molony's Military Service Pension application
courtesy Military Archives, Ireland

Ten days later she followed up with references from Francis Stuart, Maud Gonne MacBride and Kathleen Lynn and a letter which concluded,

> I make this claim and give this evidence not primarily for personal gain (although I am now a comparatively poor woman), but mainly that the Military services of the women who fought through the Irish war of Independence, may be recorded and acknowledged by the State they bravely and faithfully served. I myself am one of the least among this company.[79]

In October John Hanratty was called as an Irish Citizen Army witness on behalf of Helena Molony. Given the confused and changing command structure of the ICA in the post Rising period, it was perhaps not surprising that he was unaware of much of her work in the reconstituted South County Dublin ICA. This work was later verified by other ICA officers. The Committee explained that she came in unprepared, vague and that 'She made no case for herself after Easter'. Hanratty bluntly told them 'I cannot make it for her'. They tried to pin down definite service dates as, once active service was established, a percentage of this would be classified as military service according to the Department's definitions and a pension granted accordingly.

Hanratty claimed that Molony had left the ICA 'about 1918, there was some difference – she is the kind who would be difficult to work with'. Asked again 'Did she leave you in 1918?' Hanratty answered 'She did and she did not. It is hard to say she definitely left'. Certainly Molony identified as being a member of the ICA throughout the period. She had refused to join Cumann na mBan because of this. Given the nature of guerrilla war as well as the relative inactivity of the ICA in the period following the Rising, it is likely that she was as eligible as any of the members who were assessed as having been on active service. At one point Hanratty says 'I cannot imagine Miss Molony being anything other than active'. In the event they decide to grant her application for Easter week service and her imprisonment and leave it up to her to appeal the dismissal of the rest of her application. For pension purposes she was awarded 4 years for Easter week and 261 days out of 358 for the following year. Her claim for the rest of the period to 1923 was denied and a stark 'nil' was written in all sections of the judgement.[80]

Molony was stung by the decision and in November 1936 she lodged an official appeal, because,

> I cannot admit that my services during that terrible period were, 'nil' … I am not primarily concerned with a pension, but with the recognition of women's services rendered to the Republic.[81]

She even asked that the 'nil' be removed, without any alteration to the amount granted for pension purposes. Over the winter, both her health and financial situation worsened and she wrote again asking to know where the matter stood,

> … and when can be given effect to and money paid over. I am sorry to give trouble. I have recently suffered from illness and am forced to go away for a rest, and consequently need the money (if there is any forthcoming) for this purpose.[82]

The same month as Molony appealed her decision, Jane Shanahan, her neighbour, fellow IWWU official and colleague from the Co-op and ICA days, was called for her interview. Molony was one of Shanahan's lead referees. Shanahan entered more specific detail and attached written references in her original application. She was assessed as having been in active service for the entire period and this was entered beside each date to 1923. The visual contrast between the two women's judgements is stark but Shanahan was still only granted a small pensionable percentage for each of those years of active service. Military service was being defined very narrowly and it was an issue many of the Cumann na mBan women faced and one which Molony challenged.[83]

Throughout 1937 she sent in further letters of authentication and references and enquired regularly about the status of her appeal. In October she disputed the dismissal of much of the work done by women as non-military given that,

> In any regular army in any civilised country I never heard of such non-combatants as Army Service Corps, or Army Medical Corps, or Intelligence Dept. – being classified as non-military and I respectfully suggest in the I.R.A. 'non-military' is against the whole spirit of the Act … [i.e.] to give pensions to genuine soldiers of the Republican Army.

She concluded,

> However, I have given all evidence I am able or prepared to give and must abide by the result. I would be grateful for an early reply to this letter as my failing health makes even this small sum a necessity – except it is the intention that this money shall only be available to pay for my obsequies.[84]

This was not as exaggerated a closing line as it might have seemed – Shanahan died that January, while the process was still in train. In her capacity as Shanahan's Senior Officer, Molony immediately wrote to the Advisory Committee to see if her pension might be transferred to Shanahan's father and used for funeral expenses. This was allowed.[85] Nearly a year after Molony's initial appeal was lodged, she received a letter from the Military Pensions Board to say that a decision had not yet been reached and that she was 'under a misapprehension between military and active service'.[86] She responded swiftly,

> … the matter would appear to be simple was I (or not) a member of the Citizen Army 1914 to 1923? With regard to 'active service' it would be very difficult for anyone belonging to any section of the Republican army to avoid active service (however much they might like to) in the terrible years from 1916 to 23. Anyhow I did not avoid it.[87]

However, a week later, with her finances and health in a critical state, she sent in a one line letter and brought the process to a close; 'If it will expedite the matter of payment of the above numbered claim, I now formally withdraw the appeal lodged by me'.[88]

Molony's limited pension was issued but her story was not unique. Many Cumann na mBan members refused to give statements to the later Bureau of Military History, partly because of their treatment in the pension process. Molony herself often brushed off personal recognition, unless it reflected on the contribution of the groups of women she worked among, or illuminated a national or political point. She stood fiercely as referee and advocate for other women, but found it harder to document the specifics of much of the work that she did after 1917. In her appeal she stated 'It must be well known to members of your Board that I am not a person who is given to either bragging about their exploits or making untruthful statements'.[89]

The pension process was also stark evidence of the toll that those years had taken on the health (mental as well as physical) and personal finances of those who had dedicated all to the movement.

A WOMAN'S PLACE IS IN THE HOME
PROVIDED SHE HAS A HOME[90]

It was clear from her move into left republicanism in the 1930s that Molony had to come to terms with the fact that the national revolution to which she had devoted her life had failed to serve either the interests of workers or of women. Her mood was well captured in an interview with journalist R.M. Fox for his book *Rebel Irishwomen*. He described how a 'light came into her eyes' when she began to talk about the events leading up to 1916 but that, when talking of contemporary matters, she was 'wistful' and subdued.[91] Molony reflected sadly on the Rising,

> Perhaps the time was not ripe for success. Our people had not a widespread economic knowledge to deal with social evils. I should have hated to have Padraic Pearse as President of an Irish Republic if the misery and wretchedness of the tenements had still gone on. Our next move forward must be accompanied by clear knowledge and determination to deal with poverty, unemployment and industrial servitude. Connolly had this knowledge.[92]

James Connolly continued to be her inspiration and she used his thoughts and actions as the impetus for radical changes in Irish society. On 2 May 1937, the 21st anniversary of Connolly's execution, Molony made a major address as President of the ITUC to the 'James Connolly Commemoration' held outside the GPO. She said,

> Capitalism we are organised to down and down it we will. 21 years after they struck the first blow we are still here, and I say it with shame. I little thought that after 21 years we would be in the same plight.[93]

The *Irish Independent* reported that she defended the ideal of the worker's republic against 'ignorant, misinformed and hostile criticism' of recent months. Her opposition to the proposed 1937 constitution was evident on several grounds when she declared,

> The President and others had spoken recently of the sanctity of the home, of marriage and of private property. The working classes need no lessons on the sanctity of religion, of marriage or the home. With regard to private property they would hold that workers should have the right to acquire it. As society was organised now, five-sixths of the people were denied the right of acquiring private property.[94]

Along with other prominent public women and women's groups the IWWU campaigned for amendments to Articles 40, 41 and 45 (with its reference to the 'inadequate strength of women') of the draft constitution.[95] However, the IWWU dropped out of the campaign after some of these articles were amended, much to the dismay of the other groups. There is no evidence as to Molony's view on this.

Vocationalism was one of the influences evident in the drafting of the constitution. Molony held the same reservations and concerns as other labour leaders about the links between fascism and the corporatist or vocational system and the threat that this posed to independent trade unions. In 1938 Louie Bennett was appointed to the government's new Commission on Vocational Organisation (CVO) and was enthusiastic about its capacity to effect change. However Molony voiced her serious concerns about the corporatist tendencies shown by the CVO. At the 1939 Annual Convention she was again critical and proposed instead that the union takes its inspiration from the vision of social justice contained in papal encyclicals, such as *Rerum Novarum* and *Quadragesimo Anno*. It is unclear if this was due to a shift in emphasis in her own thinking and views on papal intervention or a recognition that such a call would be more attractive to union members than her own more radical views. Meetings were held and *Rerum Novarum* would inform future IWWU campaigns. However, debates about the role and representation of women in public life (or more accurately lack of) were also increasingly framed in this context of vocationalism. In 1934 when Molony outlined her ideas for women's technical education, they seemed to reflect this.

In 1940 Molony, along with three other IWWU officials, gave evidence to the Commission on Vocational Organisation. The hostility of the male members of the commission and its chair, Archbishop Browne, towards women's groups and claims was evident throughout her testimony. When asked, Molony listed a number of boards without female representation, one of which was concerned with daylight saving time, an issue of major concern to children. In that case, wondered a member of the commission, should children not be appointed? When Browne suggested that female employment contributed to male unemployment and was a deterrent to marriage, Molony countered that they were concerned with male unemployment,

> because we regard women as the greater part of the family and where the men are unemployed the women suffer. We are concerned with women not merely as wage earners but as human beings.[96]

It was her statement 'We all agree that a woman's place is in the home provided she has a home' that historian Joseph Lee has quoted to indicate the extent to which Irishwomen and even a 'doughty defender of women's rights' such as Molony, concurred with de Valera's vision of women in society.[97] It did not reflect the totality of her thought as Molony and the IWWU often framed demands for social justice in these terms and 'provided she has a home' was likely the significant part of that sentence for her. It is also tempting to speculate how Molony the actor (and indeed a woman often without a home herself) delivered this line and just how much of an inflexion there was on the second part. However, it was clear that the emphasis of both witnesses and commission members was very much on the importance of women as homemakers and was, as Cullen Owens writes, a 'reflection of social mores'.[98]

COMMISSION OF ENQUIRY INTO THE TRADE UNION MOVEMENT

During Molony's term as Vice-President and President of the ITUC a pressing issue facing the movement was its weakness and the need for internal reorganisation. With the prospect of government control being exerted on trade unions Molony argued that it was essential that they deal with the weakness and splits themselves before an outside authority took action. In April 1936 the ITUC established the Commission of Enquiry into the Trade Union Movement. Molony was the only woman among the twelve members appointed who comprised 'all the major names in the trade union movement at the time'. She was also appointed vice-chair.[99]

The impetus for establishing the Commission of Enquiry was twofold. Firstly there was the dispute between the Irish Transport and General Workers Union under William O'Brien and the Workers Union of Ireland. The latter had been formed as a breakaway union under Jim Larkin in 1924. Although the IWWU was unaligned, and Molony had, early on, called for an end to internal disputes, Molony was more likely to side with the ITGWU and O'Brien, whom she saw as representative of Connolly's legacy. She had been dismissive of Larkin in private since the Lockout and in later statements she called him a 'blatherskite'.[100] She was also involved in blocking Delia Larkin's readmission to the IWWU in 1918. However, it was interesting that the late de Courcy Ireland recalled that Molony was much respected by Jim Larkin. De Courcy Ireland also felt that, despite their intense disagreements, they remained aware that they were part of the same movement and were headed in the same direction.

The second issue that faced the Commission of Enquiry was the series of conflicts between Irish-based unions and those with headquarters in England (the Amalgamated unions). An increasing number of breakaway Irish unions were being formed and a dispute between the ITGWU and the Amalgamated Transport and General Workers Union was cause for concern. Molony had argued, prior to the establishment of the Commission of Enquiry, that,

> National self-consciousness was growing and finding
> expression in the desire of workers to belong to a Trade Union
> in Ireland rather than across the water.[101]

She referred to the chaos and confusion these disputes were engendering and reiterated the solution favoured by the ITGWU; the reorganisation of the trade union movement along industrial lines into ten main unions. She said that 'In the reconstruction – they would be able to build up a movement that nothing could resist'.[102] This proposal had been in existence for a long time and a large part of the motivation was national, rather than organisational, because it would entail the departure of the Amalgamated unions from Ireland. The Commission of Enquiry sat for three years and in effect worked on this proposal, which had been proposed by O'Brien.

This form of reorganisation, into ten industrial unions, raised another important issue – the existence of a separate women workers union. Molony and the IWWU were in general agreement with the reorganisation principle but could not agree to the proposal that the IWWU be merged under the category 'General Workers'. Events of the previous years had not given the IWWU any confidence to believe that the interests of women workers would be protected if this occurred. At the IWWU Annual Convention in 1937, Molony seconded the resolution,

> That this convention, recognising that the value of a union
> specifically catering for women has been proven by
> experience, is strongly opposed to any suggestion that the
> IWWU should be merged into the other unions and resolves to
> maintain the integrity of this union as a body of women in
> loyal cooperation.[103]

Molony was directed by the IWWU executive not to support any proposal which suggested such a merger. In the event she did support the proposal to reorganise into ten big unions, however she included a lengthy, revealing reservation which stated the present necessity for organising along sex lines 'owing to the fact that women are a separate economic class'.[104] The twelve-member Commission of Enquiry was not unanimous in its conclusions and as evidence of this three separate memorandums were submitted to a Special Convention in February 1939. Molony's support, albeit with a significant reservation, proved critical for the proposal also favoured by the ITGWU and O'Brien. Had she not signed it, O'Brien would have been in a minority position within the Commission.

The chaotic meeting that ensued was the last that Molony attended. She spoke strongly in favour of O'Brien's proposal (as vice-chair of the Commission of Enquiry rather than as IWWU representative) but it was defeated. In anticipation of this, a council of 'Irish Trade Unions in affiliation to the ITUC' had been formed just before the meeting and Molony was on its first committee. It was the prelude to a split that would lead to two separate congresses. However, IWWU policy towards this council changed after Molony ceased being an executive member of the ITUC. In fact, in August 1939 IWWU delegates voted against O'Brien's reorganisation proposal.

The Commission of Enquiry was one of the last major contributions Molony made as a trade unionist. As was evident from the letters she had been writing to the Military Service Pensions Board, ill-health was beginning to affect her life and work adversely. She was unable to make her keynote Presidential address to the Irish Trade Union Congress in 1937 because of bronchitis. Her health continued to deteriorate and she gradually began to withdraw from her role as a leading trade unionist. In early 1939 she attempted to resign from the Trades Council, but they persuaded her to stay on until the completion of her last term on the executive of the ITUC that summer. She was no longer a delegate after this date.

From September 1940, Molony's position in the IWWU was the subject of heated discussion and by October 1941 she had resigned on the grounds of ill-health. However, an additional factor must have been her involvement with the IRA during the Emergency, especially the role she played providing safe houses for the German spy Goertz.[105] This had brought her to the attention of the authorities and at the same time as her position was under discussion in the union she was under close Garda surveillance. Judging by intelligence records, her alcoholism had entered a chronic stage. It was a perfect storm of personal, health and political difficulties and the early 1940s would be an extremely troubled time for Molony.

Molony's contribution as a trade unionist from 1915 and later in the Free State was a substantial one. She was second General Secretary of the IWWU and kept the union alive at a critical point and went on to be one of its three central figures. She was also one of the most prominent names in the trade union movement as a whole and her election as President of the ITUC and appointment as vice chair of the Commission of Enquiry was a reflection of this. She was prepared to scale back some (though not all) of her more radical activities for this work, but consistently defended her right to hold disputed views in a hostile and conservative atmosphere. She was an important radicalising force within the IWWU, the Trades Council and the wider society. Her role as an organiser with the IWWU effected change for many women workers who otherwise would have remained unrepresented. Molony consistently raised and sought to counter the issue of female under-representation on public and trade union bodies. She was also a very public and influential voice defending the rights of women to work at a time of retrenchment. As a leading member of the Trades Council and the ITUC she initiated many schemes and galvanised colleagues to action on matters small and large. She used the memory and teachings of Connolly to inspire further action and more substantial change. Molony was also an important, if sometimes divisive, voice in the debates about the participation of labour in the Free State, and later on the unity of the trade union movement as a whole.

SOURCES

1   Fox, *Rebel Irishwomen*, p. 69.
2   John de Courcy Ireland, interview with author, 1992.
3   *Dublin Labour Year Book*, Dublin Trades' Union and Labour Council, 1930, p. 18.
4   Jane McGilligan, interview with author, 1992.
5   Cullen Owens, *A Social History of Women in Ireland*, p. 198.
6   Mary Daly, 'Women and Trade Unions', *Trade Union Century* (Dublin, Mercier, 1994), p. 109.
7   Jones, *These Obstreperous Lassies*, p. 53.
8   *Ibid.*
9   *ILPTUC Annual Report* 1929, quoted in Regan, 'Helena Molony', p. 159
10 Jones, *These Obstreperous Lassies*, p. 68.
11 *Ibid.*, p. 69.
12 Quoted in Regan, 'Helena Molony', p. 157.
13 Seámus Scully, interview with author, 1992.
14 *Irish Press, Irish Times, Irish Independent*, 30 January 1967.
15 Helena Molony, 'Technical Education and Women', *Report of the Irish Technical Education Association*, 1934, pp 34–40.
16 Annual Convention, 1 May 1929, IWWUA, ILHA.
17 *Dublin Labour Year Book*, p. 18.
18 ILPTUC 35th Annual Report, 1928–29, p. 81.
19 Helena Molony correspondence to Dublin Trades Council, 10 May 1930, IWWUA, ILHA.
20 Department of Justice, C Series, C31/34, Intelligence Reports on Women's Prisoners Defence League, 1934, NA.
21 *Irish Freedom*, January 1927.
22 Department of Justice, S Series, S3/28, Intelligence Reports on Anti Imperialist Organisations, 1928–33, NA.
23 Séamus Cody, John O'Dowd and Peter Rigney, *The Parliament of Labour: 100 Years of the Dublin Council of Trade Unions* (Dublin, 1986), p. 160.
24 *Ibid.*

25 Jones, *These Obstreperous Lassies*, p. 97.

26 Executive Minutes, 27 April 1930, IWWUA, ILHA.

27 Annual Convention Report, May 1930, IWWUA, ILHA.

28 IWWU Executive Minutes, quoted in Jones, *These Obstreperous Lassies*, p. 99.

29 Cullen Owens, *Louie Bennett*, p. 126.

30 Executive Minutes, September 1930, IWWUA, ILHA.

31 *Ibid.*

32 Memo on Revolutionary Organisations, p 24/169, Ernest Blythe Papers, UCD Archive.

33 Department of Justice, S Series, S3/28, Intelligence Reports on Anti Imperialist Organisations, 1928–33, NA.

34 Emmet O'Connor, *Reds and the Green: Ireland, Russia and the Communist Interationals, 1919–43* (Dublin, University College Dublin Press, 2004), p. 167.

35 In 'Report on The Friends of Soviet Russia', Sean MacEntee Papers, P67/522, UCDA.

36 *An Phoblacht*, 17 October 1931.

37 Executive Minutes, October 1931, IWWUA, ILHA.

38 Ward, *Unmanageable Revolutionaries*, p. 216.

39 *Republican File*, 13 February 1931.

40 Louie Coghlan O'Brien, interview with author, 1991.

41 *Ibid*, and Finian Czira, interview with author, 1992.

42 *Irish Independent*, 18–23 July 1932.

43 *Irish Independent*, 18 July, 1932. All of the subsequent quotations are from the letter pages for that week.

44 *Irish Independent*, 23 July 1932.

45 ITUC Annual Report, 1933, pp 131–2.

46 Nora Harkin, interview with author, 1992.

47 Executive Minutes, 26 October 1933, IWWUA, ILHA.

48 *Ibid.*

49 John de Courcy Ireland, interview with author, 1992. See also Penny Duggan.

50 Dublin Trades Council, Minutes, p. 59, MS 12784, NLI.

51 Finian Czira, interview with author, 1992.

52 Unsigned correspondence with author, 7 September 1992.

53 Helena Molony, 'James Connolly and Women', *Dublin Labour Year Book*, 1930, pp 31–33.

54 *Ibid.*

55 Cullen Owens, *A Social History*, p. 107, and Daly, 'Women and Trade Unions', p. 110.

56   Helena Molony, 'Technical Education and Women', pp 34–40.

57   *Ibid.*

58   Helena Molony: BMH WS 391.

59   *Ibid.*

60   Seán Ó Faoláin, *Constance Markievicz or The Average Revolutionary* (London, Jonathan Cape, 1934).

61   Department of Justice, D Series, D3/35, Intelligence Reports on Women's Prisoners Defence League, 1935–6, NA.

62   ITUC and LP Joint Committee minutes, 5 June 1935, ICTU Archives, Dublin.

63   *Ibid.*

64   Quoted in Regan, 'Helena Molony', p. 164.

65   *Ibid.*

66   *Ibid.*

67   Cullen Owens, *A Social History*, p. 268.

68   *Republican Congress*, 30 November 1935.

69   Cullen Owens, *Louie Bennett*, p. 87.

70   Quotes from Mná na hÉireann press releases and constitution, Anna MacBride White Collection.

71   Helena Molony, MSPC 11739.

72   *Ibid.*

73   *Ibid.*

74   *Ibid.*

75   *Ibid.*

76   *Ibid.*

77   *Ibid.*

78   *Ibid.*

79   *Ibid.*

80   *Ibid.*

81   *Ibid.*

82   *Ibid.*

83   Jane Shanahan, MSPC 10154 and Helena Molony, MSPC 11739. There is more valuable work to be done on the ICA women's files as the release continues.

84   Helena Molony, MSPC 11739.

85   Jane Shanahan, MSPC 10154.

86   Helena Molony, MSPC 11739.

87   *Ibid.*

88   *Ibid.*

89   *Ibid.*

90   Helena Molony, CVO, 19 April 1940, MS 925, NLI.

91   Fox, *Rebel Irishwomen*, pp 65–72.

92   *Ibid.*

93   *Labour News*, 8 May 1937.

94   *Irish Independent*, 3 May 1937.

95   Cullen Owens, *Louie Bennett*, p. 89.

96   Helena Molony, CVO, NLI.

97   Joseph Lee, *Ireland 1912–1985: Politics and Society* (Cambridge, Cambridge University Press, 1989), p. 209.

98   Cullen Owens, *Louie Bennett*, p. 99.

99   Charles McCarthy, *Trade Unions in Ireland 1894–1969* (Dublin, Institute of Public Administration, 1977), p. 143.

100   Helena Molony: BMH WS 391.

101   ITUC, Annual Report 1934, pp 125–6.

102   *Ibid.*

103   Annual Report, 1937, IWWUA, ILHA.

104   ITUC, Special Proceedings and Report of the Committee on Reorganisation, 1939, p. 13; Helena Molony, extract from *Reservation (A) to Memorandum 1 of the Final Report of the Commission on Trade Union Reorganisation*, *Field Day Anthology of Irish Writing*, Vol. 5 (Cork, Cork University Press, 2002), p. 558.

105   Regan. 'Helena Molony', p. 166.

MEMOIRIST
1941–67

Soon after her retirement from the public sphere, Helena Molony entered a quiet and mostly private phase of her life. For the first time since attending that fateful meeting in 1903, the frenetic round of agitation, of meetings, of performances on stage and platform, of military involvement, of executive meetings and congresses that had been her life, came to an end. From the mid 1940s until her death in 1967, she shared her life with Dr Eveleen O'Brien. The two women lived in a house on the North Circular Road, provided by O'Brien's employer, Grangegorman Hospital. Throughout these decades her health was still a cause for concern; aside from heart and chest problems, she was apparently still being rehospitalised to deal with her drinking. She also developed severe arthritis in the last decade of her life. However, Molony retained a lively interest in matters of social justice and was still a correspondent to the papers and authorities on matters both small and large, as well as on theatrical affairs. Over the period, prompted by the establishment of the Bureau of Military History, as well as requests from journalists and successive anniversaries of the 1916 Rising, she spent much of her time writing. Her various witness statements, typescript articles and interviews amount to what is a substantive memoir of the period. Her accounts continue to inform much of the historiography of the early period, particularly in relation to the involvement of women.

THE EMERGENCY

At the outbreak of World War Two and the start of the Emergency, Molony moved home again. She left her council house and the community in Larkfield Grove, Kimmage to live in a flat at 17 Wexford Street. IWWU minutes and Garda surveillance records reveal a woman increasingly isolated, in financial difficulty and ill health.[1] It would be several years before a calmer phase of her life began.

In the autumn of 1940 she was given 3 months leave of absence from the IWWU on the grounds of ill health. It was agreed that she would continue to represent the union at the Rosary Bead Enquiry (convened to resolve a long running strike) and an upcoming laundry conference. However when the executive sent her a cheque to cover any costs she might incur undertaking these and other representations, she returned it as it would, she felt, commit her. When she failed to return in December she was asked if she would like to stay on as a part-time official but the minutes indicate that by now, angry letters were being exchanged. On 20 February 1941 Mrs Kennedy, supported by other staff members, wished to have it recorded that 'as a long standing executive member … in her opinion, Helena Molony had always received very fair and generous treatment from the committee and staff'.[2]

While the union's records make it difficult to be conclusive about Molony's eventual resignation – and the state of her health was key – her involvement with the IRA during the Emergency and association with the Nazi spy Hermann Goertz, was also a factor.

Molony's non-union activities had always been a source of friction, especially between herself and Louie Bennett. The heightened atmosphere of the Emergency served to exacerbate this. Molony was a member of the Deportees Committee, established to help Irish people deported from England following the IRA bombing campaign. Jenny Murray, whose mother, Theresa Behan, worked for the IWWU and was a close friend of Molony's, recalled that Molony's flat, on the corner of Wexford and Camden Street, was a place where lots of 'students and young men' gathered.[3] Molony drafted a new economic and social policy for the IRA and was apparently involved with Córas na Poblachta, a new republican party, some of whose members had already been on missions to Germany.[4] England's difficulty and Ireland's opportunity were again live issues in republican circles. Even given all of this, it seems bizarre that an activist who had spoken on anti-fascist platforms and had only recently warned of the fascist tendencies of vocationalism, should be involved hiding a Nazi spy. It would appear her initial involvement came about through her close friends, the Stuarts, and a series of coincidences.

Francis Stuart, who now worked and lived in Germany, met Goertz as he planned a mission to Ireland to forge links with the IRA. In the event that he might find himself in difficulty, Stuart gave him directions to Laragh Castle, where his wife Iseult Stuart lived with their son Ian and her mother-in-law Lily Clements. Molony was a regular visitor there.

In May 1940 Goertz landed in Meath, lost his radio and then walked for miles to reach Laragh Castle. He was taken in by a surprised Iseult Stuart, who hid him and even brought him into Dublin to Clery's department store. There she bought him a suit to replace the Luftwaffe uniform he had landed in. When Goertz went on to Dublin to discuss 'Plan Kathleen', a possible invasion of Northern Ireland, he found that IRA capabilities had been greatly exaggerated. He was warned to be careful of Iseult and would later write of 'that hot and whispering atmosphere of Dublin which I utterly disliked'.[5]

Goertz managed to evade the authorities during a raid and returned to Laragh Castle, only to find that Iseult herself been arrested. Molony was staying there at the time and helped to arrange safe houses for him in Dublin.[6] From this point on, Molony was under close Garda surveillance and all of her comings and goings were monitored. Her correspondence, as well as Iseult Stuart's, was intercepted and transcribed over the period. These gave more of an insight into her personal circumstances than her involvement with Goertz, of which the authorities could only find circumstantial evidence.[7] Intelligence records reveal a change of address that coincided with Goertz's early time on the run and her first period of sick leave from the union. They also record a first connection with Dr Eveleen O'Brien,

> Miss Maloney resided in house St. Alban's, Dalkey from 1 August 1940 to 31 March 1941. This house had been let furnished for a period to Miss Mary E.O Brien … St. Alban's was used by Hermann Goertz and information is to the effect that members of the IRA also frequented and stayed there. The rent was £6 pounds per month.[8]

In April 1941 Louie Bennett reported to the IWWU executive that she had been interviewed by police officers at her home, who questioned her about Molony's movements.[9] In May 1941, after lengthy discussions in the IWWU about posts and responsibilities, Molony took over a task she had begun in 1918, that of organising domestic workers. However, less than a month later the executive agreed with her about the futility of the project.

Once more Molony took sick leave, and on 2 July 1941 an intelligence report revealed just how bad things were, reporting that she was,

> at present recovering from the after effects of heavy drinking and that she is under the care of Dr Kathleen Lynn, 9 Belgrave Road Rathmines, assisted by two nurses. It is feared by her friends that Miss Moloney will lose her position as Official of the Women Workers Union ... as a result of her latest drinking bout.[10]

It was further noted that Lynn had asked Iseult Stuart to allow her recuperate in Laragh for a few weeks, and that she would be going down on the St Kevin's bus, accompanied by a Mrs Byrne. The detailed Garda was also having a crash course in the various nicknames used among the old friends, 'Miss Moloney who has hitherto been referred to as "Chick" is now known to Mrs Stuart as "Emer"'.[11]

Molony was not only in real difficulties within the IWWU but a rift had clearly developed between her and Gonne MacBride. In the same report it was noted 'Miss Moloney and Madame McBride do not agree so well together, so that their location at Laragh Castle at the same time may have some significance'.[12] What prompted this rift is unclear. Was it to do with the events surrounding Goertz? It may have been a result of Molony's progressing addiction. Anna MacBride White had memories of one Christmas at Roebuck House when Molony disappeared and her drinking caused great embarrassment in the neighbourhood. Whatever the cause, it must have been extremely serious to disrupt their friendship and a working relationship of almost forty years. It left Molony increasingly isolated. She lost her Military Pension cheques for those months and forgot that she had received them. In later correspondence with the Pensions Board she wrote that 'illness was responsible'.[13]

Meanwhile Molony evidently remained in contact with Goertz, who was still on the run from the authorities.[14] He was in Wicklow over the summer and Garda records from the following year noted that 'Miss Maloney purchased the hut at Brittas, which was used by Goertz'.[15]

Molony never returned to the IWWU after her sick leave expired. She resigned instead. On 16 October 1941 the executive regretfully accepted her resignation on the grounds of ill health and conveyed their regret and best wishes for a speedy recovery. Whatever the circumstances, this final departure from the union was, according to Jones, an inauspicious one for someone with Molony's record of service.[16] Despite working for the union for over a quarter of a century, and the fact that she had once been General Secretary of the IWWU, she did not qualify for a full pension. At the 1941 Annual Convention, less than six months prior to her departure, it had been decided that only officials over the age of 65, who had served 25 years in the union, would be entitled to a pension. Molony was 58 at the time of her retirement and received a disability allowance of £6 per month from the union. She was placed in the invidious position of having to apply for raises over the years and on one such occasion the executive responded by referring pointedly to the circumstances of her departure.[17] Jenny Murray joined the union shortly after and it was her impression that Bennett had 'pushed Molony out'. She recalled that Molony was never mentioned in the IWWU throughout the 1940s and 1950s and it was all very 'hush hush'.[18] Indeed, she disappeared so completely from public life that several people the author contacted assumed that she had died in the 1940s.[19]

I HOPE IT WILL SOON BE ALL RIGHT

That winter Molony broke her leg and was laid up at Laragh. She subsequently stayed with Una Stack at 167 Strand Road, Sandymount.[20] Stack had been a member of Cumann na mBan and was married to Austin Stack, by then deceased. In May 1942 intelligence records noted that 'Miss E O'Brien' was also staying with Stack.[21] Further, in light of Molony's purchase of the hut at Brittas and,

> her other known connection with that alien [Goertz], it is imperative that she should be interrogated but she is not at present in a fit state to be taken into custody.[22]

An arrest was not noted but later in 1942 Molony went on holidays to Brittas Bay accompanied by two elderly ladies. The Gardaí believed them to be O'Brien and her sister. However, Mary Elliott, author of an unpublished biographical study of Eveleen O'Brien, has pointed out that the physical descriptions did not fit.[23] It is more than tempting to speculate on the identity of the 'two elderly ladies' and whether Molony was again using her famed talent at providing disguises, this time for a German spy.

Details of Molony's difficulty at finding a permanent place to live, her financial and health problems, as well as her increasing isolation from old networks, continued to emerge from intercepted personal letters. In September 1942 she wrote to Lily Clements about money that she owed but was unable to pay back. She was in need of £30 to 'raise her out of an embarrassing condition'.[24] She was unable to borrow money elsewhere and revealed 'You see I was cut off from all such influence last year. I used to be able to ask people to lend me their credit but that now is a thing of the past'.[25] Another letter to Clements concludes,

> If I can think of any plan in the next few days, I will write to you. I have not seen Iseult. I do not like ringing up Roebuck – or indeed anywhere else. I hope it will soon be all right. I will try to get Iseult to come to lunch with me some day here.[26]

Unusually, the Cziras, Sidney and her son Finian, saw little of Molony at this time. The latter recalled that when they did see her after a long absence, it was at Una Stack's home and they were introduced to O'Brien.[27] In April 1943, the Garda on surveillance duty identified Helena Molony and 'Dr Eveleen O'Brien of Grangegorman Hospital' arriving to spend a week's holiday in Brittas.[28] He went on to report that they lived very quietly and made no suspicious contacts.

That Molony had been very ill, and was slowly recovering with the help and support of O'Brien, was clear from a letter she wrote to Iseult Stuart.[29] Although she still had her own accommodation, from this time on until she moved in permanently, she was spending more and more time at the North Circular Road with O'Brien.

> 29 Charlton Rd
> Darling,
> Although I address this from above I am really staying with Dr E. for the past week. I was really very ill and my heart was in a worse way than I thought myself. Am better now. Went back to the flat to get clean clothes ... I am really on the mend but of course very depressed.
> All my love,
> Chick.

Despite a fall off in her political and subversive activities, Molony's correspondence with Iseult Stuart and Una Stack was still being intercepted. In a letter to Stack, dated July 1944, it was evident that a new and happier phase had begun in Molony's life. She had moved in to live with O'Brien on the North Circular Road and the two women were building a domestic life together:

E. came home from Mass like a drowned rat. I did not venture.
It was lashing. We have bought a new Calor Stove.[30]

It was an indication of how close the two women had
become that when Molony made her will on 9 February
1945, she made O'Brien the sole beneficiary and the
executrix.[31] For the next 22 years she lived with O'Brien in
226 North Circular Road, one of three residences built for
doctors attached to Grangegorman. The house had a large
garden at the back which led into the grounds of the
hospital. On O'Brien's retirement, the year before
Molony's death, the two women moved to a house in
Sutton owned by O'Brien.

DR EVELEEN O'BRIEN

There was an eighteen year age gap between the two
women; Molony was nearly sixty and O'Brien in her early
forties when they met. O'Brien was from a professional
middle-class family with no history of political
involvement. Born in 1901 she had grown up in Clare
where her father, a RIC Head Constable, was stationed.
She studied medicine in UCD and in 1919, while her older
brother (also studying medicine), her sister (studying arts)
and she were students, the family took a house in Coulson
Avenue, Rathgar. Molony was living a very different life
nearby in Belgrave Road at the same time. After
qualifying, O'Brien spent short periods in England and
Scotland as a locum and undertook additional training in
Neurology and Obstetrics. A piece appeared in the
Glasgow Observer of 12 September 1925 announcing that 'a
distinguished Irish Graduate, Catholic Lady Doctor' was
assisting a local practice, highlighting her 'marked ability'
and her award of first place in a special exam on mental
diseases with Richmond Hospital.[32] She was very close to
her siblings, especially her older brother who had

encouraged her to go into medicine. They used to write stories together for submission to magazines such as the *Catholic Truth Society* and the *New Irish Magazine*.[33]

Over the next five years O'Brien attained a Diploma in Public Health in UCD, a Diploma for Psychological Medicine from the Royal College of Physicians in London and worked briefly in the Children's Hospital, Temple Street, Dublin. In March 1930 she was appointed Assistant Medical Officer in St Ita's Hospital, Portrane, County Dublin, a branch hospital of Grangegorman District Mental Hospital. She remained at St Ita's for almost three years before being transferred to Grangegorman, where she worked until her retirement in 1966.

It was possible that the two women's paths had crossed earlier through Kathleen Lynn in St Ultan's Hospital, or when Molony was working to organise psychiatric nurses, but, according to anecdotal sources, they met while Molony was a patient in Grangegorman Hospital.[34] As voluntary admission was not an option at that stage, Molony must have been committed at some point, presumably in connection with her alcoholism. Overcrowding, inadequate accommodation, poor staff-patient ratios and a low rate of patient recovery meant that conditions in Grangegorman were, in the words of a previous director, 'simply appalling'.[35] If O'Brien initially looked after her, it fitted the pattern of several of Molony's friendships. Kathleen Lynn for example looked after her on several occasions and provided somewhere for her to live, as did Una Stack. Several people who knew Molony mentioned that she was looked after by O'Brien.[36] However, Finian Czira, son of one of Molony's oldest friends, was candid about the fact that the two women were in a relationship.[37]

From the point of view of O'Brien's colleagues and family the arrangement was controversial. This was even without details of the Goertz affair being common knowledge. Professor Ivor Browne, whose career in Grangegorman overlapped with O'Brien's, volunteered in an interview with Elliott that O'Brien had,

> adopted an old lady who was in Grangegorman and had something to do with the 1916 Rising. She took her to live with her and looked after her until her death and ... everyone was surprised by this.[38]

O'Brien's family were particularly upset that, soon after she met Molony, she asked her brother and nephew, both then living at 226 North Circular Road, to leave the house and find their own accommodation. Her siblings (their parents were dead at that stage) were horrified when Molony moved in. As Elliott has commented 'it is ... possible that Eveleen may have been rebelling against a gendered construction of her role within her own family'.[39] O'Brien remained estranged from her family until after Molony's death in 1967. A surviving family member recalled in an interview that she broke not only with her family but with all her friends. His view [was] that Helena ruined his aunt's quality of life, was taking advantage of her and he also said she was 'in and out' of Grangegorman.[40] He described Molony as a 'nasty, cunning, vicious and vindictive woman who had inveigled her way into O'Brien's house and turned her against her family'. However, he also went on to say that O'Brien thought Molony was 'simply marvellous'.[41] Margaret Buckley, who had been in Inghinidhe na hÉireann, the Women's Prisoners' Defence League and the IWWU, said rather pointedly of Molony that 'she always fell on her feet'.[42] Other union members, including Jenny Murray, had a significantly more affectionate memory of her. She felt that accounts of Molony's drinking ought to be viewed in light of the conservatism of the IWWU, and the prevailing attitude towards women who drank.[43] The contradictions may well have their roots in prevailing social norms and personality clashes as well as the nature of Molony's addiction. There is probably an element of truth in all of the opinions.

It would seem that Molony did begin to recover her strength as a result of the care and security the relationship provided, but also that the two women led a relatively contented and supportive shared life over twenty three years that they were together. After meeting Molony, O'Brien's career developed internationally and Elliott has noted that she,

> and her contemporaries, making their way in a male-dominated Ireland, may not have had the support of a network of like-minded women which was of such importance to the early pioneers of women's rights. Perhaps this is what her relationship with Helena Molony provided for her.[44]

O'Brien's will was instructive and reflective of the context in which she and Molony met in the 1940s. O'Brien, who survived Molony by almost fifteen years, bequeathed her savings to her nephew and instructed that the remainder of her estate (which included the house in Sutton) was to be sold. The money realised was to be held in trust by the Catholic Archbishop of Dublin,

> for such Charities devoted exclusively to the needs of necessitous, secular Unmarried Women of Ireland from and over the age of 65, as he in his absolute discretion shall decide.[45]

She must have seen this need time and time again in Grangegorman and then, through her relationship with Molony, become even more aware of the consequences of lack of a proper pension and family support. In fact, when Molony died in 1967, she had just over £91 in savings and £4, eight shillings and nine pence owing on her Military Pension entitlements. Her funeral costs were £82, six shillings and six pence.[46] The specification of 'secular' in O'Brien's bequest is interesting and may have been evidence of Molony's influence; while the terms under which it was to be dispensed (at the discretion of the Archbishop), an indication of O'Brien's own continuing devout Catholicism. It was a poignant legacy both in the context of her personal and working life but may have compounded the bitterness O'Brien's family felt towards Molony.

BUREAU OF MILITARY HISTORY

In March 1949 Helena Molony was visited at her home on the North Circular Road by Jane Kissane, an investigating officer from the Bureau of Military History. The purpose of this visit was to take down her account of the Rising and the events leading up to and after it. The Bureau had been established in 1947 to 'gather primary source material for the revolutionary period in Ireland from 1913 to 1921'.[47] Investigating officers spent ten years gathering witness statements and other material. Their initial lists were drawn up from the Military Service Pensions files and as Molony, a 1916 veteran, was one of the 'elite of the republican movement' she was an early witness.[48] Collecting went on into the late 1950s and, out of a total of 1,773 statements gathered, Molony was one of only 146 women who provided statements and one of only a handful of female combatants.

Despite controversies related to the Bureau's establishment, procedural decisions and the later closing of the archive until 2003, its investigating officers followed 'good practice'.[49] They were schooled in oral history techniques and were not seeking to reconcile different or contradictory accounts. Safeguards included interviewer notes on both the process of collection and the state of mind of the interviewee, all of which provided a valuable context for the information provided. Witnesses were also entitled to stipulate conditions which were marked on the cover of the form. Molony initially gave a lengthy statement covering the period 1903 to 1921 and also donated relevant material. This included copies of *Bean na hÉireann*, photographs, items of correspondence and a miscellaneous collection of documents.[50]

Helena Molony and Maud Gonne MacBride, 1940s
courtesy Imogen Stuart

Once a witness statement had been taken, it was transcribed and the investigating officer then returned to read the statement aloud, before asking the witness to verify and sign it. Following this it would be officially entered into the Bureau. Kissane duly returned to 226 North Circular Road in June 1949, to get Molony's verification and signature. However, as the transcription was read back to her, Molony was horrified by what she heard and refused to sign, saying she felt it was just 'a gabble'.[51] Molony set to work rewriting and over the following months she worked on the first half of her 70 page statement. She annotated the original, deleted some parts and added more detail in others. The process of rewriting her statement galvanised her. One of the sections which she reworked concerned the 1910 school meals scheme. This prompted her to write to Maud Gonne MacBride about it. Gonne MacBride replied,

> 21 Dec 1949, 83 today!
> Helena dearest –
> Iseult brought me your letter on the schools – you are quite right more should be done for the children. Why don't you write on the matter *you* are thinking of to the paper? Your thought is more up to date than mine, and you have more information.
> Love etc.[52]

It is perhaps significant that she relied on Iseult as a go-between; it suggested that the two women were in contact but were not as close as they had been before the rift of the early 1940s.

While Molony worked on the first half of her statement, Kissane corrected syntax and grammar, removed some repetition and generally tidied up the second half. In May 1950, with the two revised sections completed, Kissane returned to Molony who was happy this time with what was read out to her. She signed the revised statement of 60 pages on 19 May 1950, without stipulating any conditions.

It was entered into the Bureau of Military History as Witness Statement 391 on the following day. She also attached as an appendix, two letters which she had written to Seán Ó Faoláin in August and September 1934, concerning his biography of Constance Markievicz.

Molony's final statement is a vivid and detailed account of many of the events leading up the Rising and after. It is one of the longer of the witness statements in the Bureau's collection and was organised under a total of 21 headings that varied in length from one to eight pages. Sections covered everything from her introduction to the Inghinidhe, details of their activities and of *Bean na hÉireann*; her introduction to a stage career; her 1911 arrest; her work in the Co-op and a detailed lead up to the Rising in which months are unclear but events are outlined accurately. Her actor's voice and playwright's ear are evident in many of the exchanges that she recalled. One can almost hear her performing and dramatising key moments for Kissane. The reader is brought into the back room of the Co-op on Eden Quay; we learn the intimate detail that she left all of her clothes there and so had to borrow underclothes in the immediate aftermath of the Rising. On Easter Monday she brings us from Liberty Hall, out onto Dame Street and on up to Dublin Castle 'the middle of the excitement' and then into City Hall. We sit with her under bombardment that night and are then led out through the broken windows as the garrison falls. She again stressed the status of women in the Irish Citizen Army,

> Actually, the women in the Citizen Army were not first aiders, but did military work, except where it suited them to be first-aiders. Even before the Russian Army had woman soldiers the Citizen Army had them.[53]

It is interesting that she gave an extremely detailed account of the events around the first anniversary of the

Rising in 1917. At eight pages it was one of the longest sections and may be an indication of how important she felt it was and how central her role was in it. However Molony did not just record her own activities. The other eight page section of her statement concerned Constance Markievicz who, she wrote, was 'in danger of being misunderstood'.[54] Molony's 1934 correspondence with Ó Faoláin has been described by Eve Morrison as 'Probably the most openly "feminist" statement in all of the collection'.[55]

Molony devotes very little space or detail to events after 1917. In fact the period June 1917 to 1921 (the end date of the Bureau's investigations) only took up two and a half pages. Kissane noted that,

> Witness's memory is not too good. I am of the opinion that she failed to remember many of the activities in which she took part and that in this respect her statement does not do her justice.

She also noted that 'When signing she said that if she remembered anything else of importance she would give me a supplementary statement'.[56]

Consequently, whilst the relative lengths of different episodes are interesting, perhaps rather than having a wider significance, they illuminate what she could recall in detail in 1949/1950. In both versions she struggled to recall certain details and in another early draft, possibly prepared before the interview, she wrote 'my brightest memories are of the Inghinidhe days and the fact that I was the 1st political prisoner since the Land League days'.[57] However, even a partial statement of her activities in the period is remarkable, as is the level of detail. Apart from confusion over specific dates and months, characteristic of oral history of this nature and of other statements, there are very few identifiable errors or inaccuracies.[58]

Molony subsequently donated the first version of her witness statement, with her own handwritten annotations, to the museum at Kilmainham Gaol. The two versions are very similar but the contrasts between them are fascinating. While many of the changes served to successfully tighten the script and its phrasing, some of the original version is fresher and more immediate. It also contains more detail about certain events. Her final statement was slightly more self-conscious; she was aware maybe that she was also writing a wider history of the Inghinidhe and later events. The original was also more evidently a transcript of an interview, where the interviewee struggled to recall certain facts, repeated herself and directly addressed the interviewer. The very process of memory was visible as the connections and realisations Molony made during the course of the interview were scripted.

STATEMENT OF MISS HELENA MOLONY,
226, North Circular Road, Dublin.

My first political interest was in Inghínidhe na hÉireann. I was a complete outsider up to that time; and it was my brother I pestered. He was five or six years older that I was. He said: "Join the Inghínidhe". Then I plucked up courage, and went and joined the Inghínidhe na hÉireann. That was 1903.

Helena Molony's annotated draft statement for
the Bureau of Military History
courtesy Kilmainham Gaol Museum, KMGLM 2011.0283.01

There are noticeable omissions in the second, final statement, many of which relate to personal details. Perhaps, as she rewrote, she felt she was being indiscreet. The first concerned Maud Gonne MacBride and John MacBride's controversial separation. In the original version she had talked extensively about how the Inghinidhe made a decision not to talk of this and how it was damaging to the cause of Ireland. She deleted this and in her rewritten version explained, more discreetly, how,

> Through unhappy private affairs, Madame Gonne MacBride had to spend most of her time in France, as her son would be likely to pass out of her care if she brought him to Ireland.[59]

The second omission concerns her own supposition about the death by drowning of Anna Parnell. She also removed references to her own illness of 1914, simply saying 'I spent the whole of 1914 in France'.[60] Another deletion concerned the detail of a case she oversaw as a Rathmines District Court judge in the Sinn Féin courts involving a young man with elderly parents who was 'a bit wanting' and had assaulted his father.[61] In her final statement she instead stated that she dealt with minor cases and followed this with a wider political point about the significance of the courts.

Molony's testimony, like so many others, was coloured by her experience with the Military Service Pensions Board. In fact many of the Cumann na mBan women had refused to testify, partly because of their treatment.[62] The dismissal of her claim for the 1917 to 1923 period still rankled and she referenced this in her original statement (but removed it from the final version) when she said,

> I never worked for the Republic or national cause in my life for a salary. I would have got a good pension if I had. I have a pension of £23.10.11 per year. It is strange that if you were a salaried employee, you would get a better pension.[63]

Given the lack of recognition that Molony had received for her role in the early years of the twentieth century, it is perhaps apt that her Bureau of Military History witness statements and other writings, with their clarity of vision and strength of writing, continue to intrigue and inform contemporary historians and readers.

BUREAU OF MILITARY HISTORY 1913-2
BURO STAIRE MILEATA 1913-21

No. **W.S.** *391*

ROINN COSANTA.

BUREAU OF MILITARY HISTORY, 1913–21.

STATEMENT BY WITNESS

DOCUMENT NO. **W.S.** 391

Witness
Miss Helena Molony,
226 North Circular Road,
Dublin.

Identity
Honorary Secretary of
Inghini na hEireann 1907-1914.

Subject

(a) National activities 1903-1921;

(b) City Hall, Dublin, Easter Week 1916.

Conditions, if any, stipulated by Witness

Nil

File No. S.164

Form B.S.M. 2.

Bureau of Military History, Witness Statement 391
courtesy Military Archives, Ireland

In the years following the submission of her Bureau of Military History witness statement, Helena Molony seemed to recover and she emerged from 'the complete obscurity' of the previous decade.[65] She began to correspond more regularly, with renewed vigour, and her letters had a significant impact on those who received them. She continued to write about the period of the revolution, but also campaigned for various ideas and made suggestions about contemporary events. She kept an affectionate and watchful eye on the affairs of the Abbey Theatre and the IWWU. Her memory also seemed to improve as she recounted episodes (such as the trip from Lewes prison to the House of Lords, not contained in her BMH witness statement) with great clarity and in detail. In June 1952 she even came across an uncashed pension cheque which had been lost back in the dark days of July 1941. Her circumstances were still straightened and she wrote immediately to the Military Pensions Board to see if she could cash it, saying that 'when one has little money, the sum of £1 is important'.[66]

Periodically articles appeared in the national press which detailed her contribution, but she did not like this attention and said, 'I like to avoid lime light these latter days since I have joined the queue waiting for the Jordan or Styx ferry'.[67] For the previous fifteen years Molony had been mentioning how close she was to death; in fact she would go on to live another fifteen. In 1951 Cathal O'Shannon, a journalist and old colleague from her trade union days, received a letter from her in which she suggested ways of fundraising for a new Abbey Theatre after fire destroyed the original. The letter appeared as an article that August in *The Irish Times*. A quote from Molony referred to her own time in the Abbey's Second Company when,

> Military and social problems overshadowed artistic and
> cultural ones and, I think have continued to do so for the last
> twenty-five years. Perhaps this Abbey fire may swing us back
> to the artistic values?[68]

Perhaps it was an indication of her own interests 'swinging back' to the world of the arts. In a subsequent letter to O'Shannon thanking him for the 'splurge' about her, she floated the idea of a National Concert Hall as she wanted to find 'means of helping music, the sister art of Drama, into the place it should hold in Ireland'. Ballet was another concern and she was full of praise for the 'original and constructive' Ria Mooney, who she felt would be a better Abbey Director than the incumbent Ernest Blythe. He was an old adversary of Molony's from the Civil War days, whose,

> politics and latter day historical record are unspeakable, as I
> have said so, with as much emphasis as I was capable of, from
> soap boxes in various parts of the city and the country.

Blythe had been scathing about women's involvement in the independence movement and Molony, despite her mission to rescue him in 1916, knew he would not take any suggestion from her kindly. She suggested that O'Shannon make it instead and that should he put his shoulder 'to the wheel of artistic progress, I know it will go whirring around'. She signed off saying that, like Bridget Gillen from W.B. Yeats' *Cathleen Ní Houlihan* (a character she played many times), 'I always have my head full of plans!'[69]

Molony and O'Brien were by now very settled into their life together on the North Circular Road. They holidayed regularly in Ireland with Una Stack and also stayed in Virginia, County Cavan in a quiet hotel overlooking a golf course and a lake. Molony seemed to have made a substantial recovery with the care of O'Brien and the maid who worked in the house. She experienced a stable home life, perhaps for the first time since her brother and his wife left for America when she was in her twenties.

Seemingly O'Brien's own working life was not easy. Aside from the poor conditions for patients in Grangegorman, her relationship with her immediate superior was difficult. Although she was Acting Medical Superintendent for three months annually, her prospects for permanent promotion were limited, partly because of gender.[70] However, she went on many international research trips in this period. She published extensively and presented papers on international best practice in the area of mental health, as well as the Irish experience. 'Mental Hospitals in America' was published in the *Irish Journal of Medical Science* in 1949 following a trip to the US. The same year she also attained a Diploma in Public Administration in UCD. She went on several international study tours as well as receiving a World Health Organisation fellowship to do research in Britain. She presented on 'National Mental Hygiene-Éire' at the European Congress for Mental Health and also published in the *Irish Medical Association Journal* on her 1953 visit to a branch of the innovative Gheel community in Belgium.[71]

Molony may not have travelled with her on these trips but she kept busy writing. She also had time to pursue other practical interests such as carpentry, beekeeping and cheese-making.[72] She kept in close contact with a small circle of friends, mostly those from the Inghinidhe days. She would regularly visit the Cziras as well as Iseult Stuart and her extended family in Laragh. Imogen Stuart, then daughter-in-law of the Stuarts, recalled her coming down on the bus. She was a 'sweet, generous, funny person' whom the children called 'Auntie Chick' and who knew better than to talk politics with Iseult, who was easily bored.[73]

Helena Molony at a sale of work in St Brendan's, Grangegorman, 1962
courtesy Kilmainham Gaol Museum

Molony's brushes with death and her ongoing recovery
affected her outlook. O'Brien certainly became more
republican during their time together and it is probable
that the influence worked both ways. Molony increasingly
emphasised the spiritual aspect to the struggle for a just

society, particularly in the IWWU. Francis Stuart and Máire Comerford both recalled how she became more religious and, in fact, Comerford felt she had lost her revolutionary spirit.[74] In 1952 Louie Bennett received 'an amazing letter' from Molony whom she had not heard from for years. She described her as,

A woman who was a prominent figure in the 1916 Rising and the Black and Tan period ... She was one of the people who pulled me into the Labour movement ... Afterwards she and I worked hard together but she was an unfortunate unhappy person.

In her letter Molony had deplored 'the modern materialist spirit' and suggested to Bennett that women such as themselves should take the lead in reinstating spiritual values into the country,

... we were sinners in our youth but we did cling to spiritual values, we were inspired by them. It's time the veterans who lived and worked with those values in the depths of their being – it is time they spoke out and called for a revival ...

She suggested the IWWU call on their patron saint and arrange for a Festival of Prayer and Appeal on St Brigid's Day, with ceremonies in Catholic and Protestant churches to 'arouse devotion to spiritual values which are essential to culture as well as to living standards'.[75] A resolution along these lines, proposed by Molony, was passed at the next IWWU Annual Convention and the tradition of a St Brigid's mass was established. Although Molony had often spoken of the moral code of Christianity as a basis for social justice, and St Brigid had been patron saint of both the Inghinidhe and the IWWU, it was a significant shift in her emphasis, both personal and political. What had not changed was her insistence on effecting change and she was dismissive of a contemporary 'sentimental humanitarianism'.[76] Throughout the decade it was rebalanced somewhat by a return to the more economic left wing analysis she had held throughout her life. Perhaps it also spoke of a woman still coming through difficult times. O'Brien's nephew and others maintained that Molony continued to drink and was rehospitalised on occasion during this period.[77]

In 1953 Maud Gonne MacBride died, exactly fifty years after Molony had first heard her speak and been inspired to join the Inghinidhe. Molony was among the principal mourners at the funeral and that morning, she and Micheál Mac Liammóir paid tribute to Gonne MacBride on RTÉ Radio.

Molony wrote several articles for the commemoration of the Rising in 1956 and presented the IWWU with an oil portrait of Constance Markievicz. In one typescript piece about James Connolly she was particularly critical of the contemporary labour movement. Her analysis was very different to the spiritual approach she had proposed for the IWWU four years previously, and closer to views she had espoused all her life. 'Nor can I see within the Labour movement of today any great urge to end Capitalism but only a desire to get a larger share out of it – a totally different thing', she wrote.[78] Wages had been raised and conditions had improved but she pointed out that the fundamental economic framework had not altered. She catalogued other social problems and continuing emigration and wrote about the,

> depressing fact ... that thousands of our best young citizens seem glad to fly the country as soon as they arrive at maturity ... The slum problem has not been entirely dealt with ... Schools are still overcrowded and badly equipped and understaffed ... At no time were we more in need of the inspiration and enthusiasm which James Connolly gave us as we are at present ... I would be more hopeful if the Trade Unions in their claims for increases did not base them on the rising cost of living so much as on the worker's moral right to share in the profits they create ... As long as we have wage-

slaves, on the one hand ... and property owners on the other ... [things will not change].[79]

In 1960 Molony was 'rehabilitated' in the IWWU. Perhaps significantly, this occurred after Louie Bennett's death in 1956. Molony attended the 1960 Annual Convention and wrote enquiring about her dues as a retired member and hospital benefits. However the association was more important to her than benefits and on 7 May she wrote 'I would like to feel that I was in *live* membership, for sentimental reasons. I do not wish to feel I am an outsider to my old loved union'. The executive wrote to say that they had made her a life member and she replied to IWWU General Secretary, Kay McDowell,

> A thousand thanks for your letter. Will you thank the Executive for the honour they have given me, and more for the affection and regard they have shown me ... Your letter made me very happy, as I would not like to be an outsider among the company of sisters of IWWU where I lived so happily and for so long.[80]

They soon felt the force of her insider status. The following year she wrote to the executive about the (now annual) mass for St Brigid, saying that the original spirit had been lost and she felt that the union was regarded as a 'wage raising slot machine'. This attitude was destroying 'idealism, loyalty and enthusiasm for our traditional role of raising life standards of women and the establishment of social justice'.[81] The executive replied and regretted the fact that they did not see what could be done about the general apathy towards the service. In 1962 Molony wrote again and insisted that if no action were taken she would bring the matter to the pages of the national press. What happened after that is unclear – what is evident is that at nearly 80 years of age she was still prepared to fight for what she believed in. Kay McDowell later remarked that Molony and Bennett were 'two of a kind', both hard-headed women, and that this accounted for some of the tensions between them throughout the decades.[82]

Sporadic mentions of Molony continued to appear in the national press. In November 1961 the social column of the *Irish Independent* announced that An tUachtarán, Éamon de Valera had received Miss Helena Molony, Dr Eveleen O'Brien and Miss Máire Comerford at the Áras. Following a radio interview she corresponded with Cathal O'Shannon and gave him a vivid account of the bizarre episode surrounding the 1916 House of Lords arraignment hearing. She described how she and the other women prisoners were taken out to a fashionable London restaurant by the MP Alfie Byrne.

An interview which she gave to *The Irish Times* Candida columnist, to mark her 82nd birthday, gives a clear contemporary snapshot of Molony in 1965. It showed the extent to which she was thriving and enjoying herself in these later years of her life. She had celebrated her birthday with a visit to the pantomime and was still concerned with the lack of involvement of women in public life, with the state of education and of the Abbey Theatre, as well as being full of practical suggestions. Arthritis was her main ailment and,

> Although the days when she enjoyed long-distance walking in the Pyrenees based in a house belonging to her friend Maud Gonne, are long past, she has the complexion of a girl and her mind is as lively as her memory … [On the Abbey] 'It's standing a bit still now' she thinks. She admits to being disappointed that Irish women of today do not show any ambitions for getting into public life. There is far less poverty – nothing compared with her early days – but she would like to see revolution in education and she thinks the free fuel should be delivered to the old people who she knows have often to pay two shillings to have it delivered to the door. 'Why don't the Army deliver it in their lorries?' she wants to know.[83]

Helena Molony
courtesy Imogen Stuart

In 1966 O'Brien retired from Grangegorman Hospital and
the two women moved to a house in Sutton bought by
O'Brien, 'Lurganare', on Strand Road. Throughout that
year, the 50th anniversary of the 1916 Rising, Molony was
interviewed extensively for radio, for newspaper articles
and books on her role in both the Lockout and the Rising.
When Cathal O'Shannon went to her home to make audio

recordings for Claddagh Records and the BBC Home Service, he recalled just how painful her arthritis was. However,

> Helena was at her best and brightest that afternoon in spite of her suffering. She was intensely interested in telling and at some of her recollections gaily humorous. How well she did all that for more than an hour surprised and delighted the recording team.[84]

Molony attended several major state functions in her wheelchair, her medals pinned to her coat. As one of the surviving combatants she was given VIP status and appeared on the front page of the *Evening Press* at the opening of the Garden of Remembrance. She was pictured at the opening of the new Liberty Hall and at the Abbey Theatre as Taoiseach Seán Lemass unveiled a plaque, honouring Molony and fellow Abbey members and staff who had fought in the Rising.

Helena Molony only saw out the 50th anniversary of the Easter Rising by 29 days, but lived to see her contribution recognised and celebrated. She died at home in Sutton, two weeks after her 84th birthday on 29 January 1967, of a cerebral haemorrhage. Eveleen O'Brien was present and Molony's death certificate recorded that she was single and a retired secretary.[85]

Her death was front page news in all of the national newspapers. She was described as 'Heroine of the 1916 Rising' and 'an outstanding figure in the events leading up to and embracing the 1916 Rising, a pioneer woman trade unionist and former Abbey actress'. Her obituary notices contained the statement by President de Valera,

> Helena Molony was one of the great patriotic women of our time. With James Connolly and Countess Markievicz she worked for Irish freedom, for the Irish worker and for the poor. She stood firmly for the rights of women and their political equality with men in our society. She was admired and loved by those who knew her as a noble Irishwoman who

had deeply at heart the welfare of our nation and its people. May she long be remembered amongst us. I bhflaitheas Dé go raibh sí.[86]

Helena Molony in 1966 at the Abbey Theatre unveiling by An Taoiseach Seán Lemass of a plaque commemorating Company and Staff who participated in the 1916 Rising
courtesy Abbey Theatre Archive

There was a measure of irony in the fact that de Valera wrote this tribute. In the 1920s and 1930s Helena Molony had opposed him weekly on public platforms on these very issues – the rights of workers and in particular women workers – as well as the direction the state was taking under Fianna Fáil administrations. However, in the immediate aftermath of the 50th anniversary celebrations of the 1916 Rising, it was her contribution to the national cause and her close friendship with James Connolly, Constance Markievicz and Maud Gonne MacBride which attracted most attention.

Her funeral took place on 31 January 1967 and was attended by Éamon and Síle de Valera, representatives of the Minister for Defence and the Eastern Command, Ruairí Roberts and Fintan Kennedy, General Secretary of ICTU and the ITGWU respectively. Barry Desmond was there for the Labour Party, and Phil O'Kelly and Gabriel Fallon from the Abbey Theatre. Also present were Thomas J Byrne of the Dublin Brigade of the IRA, veterans of the Irish Citizen Army, representatives of the IWWU and Clann na Gael girl scouts. There was an ICA guard of honour, an Army firing party and a bugler who played the Last Post. The *Irish Independent* added that 'a cluster of Helena's nearest friends wept quietly'.[87]

She is buried in the Republican Plot in Glasnevin Cemetery under a small, plain gravestone which reads,

Helena Molony 'Emer' 29th Jan. 1967
A Gallant Irishwoman and Beloved Friend.
May the angels guard her sleep.[88]

A/cs. GEN. 20.

PAYMENT OF SUMS DUE AT DEATH

Form of declaration prescribed for the purposes of Section 8 of the
Superannuation Act, 1887.

———

I...Eveleen.O'Brien.formerly.of.29.Charleston.Road.Dublin.and.now

of..Lurganare,.Strand.Road,.Sutton,.Co..Dublin,.Medical.Doctor,

do solemnly and sincerely declare that....Helena.Molony...............

....

of...formerly.of.29.Charleston.Road.aforesaid.and.lately.of.Lurganare
Strand Road aforesaid, Spinster,

died on the....29th...day of.........January,.........1967... and

(a) Here state whether the deceased made a Will and, if so, whether it is or is not intended to prove same. If the deceased died intestate state so and whether it is intended to take out grant of administration.

that (a)...deceased.made.a.will.dated.9th.February.1945,.As...

deceased's.assets.do.not.exceed.the.sum.of.£100.0.0.it.is.not

intended.to.extract.a.Grant.of.Probate.to.the.will.of.deceased
I.am.the.Executrix.appointed.by.said.will.and.sole.beneficiary
thereunder.

(b) Insert name of deceased.

The whole amount due to the said (b)...Helena.Molony..............

....from Public Funds does not exceed £500

N.B.S. The relations left by the said (b).................................

(c) Here state names, addresses, ages and relationship of survivors.

are as follows :— (c)...

....

....

....

And I make this solemn declaration conscientiously believing the
same to be true, and by virtue of the Statutory Declarations Act,
1938.

Eveleen O'Brien   { Signature of person
                           { making declaration.

Declared before me by......Eveleen.O'Brien.............................

Application by Eveleen O'Brien following Molony's death for
payment of her outstanding Military Service Pension
courtesy Military Archives, Ireland

SOURCES

1   Jones, *These Obstreperous Lassies*, pp 161–5, and G2/3364, Military Archives of Ireland (MAI), quoted in Mary Elliott, 'Inheriting New Opportunities: Eveleen O'Brien' (1901–1981), MA in Women's Studies Thesis, Faculty of Arts, University College, Dublin, August 2003, and reproduced in McGarry, *Abbey Rebels*.

2   Executive Minutes, February 1941, IWWUA, ILHA.

3   Jenny Murray, interview with author, 1995.

4   McGarry, *Abbey Rebels*, p. 259.

5   *The Irish Times*, 10 August 2013.

6   Enno Stephan, *Spies in Ireland* (London, MacDonald and Co, 1963), p. 130.

7   Garda report, 8 May 1942, G2/3364, MAI, reproduced in McGarry, *Abbey Rebels*, p. 262.

8   *Ibid.*

9   Regan, 'Helena Molony', p. 166.

10 Garda report, 2 July 1941, G2/3364, MAI, reproduced in McGarry, *Abbey Rebels*, p. 261.

11 *Ibid.*

12 Quoted in Elliott, 'Eveleen O'Brien', p. 44.

13 Helena Molony, MSPC 11739.

14 Whyte's Auction Catalogue, 261. 1, Letter from Hermann Goertz, Helena Molony Archive, 9 March 2014.

15 Garda report, 8 May 1942, G2/3364, MAI, reproduced in McGarry, *Abbey Rebels*, p. 262.

16 Jones, *These Obstreperous Lassies*, p. 204.

17 *Ibid,* p. 165.

18 Jenny Murray, interview with author, 1995.

19 John de Courcy Ireland, interview with author, 1992.

20 Garda report, 8 May 1942, G2/3364, MAI, reproduced in McGarry, *Abbey Rebels*, p. 262.

21 *Ibid.*

22 *Ibid.*

23 Elliott, 'Eveleen O'Brien', p. 44.

24 Helena Molony to Lily Clements, September 1942, G2/3364, MAI, quoted in Elliott, 'Eveleen O'Brien', p. 46.

25 *Ibid.*

26 *Ibid.*

27 Finian Czira, interview with author, 1992.

28   Garda report, April 1943, G2/3364, MAI, quoted in Elliott, 'Eveleen O'Brien', p. 44.
29   *Ibid.*
30   *Ibid.*
31   Helena Molony, MSPC 11739.
32   *Glasgow Observer*, 12 September 1925.
33   Elliott, 'Eveleen O'Brien', p. 33.
34   Interview with Dr Thomas O'Brien (nephew of Eveleen O'Brien), quoted in Elliott, 'Eveleen O'Brien'.
35   Interview with Professor Ivor Browne, quoted in Elliott, 'Eveleen O'Brien'.
36   Francis Stuart, Séamus Scully and Jenny Murray, interviews with author, 1991–1995.
37   Finian Czira, interview with author, 1992. He specifically mentioned that 'she got pally with Dr O'Brien and fell in love with her'.
38   Interview with Professor Ivor Browne, in Elliott, 'Eveleen O'Brien', p. 45.
39   Elliott, 'Eveleen O'Brien', p. 46.
40   Interview with Dr Thomas O'Brien, in Elliott, 'Eveleen O'Brien', p. 43.
41   *Ibid.*
42   Jenny Murray, interview with author, 1995.
43   *Ibid.*
44   Elliott, 'Eveleen O'Brien', p. 54.
45   *Ibid,* p. 47.
46   Helena Molony, MSPC 11739.
47   Guide to the Collection, Bureau of Military History, http://www.bureauofmilitaryhistory.ie/
48   Eve Morrison, 'Bureau of Military History witness statements as sources for the Irish Revolution', historical essay, http://www.bureauofmilitaryhistory.ie/abouthistoricalessays.html.
49   *Ibid.*
50   Letter from BMH acknowledging receipt of items from Helena Molony, 30 March 1949, Box 59 (3), IWWUA, ILHA.
51   Helena Molony: BMH WS 391. Investigating officer's notes.
52   Letter from Maud Gonne MacBride to Helena Molony, 21 December 1949, Hugh O'Connor Collection, NLI.
53   Helena Molony: BMH WS 391.
54   Helena Molony: BMH WS 391.
55   Morrison, BMH historical essay.

56   Helena Molony: BMH WS 391.

57   Helena Molony, Draft WS Kilmainham.

58   Morrison, BMH historical essay, see also Chapter 4, note 9.

59   Helena Molony: BMH WS 391.

60   *Ibid.*

61   Helena Molony, Draft WS Kilmainham.

62   Eve Morrison, 'The Bureau of Military History and Female Republican Activism, 1913–23', in Maryann Gialanella Valiulis (ed), *Gender and Power in Irish History* (Dublin, Irish Academic Press, 2009), pp 59–83.

63   Helena Molony, Draft WS Kilmainham.

64   Cathal O'Shannon, correspondence with Helena Molony, COS, ILHA.

65   Louie Bennett correspondence, private collection.

66   Helena Molony, MSPC 11739.

67   Cathal O'Shannon, correspondence with Helena Molony, COS, ILHA.

68   *The Irish Times*, July 1951.

69   Cathal O'Shannon, correspondence with Helena Molony, COS, ILHA.

70   Elliott, 'Eveleen O'Brien', p. 34.

71   *Ibid*, p. 60.

72   Finian Czira, interview with author, 1992.

73   Imogen Stuart, interview with author, 1993.

74   Francis Stuart, interview with author, 1991; Margaret Ward, letter to author, 1992.

75   All preceding quotes from Louie Bennett correspondence, 1952, Box 55 (9), IWWUA, ILHA.

76   Helena Molony, Letter to Helen Chenevix, Box 55 (9), IWWUA, ILHA.

77   Imogen Stuart, interview with author, 1993; Elliott, 'Eveleen O'Brien', p. 45.

78   Helena Molony 'James Connolly', Typescript article, Hugh O'Connor Collection, NLI.

79   *Ibid.*

80   Correspondence with Helena Molony, Box 55 (13), IWWUA, ILHA.

81   *Ibid.*

82   Jenny Murray, interview with author, 1995.

83   *The Irish Times*, Candida column, January 1965.

84   Cathal O'Shannon, 'Recording the Voice of Helena Molony', *Evening Press*, 3 February, 1967.

85   Death certificate, Helena Molony, 29 January 1967, PRO, Dublin.

86   *Irish Press, Irish Times, Irish Independent*, 30 January 1967.

87   *Ibid.*

88   Special thanks to Fán Regan for finding the plot.

Helena Molony, undated
private collection

LEGACY

In November 2015 the Abbey Theatre launched its Rising centenary programme and in their promotional video used Molony's words from her interview with R.M. Fox published in 1935,

> 1916 has been represented as a gesture of sacrifice. It is said that those in it knew they would be defeated. I know how we all felt. We thought that we were going to be part of this big thing, to free our country. It was like a religion, something that filled the whole of life. Personal feelings and vanities, wealth, comfort, position, these things did not matter. Everyone was exalted, caught up in the sweep of a great movement. We saw a vision of Ireland. Free, pure, happy. We did not realise this vision. But we saw it.[1]

It was a brilliant choice. Her words are historically illuminating and challenge the received notion and continued presentation of the 1916 Rising as a blood sacrifice. Molony herself was keenly aware of the transformative potential of the Rising's anniversaries and from the first commemoration, which she herself initiated, she used it to try to effect radical change in contemporary society.

The irony, especially in the light of Molony's own life and thought, was that the theatrical content of the programme and its hashtag, #WakingtheNation, prompted one of the most energetic and cathartic movements and discussions in recent years around the representation and place of women as actors, writers and producers in Irish theatre under the banner 'Waking the Feminists'. Given that Molony and her colleagues had spent the first half of the last century seeking to do just this, it underlined the fact that her legacy is more relevant than ever.[2]

Molony consistently promoted the rights of women to an equal place in all aspects of Irish society. Representation was a critical part of the process, whether that be on political platforms like the post-Rising Sinn Féin executive, trade union committees, government commissions or army command structures. She was regularly a lone voice in many of these settings up to 1940 and was all the more important because of that.

Perhaps the sense that much – not all by any means – of what she said and wrote was resolutely modern, is one of the reasons that she has re-emerged as an intriguing figure in this Decade of Centenaries, as evidenced by the Abbey Theatre debates. From her assertion in 1909 that women's interests need not be bounded by 'frying pans and fashion plates' to her disappointment in 1965 that modern women did not show any ambitions for getting into public life, Molony is a vivid example of one of those who, in that exhortation of archivist and historian Catríona Crowe, 'complicate the narrative'.[3]

Molony's work and life sat at the intersection of three great movements in early twentieth century Ireland; socialism, feminism and nationalism and she spent her life working to combine them in the most practical way possible.[4] She was to be found at so many of the iconic moments of the early period; among them, making up Larkin on Bloody Sunday 1913, in the Co-op on Eden Quay with the Proclamation under her head Easter Sunday night 1916; in Kilmainham for the executions; the list goes on.

In the historiography of those movements she is also in an intriguing and contested position, not least because of how clearly and how well she wrote about that intersection. Her legacy is very much in her writing. Her articles, interviews and her carefully-crafted paragraphs and dialogue, written with an eye to the audience, are eminently quotable and punctuate, illuminate and have filtered their way into many histories of the period, particularly those concerned with the women's nationalist movement, trade unionism and social history.[5]

And yet so much of her work was, in her own words, 'just what came to our hands day to day'. Away from the statements and the iconic moments, it was her daily organising work and her regular appearances on various stages that built up into the pattern of a life's work. For much of the period of the Free State, she was a busy trade union official, attending meetings, organising, negotiating, agitating and representing the members. This spoke to another significant aspect of her personality, which was her ability to draw people into the causes she worked for, and her role both as a connecting and a radicalising force within those movements. She had a reticence about talking about her own activities and tended to ascribe much of her work to her powerful mentors, such as Connolly and Gonne MacBride or framed it (as many of that community of women did) through a collective 'we'. Such reticence makes her draft and final witness statements from the Bureau of Military History even more valuable. In the differences between these versions, there is evidence of the struggle between the self who loved anecdote, intrigue, humour and performance (which was in many ways the actor in her), and the self who was the publicist and historian for 'the movement'.

Molony was a complicated character and a darker side was particularly evident in the early 1940s, both in terms of her alcoholism and also the bizarre episode with Goertz. As someone who was avowedly proud of her propagation of physical force nationalism and of her status as a 1916 combatant, Molony had a reassuringly humane reaction toward the reality of that violence. In *Rebel Irishwomen* in 1935 and again in her Bureau witness statement of 1950, she recalls her relief that the policeman she fired at, in the 'excitement' following the shooting dead of a policeman by Seán Connolly at City Hall, was unhurt and 'skipped' out of the way unharmed.[6] In her Military Pension application there is a palpable sense of trauma as she recounts speaking at a meeting on O'Connell Street and incidents of shootings occurring right beside her. It is also perhaps significant that Molony was not a combatant after 1916, although she was clear about the fact that many of her non-combatant activities were still military.

Finally, the issues of low wages, insecure terms of employment and lack of adequate social housing that she prioritised as a trade unionist are all as relevant in contemporary Irish society as they were in 1916 or in the 1920s and 1930s. However, perhaps an apt place to end this story is with a quote from Louie Coghlan O'Brien, who had encountered Molony when she was a very young woman in the 1930s. She said of Molony and the others,

> they didn't know this thing about being oppressed – it never occurred to them to apologise for their outrageous behaviour … [she was] full of energy and confidence … Never struck them to be afraid, [they] just did it.[7]

SOURCES

1   Fox, *Rebel Irishwomen*, p. 120.
2   Nell Regan, www.wakingthefeminsts.org, 18 November, 2015.
3   *Bean na hÉireann*, June 1909; *The Irish Times*, Candida column, January 1965; Catríona Crowe to author, November 2015.
4   Regan, 'Helena Molony', p. 141.
5   See for example Sinéad McCoole's *Guns and Chiffon*, the title of which is taken from Molony's Kilmainham WS; Senia Pašeta's *Irish Nationalist Women, 1900–1918* where a substantial number of the chapter headings are quotes from Molony's two WS; Rosemary Cullen Owens, *A Social History of Irish Women* where Molony's comments are used to illustrate the situation of women in the 1930s Free State.
6   Fox, *Rebel Irishwomen*, p. 70; Helena Molony, BMH WS 391.
7   Louie Coghlan O'Brien, interview with author, 1991.

ARCHIVES
National Library of Ireland
William O'Brien Papers
Sheehy Skeffington Papers
Earnán de Blaghd Papers
Sydney Gifford Czira Papers
Hugh O'Connor Collection
Rosamond Jacob Diaries
Joseph Holloway Papers
Anna Parnell correspondence
Helena Molony correspondence
Minutes of Commission of Vocational Organisation
Abbey Theatre Press Cuttings,
Dublin Trades Council Minutes.
Thom's Directory of Ireland, 1883–1981

Irish Labour History Archive
Cathal O'Shannon Collection
IWWU Archive

UCD Archive
Ernest Blythe Papers
Sean MacEntee Papers

Military Archives, Ireland
Military Service Pensions Collection
Helena Molony 11739
Jenny Shanahan 10154
Bureau of Military History
Ernest Blythe WS 939
Christopher Brady WS 705
Ina Connolly Heron WS 919
Nora Connolly O'Brien WS 286
Sidney Czira, WS 909
Nellie Donnelly (nee Gifford) WS 256
Alice Ginnell WS 982

Rosie Hackett WS 546
Bulmer Hobson WS 1365
Seamus Kavanagh, WS 1670
Kathleen Lynn WS 357
Maud Gonne MacBride WS 317
Maeve Cavanagh MacDowell WS 258
Helena Molony WS 391
Annie O'Brien WS 805
Frank Robbins WS 585
Liam Roche WS 1698

Abbey Theatre
Playlists, 1912–26
Programmes, 1912–26

RTÉ
'The Green Jacket' (1960)
'Women of the Rising' (1963)
'Portraits 1916' (1965)

Fawcett Library, London
Audio interview with Máire Comerford

Kilmainham Gaol Museum
Helena Molony Collection

Private
Anna MacBride White collection

National Archives
Department of Justice Intelligence Reports, C/ D and S series

Public Records
CSO RP 1916

ICTU
ILPTUC Annual Reports
ITUC Annual Reports
ITUC and LP Joint Committee minutes

Interviews with author
Louie Coghlan O'Brien, 1991
Finian Czira, 1992
John de Courcy Ireland, 1992
Jane McGilligan, 1992
Jenny Murray, 1995
Séamus Scully, 1992
Imogen Stuart, March 1993
Francis Stuart, 1991
Prionnsias MacAonghusa, 1993

Newspapers and periodicals
Irish Press
The Irish Times
Irish Independent
Evening Press
The Evening Herald
Evening Telegraph
Daily Express
Saturday Evening Post
Bean na hÉireann
The Irish Citizen
The Irish Worker
Irish Freedom
The Stage
An Phoblacht
Republican File
Glasgow Observer

Books and Articles
Henry Boylan's *Dictionary of Irish Biography* (Dublin, Gill and Macmillan, 1988).
J. Bowyer Bell, *The Secret Army: History of the IRA, 1916–79* (Dublin, Poolbeg, 1989).
Andrew Boyd, *The Rise of Irish Trade Unions 1729–1970* (Tralee, Anvil Books, 1972).

Séamus Cody, John O'Dowd and Peter Rigney, *The Parliament of Labour: 100 Years of the Dublin Council of Trade Unions* (Dublin, Women's Community Press, 1986).

Rosemary Cullen Owens, *Smashing Times: A History of the Irish Women's Suffrage Movement 1889–1922* (Dublin, Attic Press, 1984).

Louie Bennett (Cork, Cork University Press, 2001).

A Social History of Women in Ireland, 1870–1970 (Dublin, Gill and Macmillan, 2005).

Mary Daly, 'Women in the Workforce from Pre-Industrial to Modern Times', *Saothar* 7 (Dublin, ILHS, 1981).

'Women and Trade Unions', *Trade Union Century*, edited by Donal Nevin (Dublin, Mercier Press, 1994).

Roy Foster, *Vivid Faces: The Revolutionary Generation in Ireland, 1890–1923* (London, Penguin, 2014).

Desmond Greaves, *The Life and Times of James Connolly* (London, Lawrence and Wishart, 1972).

Donal Nevin (ed), *James Larkin: Lion of the Fold* (Dublin, Gill and Macmillan, 2006).

Trade Union Century (Dublin, Mercier Press, 1994).

Sidney Gifford Czira, *The Years Flew By*, edited by Alan Hayes (Galway, Arlen House, 2000).

James Hogan, *Could Ireland Become Communist? The Facts in Full* (Dublin, Cahill & Co., 1935).

R. Hogan, R. Burnham and D. Poteet (eds), *The Rise of the Realists* (Dublin, Dolmen Press, 1979).

Mary Jones, *These Obstreperous Lassies: A History of the Irish Women Workers' Union* (Dublin, Gill and Macmillan, 1988).

Declan Kiberd, 'Inventing Ireland', *The Crane Bag*, Vol. 2 (Dublin, Blackwater Press, 1984).

David Krause (ed), *The Letters of Sean O'Casey 1910–41*, Vol. 1 (London, Cassell, 1975).

Ann Matthews, *The Irish Citizen Army* (Cork, Mercier Press, 2014).

Lucy McDiarmid, *At Home in the Revolution* (Dublin, Royal Irish Academy, 2015).

Fearghal McGarry, *The Rising: Ireland, Easter 1916* (Oxford University Press, 2011).

The Abbey Rebels of 1916: A Lost Revolution (Dublin, Gill and Macmillan, 2015).

Charles MacCarthy, *Trade Unions in Ireland 1894–1960* (Dublin, Institute of Public Administration, 1977).

Mac Curtain, Margaret and Donncha Ó Corráin (eds), *Women in Irish Society: The Historical Dimension* (Dublin, Arlen House, 1978).

Marie Mulholland, *The Politics and Relationships of Kathleen Lynn* (Dublin, Woodfield Press, 2002).

Anna MacBride White and A. Norman Jeffares (eds), *The Gonne-Yeats Letters, 1893–1936: Always Your Friend* (London, Pimlico, 1992).

Anne Marreco, *Rebel Countess* (London, Weidenfeld and Nicolson, 1967).

Arthur Mitchell, *Labour in Irish Politics, 1890–1930: The Irish Labour Movement in an Age of Revolution* (Dublin, Irish University Press, 1974).

Helena Molony, 'Technical Education and Women', *Report of the Irish Technical Education Association* (Dublin, 1934), pp 34–40.

'James Connolly and Women', *Dublin Labour Year Book*, (Dublin, Dublin Trades Union and Labour Party, 1930), pp 31–33.

Therese Moriarty, *Work in Progress: Episodes from the History of Women's Trade Unionism* (Belfast and Dublin, ILHS/Unison, 1994).

'Larkin and the Women's Movement', in Donal Levin (ed), *James Larkin: Lion of the Fold* (Dublin, Gill and Macmillan, 2006), pp 93–101.

'Delia Larkin: Relative Obscurity' in Donal Levin (ed), *James Larkin: Lion of the Fold* (Dublin, Gill and Macmillan, 2006), pp 428–438.

Eve Morrison, 'Bureau of Military History witness statements as sources for the Irish Revolution', in *Guide to the Collection*, http://www.bureauofmilitaryhistory.ie/abouthistoricalessays .html.

'The Bureau of Military History and Female Republican Activism, 1913–23', in Maryann Gialanella Valiulis (ed), *Gender and Power in Irish History* (Dublin, Irish Academic Press, 2009), pp 59–83.

Máire Nic Shuibhlaigh, *The Splendid Years*, (Dublin, James Duffy, 1955).

Diane Norman, *Terrible Beauty: A Life of Constance Markievicz, 1868–1927* (Dublin, Poolbeg Press, 1988).

William O'Brien, *Forth the Banners Go* (Dublin, Three Candles Press, 1969).

Emmet O'Connor, *A Labour History of Ireland 1824–2000* (Dublin, UCD Press, 2011).

Reds and the Green: Ireland, Russia and the Communist Internationals, 1919–43 (Dublin, UCD Press, 2004).

Seán Ó Faoláin, *Constance Markievicz or The Average Revolutionary* (London, Jonathan Cape, 1934).

Senia Pašeta, *Irish Nationalist Women, 1900–1918* (Cambridge, Cambridge University Press, 2013).

Henry Patterson, *The Politics of Illusion: A Political History of the IRA* (Serif Publishing, 1981).

Nell Regan, 'Helena Molony', in Mary Cullen and Maria Luddy (eds), *Female Activists: Irish Women and Change* (Dublin, Woodfield Press, 2001), pp 141–168.

As ed. 'Helena Molony from: Reservation (A) to Memorandum 1 of the Final Report of the Commission on Trade Union Reorganisation (1939)', *Field Day Anthology of Irish Writing*, Volume 5 (Cork, Cork University Press, 2002), p. 558.

'Striking Bravery: Women and the Lockout', *The Irish Times*, 11 September 2014.

'A Tigress in Kitten's Fur', *The Irish Times*, 23 May 2013.

Lennox Robinson, *Ireland's Abbey Theatre, A History 1898–1951* (London, Sidgwick and Jackson, 1951).

Enno Stephan, *Spies in Ireland* (Harrisburg, VA, Stackpole Books, 1965).

Francis Stuart, *Black List Section H* (Dublin, Lilliput Press, 1995).

Dublin Labour Year Book (Dublin, Dublin Trades Union and Labour Council, 1930).

Jacqueline Van Voris, *Constance de Markievicz in the Cause of Ireland* (Cambridge, MA, University of Massachusetts Press, 1967).

Margaret Ward, *Unmanageable Revolutionaries, Women and Irish Nationalism* (Dingle, Brandon Books, 1983).

Maud Gonne: Ireland's Joan of Arc (London, Pandora, 1990).

Padraig Yeates, *Lockout: Dublin 1913* (Dublin, Gill and Macmillan, 2000).

THESES AND UNPUBLISHED ARTICLES

Mary Banta, 'The red scare in the Irish Free State, 1929–37' (MA, UCD, 1982).

Theresa Breathnach, 'Matthew Walker: Nationalist Printer 1846–1922', presented to Face Forward Typography Conference, (Dublin, 2015).

Penny Duggan, 'Helena Molony: Actress, Feminist, Nationalist, Socialist and Trade Unionist. Working Paper No 14' (Amsterdam, International Institute for Research and Education, 1990).

Mary Elliott, 'Inheriting New Opportunities: Eveleen O'Brien, 1901–1981' (MA, UCD, 2003).

Nell Regan, 'Helena Molony: The Formative Years' (BA minor thesis, UCD, 1991).

INDEX

Abbey Theatre 29, 79, 90–1,
93–4, 96–101, 103–7, 111–
4, 124–5, 130, 132, 143–4,
152, 162–3, 167, 173–5,
177–8, 183, 188–9, 253–4,
260, 262–4, 271–2
Allgood, Sara 40, 90, 97, 99

Bennett, Louie 14, 29–30, 72,
102, 140, 158, 169, 171,
184, 186, 189, 196, 198,
199, 201, 204, 206, 208,
211, 223, 235–6, 238, 257,
259
Blythe, Ernest 126–7, 254
Bureau of Military History
17, 25, 27–30, 32, 53, 62,
112, 129, 221, 234, 245,
247–50, 252–3, 273–4
Bushell, Ellen 143–4
Byrne, Alfie 111–2, 142, 260

Carney, Winnie 119, 130,
142, 144, 145
Cavanagh, Maeve (later
Cavanagh MacDowell)
121, 143, 162, 207
Chenevix, Helen 72, 169,
184, 196, 204
Clarke, Kathleen 162, 213
Clarke, Tom 84, 124
Clements, Lily 235, 239
Coghlan, Louie (later
O'Brien) 27, 31–2, 69, 274
Comerford, Máire 36, 151,
186, 257, 260
Connolly, James 14–6, 25,
27, 60, 65, 80, 87, 89, 93–4,

96, 102–3, 110, 112–3, 121–
4, 126, 128–30, 132–4, 139–
40, 153, 155–56, 168, 178,
193, 205, 208, 210, 222,
225, 229, 258, 262, 264, 273
Connolly, Nora (later
Connolly O'Brien) 126–7,
215
Connolly, Seán 14, 90, 92,
95, 103, 125, 130–3, 274
Cumann na mBan 26, 108–
10, 119–21, 154–55, 160,
162, 164–5, 177, 215, 218,
220–1, 239, 251
Cumann na dTeachtaire 248
Czira, Finian 27, 32, 36, 201,
242

de Courcey Ireland, John 27,
205, 225
de Valera, Éamon 160–1,
201, 213, 224, 260, 260, 264
Despard, Charlotte 165, 200
Dublin Trades Council, also
Dublin Trade Union and
Labour Council 27, 62,
144, 191, 195–6, 199, 201,
203, 205, 207, 227–8

Ervine, St John Greer 98,
106, 111, 117, 143

ffrench Mullen, Madeline
65,84, 120, 137, 155, 158,
161, 166, 175
Fox, RM 27, 221, 271

Gifford, Grace (later
Plunkett) 65, 160, 164
Gifford, Muriel 65, 85
Gifford, Nellie 101, 111–12,
120
Gifford, Sidney ('John
Brennan', later Czira) 27,
32, 46–7, 49–51, 65, 68–9,
79, 82–6, 92–3, 104, 201,
207, 214
Goertz, Hermann 29, 228,
235–39, 242, 274
Gonne, Iseult (later Stuart)
104–6, 168, 207, 235–7,
240, 247, 255
Gonne MacBride, Maud 25,
27, 35, 39–41, 45–47, 54,
65–6, 77, 80, 88, 90, 94,
104–6, 110, 141, 162–3,
165, 168, 207, 214–5, 218,
237, 246–7, 251, 258, 260,
264, 283
Gregory, Augusta 93, 98,
100, 167
Griffith, Arthur 43, 48, 160–
1

Hackett, Rosie 113, 119, 126,
155–7, 164
Hobson, Bulmer 31, 48, 53–
4, 68–70, 74, 87, 123, 201

Inghinidhe na hÉireann 13,
25–6, 39–41, 43–51, 53–56,
59–62, 65–6, 71–2, 80, 84–
5, 87, 90–1, 102, 120–1,
128, 160, 214, 243, 248–51,
255, 257–8
Irish Citizen Army 11, 25,
29–30, 72, 108, 110, 119,

121–4, 126, 129–30, 133,
135, 146–9, 152–3, 156,
162, 165–6, 169, 175, 215–
20, 248, 264, 280
Irish Labour Party 63, 100,
110, 113, 156, 173, 191,
225–7, 255, 264
Irish Labour Party and
Trades Union Congress,
later Irish Trades Union
Congress 171–4, 183–4,
186, 190–1, 193–4, 205,
211–4, 222, 224–5, 227–8
Irish Republican Army 68,
166–7, 195, 199, 201, 215,
228, 235–6, 264
Irish Transport and General
Workers Union 63, 100,
110, 113, 156, 173, 191,
225–7, 264
Irish Women Workers'
Union 14, 126–7, 72, 112–
3, 120, 140, 152, 160, 163,
168–9, 171–2, 178, 183–91,
196, 198–204, 210–14, 219,
222–8, 232, 234–8, 243,
253, 257–9, 264

Jacob, Rosamond, 29–30, 36,
80–7, 95, 104, 112, 161

Larkin, Delia 14, 29, 94, 102,
112, 119
Larkin, James 63, 85–6, 88–9,
100–3, 110, 191, 210, 225,
273
Lemass, Seán 206, 210–1,
214, 262–3
Lynn, Kathleen 14, 30, 72,
102, 104–5, 109, 120, 122,

129, 131–7, 139–40, 143, 152, 158–62, 164, 166, 171, 174–5, 178, 218, 237, 242

MacBride, Seán 10, 199
MacDermott, Seán 70, 27, 124
Markievicz, Casimir 9, 79, 91–2, 95
Markievicz, Constance 14, 18, 27, 49–50, 53–4, 59, 65, 67–9, 71–2, 78–9, 82–5, 87–8, 92–3,100–2, 105, 109–10, 119–21, 123, 126, 132, 138, 152, 159, 161–3, 194, 201, 209–10, 215, 248–9, 258, 262, 264
Military Service Pensions 215–20, 227, 238, 245, 251, 253
Molony, Helena
Early life and family
35–6
Personal life
Bulmer Hobson 31, (33), 69–70, 201; Eveleen O'Brien 32, (33), 233, 240–1, 245
Ill-health, depression and alcoholism
15, 36, 85–7, 104–6, 201, 216, 219–21, 227–8, 233, 237–8, 242–3, 251, 260, 262, 274
Separatist nationalist involvement, propaganda and military
Introduction to Inghinidhe na hÉireann 39–44; made Hon Secretary of 45; editorship of *Bean na hÉireann*, 47–62; early

position on physical force 51–53, 55–56; on Fianna Éireann's foundation and early activities 53–54, 58, 59; role in Irish Citizen Army and 1916 Rising 119–134; on role of women in ICA 30, 120–22, 215, 218–9, 221, 248; imprisonment in 1911 80, 83, 87 and after 1916 Rising 135–4; role in 1917 Commemorations 153–8; activities in War of Independence 163–66; Civil War 173–78; leading left republican 194–204; Republican activities in World War II and involvement with Hermann Goertz; 29, 228, 234–40; 50th Anniversary of the Rising, 26, 261–2, 264
Acting career
Seeds of 44–5, 90–2; on acting career and the Abbey Theatre 91, 96, 106, 114, 143, 189, 253; member of Abbey Company 79–80, 93–4, 96–8, 106, 108, 113; high points 79, 98–9, 177, 188–9; retirement 183, 188–9; use of for political purposes 77, 101, 127–8, 189
Trade union career
Development of socialism 62–6; job offers from James Connolly 80, 93–4, 96, 112; and 1913 Lockout 100–4; as General Secretary of IWWU 112–4, 152, 168–9; post 1918

position and work in
IWWU 184–91; Executive
member of Trades Council
191–3, 205; role in 'Red
scare' 195–204; role in
Conditions of Employment
Bill debates 210–5; National
Executive of ILPTUC/ITUC
and President; 171, 184,
205–6, 222; Vice Chair of
Commission of Enquiry into
Trade Union Movement
224–7; retirement 183–4,
233, 238
Feminism
Bean na hÉireann 48, 50, 56–
60; debates and co-
operation with suffrage
movement 30, 42, 60, 66, 83,
88–9, 96–7, 103, 108–9, 199,
208; and working women
15, 63, 140, 169, 184–7, 204,
209–9, 228, 264; and
women's political agency
209–10, 215, 248–9; 161;
Conditions of Employment
Bill 210–15; on equal status
of women soldiers 30, 120–
2, 215, 218–9, 221, 248; 1937
Constitution 214, 222–3;
Commission on Vocational
Organisation 223; on the
equal representation of
women in public life 172,
178, 189, 223, 228, 260, 272
and through Cumann na
dTeachtaire 248, and Mná
na hÉireann 214–5
Molony, Frank 35–6, 39, 45,
54, 66, 80, 82, 93–4

Mná na hÉireann 214–5
Nic Shiubhlaigh, Máire 27,
40–1, 90–1, 154, 167
Norgrove, Annie 130, 134–5
Norgrove, Emily 130, 133
Norgrove, George 133
Norton, William 212–3

O'Brennan, Lily 164–5
O'Brien, Eveleen 15, 28–9,
233, 236, 239–45, 254–6,
258, 260–2, 265
O'Brien, William 65, 123,
144–5, 212, 225–7
O'Casey, Sean 188
Ó Faoláin, Seán 15, 18, 35,
209–10,
O'Shannon, Cathal 173,
253–4, 260–1

Parnell, Anna 60–2, 83, 251
Perolz, Marie 71, 90, 106,
112, 120, 123, 128, 142,
152, 158, 160
Plunkett, Countess 140, 160,
171
Plunkett, Count 160–1
Plunkett, Fiona 154–5
Plunkett, Joseph Mary 50

Robinson, Lennox 91–2, 97,
103, 107, 124, 175, 177
Ryan, Nell 140, 142, 145, 159
Ryan, Frank 199, 207

Saor Éire 15, 199–200, 206
Shanahan, Jenny 113, 122,
126, 129, 130, 132–3, 135,
155–6, 207, 219–20,

Sheehy Skeffington, Frank
61, 87, 132
Sheehy Skeffington, Hanna
57, 59–60, 102, 159–60,
162, 170–1, 200, 213
Sinn Féin 14, 48, 59, 84, 143,
155, 158, 160, 162–4, 170,
172–3, 178, 194–5, 251, 271
Stack, Una 239–40, 242, 254
Stuart, Francis 27, 32, 168,
175, 207, 218, 235, 257
Stuart, Imogen 206, 246, 255,
261

Women's Prisoners'
Defence League 151, 163,
165, 177, 184, 194, 198,
200–1, 204, 212, 243
Wyse Power, Jenny 40, 82–
4, 160, 213

Yeats, William Butler 44, 55,
77, 80, 90, 94, 104–6, 111,
141, 167, 254
Young, Ella 128–9, 136